Advance

D1491142

"**Soul to Soul Parenting** is an inspiring and empowering book for parents who desire to raise spiritually conscious children on a daily basis in their own home. Annie encourages all parents to trust themselves to model authenticity, self-love, inner-knowing, deep joy and much more for their children so that they may actively participate in the shift to higher consciousness occurring in our world today."

— Sonia Choquette, *NY Times* best-selling author

"**Soul to Soul Parenting** offers a breathtaking new view of what it means to be a parent. This remarkable book assists both parents and children to see themselves in a new light as they offer a higher vibration of love to each other and to the world at large. Annie Burnside lovingly inspires parents to create conscious families who want to deeply understand their infinite and eternal nature. This is an exciting new framework for spiritual parenting in the twenty-first century that enables our heartfelt connections to prosper."

— Dannion and Kathryn Brinkley, best-selling authors of *Secrets of the Light: Lessons from Heaven*, parents of six amazing young adults

"Annie Burnside's **Soul to Soul Parenting** is a must read! It's as essential as drinking water and breathing. The power and potential of a conscious family extends far beyond the walls of your home...it impacts the entire world. This book will give you the tools, strategies, and support to make conscious choices of love, compassion, forgiveness, and gratitude."

— Dr. Darren Weissman, best-selling author of *Infinite Love and Gratitude* and *Awakening to the Secret Code of Your Mind*

"With deep insight and infinite compassion, Annie Burnside teaches us how parents are 'God's caretakers' of our precious children, guiding the formation not only of their bodies and minds, but helping to grow their hearts and souls. Make Annie's wisdom your own, and give your children the gift of a soulful life that enriches and ennobles them, and leads to the evolution and transformation of our planet."

— Rabbi Wayne Dosick, Ph.D., best-selling author of *Golden Rules* and *Empowering Your Indigo Child*

"During times of confusion and anxiety, it is imperative that we find and cultivate tools that help us to stay centered in what is true and meaningful. And parents, even those who consider themselves to be spiritually aware, need all the help they can get in maintaining that focus amidst the challenges of family life. **Soul to Soul Parenting** is just such a tool for those seeking to help their families not just survive, but thrive. Written with grace, warmth, openness and humor, reading this book felt like opening the diary of a wise and wonderful friend. One comes away feeling encouraged that creating a family life of awareness can be both effortless and fun. This book is a gift."

— Beth Nonte Russell, author of *Forever Lily*

"Soul to Soul Parenting is a divinely inspired gem of a book filled with practical wisdom that should be in the home of any parent who wants to know how to raise spiritually conscious children. I highly recommend this book!"

— Susan Wisehart, marriage and family therapist, nationally certified school psychologist, and international best-selling author of *Soul Visioning: Clear the Past, Create Your Future*

"This book is a must read for everyone who is a parent. The definition of 'family' is evolving. Annie Burnside's words will inspire you to communicate, nurture, and thrive."

— Jenniffer Weigel, Emmy-Award winning journalist and author

"Annie Burnside has captured the essence of raising conscious, healthy children. The importance of parenting from the inside out rather than from a set of imposed rights and wrongs is exactly what we need to raise the awareness of our society as a whole. Her book is infused with her heart, her soul, and her personal journey. The reader will receive an experience of transformation along with a very practical guide of how to apply these principles in their family lives. This book is a gem."

— Marion Light, founder of Women in Bloom, Transformational Retreats for Women

"For creativity to emerge fully, the soul must be well-tended. Annie Burnside's spiritually intelligent approach encourages the vibrant and joyful unfurling of creativity, intuition, and above all love. I recommend **Soul to Soul Parenting** to those who want to nurture their children's soul connections and deepen the connection to their own souls as well."

— Robyn McKay, Ph.D., coach for creative and intuitive people

Parenting

A Guide to Raising a Spiritually Conscious Family

ANNIE BURNSIDE, M.Ed.

Dedication

I dedicate *Soul to Soul Parenting* to parents and children everywhere.

• • • • •

Soul to Soul Parenting®
A Guide to Raising a Spiritually Conscious Family

S E C O N D   E D I T I O N

ISBN: 978-1-936214-14-3

Library of Congress Control Number: 2010926897

Edited by Lisa Pliscou.

For information on quantity discounts, wholesale orders, and rights contact:
nancy@wyattmackenzie.com

Wyatt-MacKenzie Publishing, Inc.
15115 Highway 36, Deadwood, Oregon 97430
541-964-3314 ★ www.wyattmackenzie.com

TABLE OF CONTENTS

Part One

Part Two

Soul to Soul Parenting Vehicles
for Integrating Spirituality into Daily Family Life

Part Three
Soul to Soul Parenting Spiritual Themes

Part Four

The author adds her personal notes, experiences, exercises and more in sidebars such as these.

Part One

....

Introduction

The Journey

Blazing a Spiritual Path
for Your Own Family

A spiritually conscious family is not a perfect family, but rather a wide-awake family; meaning one that is fully aware of its co-creative capacity with the Universe to shape what occurs in their own reality.

INTRODUCTION

Six years ago, I woke up one morning and knew deep in my heart that I would begin to teach my children the truth of their divine heritage. As a family, we had always used a soulful language in our home, but this was different. I'd been studying spirituality and consciousness for about fifteen years, and other than my family, this course of study was my greatest passion and joy. I intuitively knew in that moment while lying in bed that the time had come to commit myself to bring my entire family along with me on this beautiful journey that awakened me so lovingly and gently to my true eternal existence. While my husband had always shown support and interest in my spiritual exploration, we had not yet claimed spiritual companionship as central to our life together as a family. This book is our story.

But before I begin *our* story, I'd like to briefly share my own, for it is my personal spiritual journey and subsequent awakening that created a fire deep inside of me to embrace a spiritually conscious parenting model. Today I am an everyday, modern mother of three children who enjoys worldly pleasures such as coffee with friends, pop music, and baseball games, and who *also* infuses a vibrant consciousness and divine perspective into every aspect of her life. But even when I was a child, I knew that there was much more than met the physical senses. I intuitively felt that there was more to the story than a God in the sky whom I was supposed to worship and fear, heaven and hell, and sin. I knew in my heart that there was something beautiful *out there* that deeply, deeply loved me, and that I was somehow connected to that eternal source.

In this book I integrate my personal spiritual journey into a comprehensive guidebook for other parents by highlighting the nondenominational, conscious spirituality that we've created in our own family unit. It's sustained and grows by allowing each individual family member to experience impenetrable intimacy with the voice of his own soul. This conscious connection with one's truth cultivates authentic relationships and experiences both within the family structure and in the world at large. Through our example, I hope to provide insight and guidance for parents who desire more depth in the interactions with their children. I hope to inspire other parents to trust themselves as they tap into their *own* intuitive wisdom to teach their *own* children about the divinity of life. I encourage parents to open the doors to spiritually evolve together as a family knowing that it doesn't take place all at once, but is a conscious evolution that occurs over the course of many years.

I wrote this book because I feel that many parents today are searching for an updated model of family spirituality. As can be seen by the enormous growth of the self-help/inspirational/spiritual book and media market over the past twenty years, a spiritual shift is occurring, not only in the United States, but also throughout the world. With this shift, more parents want to share a spiritual path with their children either within or outside of a specific religious tradition. This book is not about creating the *perfect* family, an impossible task, but rather invites parents to create a *conscious,* accountable family where two-way lines of communication are open between all family members as each individual strives to view life experiences from an expanded perspective.

The spiritual presentation I offer you on these pages is not a top-down model. I simply share my experiences with you as a spiritual journeyman, wife, mother, sister, daughter, friend, teacher, and soul nurturer. Ultimately, it is your experiences that will lead you to create a conscious family that embraces personal spiritual truth. I hope to provide a basic framework and inspiration for the creation of a more spiritually conscious family environment, but the details of what works for your family will be left entirely up to you and your family as a whole. Personal creativity and ownership make any type of expansion and awakening real. Despite what we've been taught by many throughout thousands of years, it is my passionate belief that there is not one singular, right path to expand consciousness and spiritually awaken.

I have no desire to decide for you which language is right to use with your family. I speak a broad spiritual language that feels right in my soul, but you are the master of your own spiritual path; you must speak a language that feels comfortable to you and yours. If it resonates to use the spiritual language that I offer, then I enthusiastically invite you to do so. At times, if it indeed feels right to teach the nondenominational, universal spiritual themes utilizing a more secular language, then by all means follow that impulse. The important message here is that parents become *willing* to be the catalyst for expanded perceptions in their own family. I have no desire to leave anyone out of this all-important discussion. We are at a place in history where we must begin to focus on broadening our own narrow perceptions of humanity and reality. Whether you view the world from a more sacred or secular perspective, this expanded vision begins in the home. It is my heartfelt belief that our expanded perception of life, our children's expanded perception of life, and our collective expanded perception of humanity as a whole will change our world.

A spiritually conscious family is not a perfect family, but rather a wide-awake family; meaning one that is fully aware of its co-creative capacity with the Universe to shape what occurs in their own reality. A conscious family fully understands the power of individual choices, beliefs, and perceptions which lead to natural consequences. Conscious parenting requires paying more attention to bringing your children to a deeper understanding of such large universal concepts as self-love, truth and perception, forgiveness, authenticity, free will, compassion, true joy, purposeful variation and

A universal soul language, embracing connectedness, nonjudgment, tolerance, and gratitude, is now being spoken by many individuals around the world. It's just beginning to percolate as a grass-roots movement to perceive the world in a different way. Those parents who embrace this new reality desire to share it with their children to build a more fulfilling family environment and expose their children to a broad spiritual perspective. Based on this now perceptible shift, as well as on my discussions with many parents both in my private and professional life as a soul nurturer, I feel that the time is ripe to begin integrating and applying personal spiritual exploration into modern family life. Through this book, I hope to empower parents to live not only side by side by side but also soul to soul with their children.

diversity, and gratitude, so they can realize their highest potential by consciously utilizing their infinite and eternal spiritual nature. This book will assist parents in applying a life-changing message of love and universal connectedness that can be integrated into modern society.

No matter what a parent's current religious affiliation, I hope to model through our family experiences what it means to live mindfully and consciously in an often hectic world. I provide a curriculum for parents as they seek to share universal, spiritual life themes with their children. I share my spiritual parenting methods and ideas such as visual cues, family discussions, examining nature, greater intimacy, family rituals, role-play, imagination, and utilizing art forms so that other parents have a starting point as they seek to enhance their family's spiritual practices within the home.

Conscious parenting is open to all who desire it. No matter what the specifics of a family unit, whether it be two parents in the home or one, two children or four, rich or poor, soul to soul parenting is possible and within reach for each and every parent. Parents are encouraged to awaken more fully to their own authenticity and thereby give their children permission to do the same.

The core curriculum tools that this book offers include twenty-two **Soul to Soul Parenting Vehicles** and **Soul to Soul Parenting Spiritual Themes** which can be used to infuse new spiritual practices into daily family life, forming a foundation of spiritual companionship among family members and deepening understanding of the often unseen, yet deeply felt aspects of life. These universal spiritual themes become the basis for not only rich family discussions, but also for a whole new perspective on reality. The vehicles which represent the methods, and the spiritual themes which share the family curriculum, are meant as possibilities and examples for families as they move towards the reality of a more spiritually conscious home in their own unique way.

You'll notice that I use the terms *God, Spirit, Divine Essence, Consciousness, Universe,* and *All That Is* interchangeably throughout this book. To me, they all refer to the same Magnificent Force that infuses and surrounds all things. Again, I encourage you to use the language that works best for your family.

I invite parents to utilize their intuition, imagination, passion, and deep love for their children to create a consciousness within their family that can be applied to all relationships and life situations. My intention is for whole families to become more aware of the eternal nature we all possess and the divine presence that connects us all.

As for me, I am simply a *normal* mother who experienced a spiritual awakening and created the means through which to effectively share the fruits of that awakening with my children. I believe that all parents have the capacity within them to create a thriving spirituality and consciousness within their home if it is their deep desire to do so. While the model of my family's spiritual shift may indeed blaze a trail for others as they head down a new spiritual path, every family's spirituality is personal and must be tailored to fit their own beliefs and needs. The spiritual process is an inner journey often precipitated by external catalysts. It rarely occurs instantaneously, but rather is a continual interior uncovering. There is not one grand moment of total enlightenment, but instead a series of luminous moments that begin to occur more frequently over one's lifetime, gradually shaping an expanded perspective of reality. It becomes a parent's role to model, hold space, and support her children on their own journey of self-discovery.

> *As for me, I am simply a normal mother who experienced a spiritual awakening and created the means through which to effectively share the fruits of that awakening with my children.*

> Neither this book nor my work as a soul nurturer stems from my being an expert on parenting or spirituality. In fact, my intention in writing this book is to inspire other parents to become the spiritual experts of their own families as they lead their children to contemplate things of a more spiritual nature and broaden perspective.

After reading the book, it will be up to the parent as to how they want to begin this journey of the heart and soul with their children. Parents are invited to utilize the *Parent Contemplations* at the end of each chapter to reflect on their own experiences and beliefs so that they can choose a path that *feels* right for their family. These are designed to offer parents in-depth reflection of the material before introducing it to their children. It will also be up to each parent to decide how best to utilize the suggested activities, books, movies, and songs as integrative materials at the end of each spiritual theme. There's no one right way or perfect time frame in which to implement this material.

All families face their own challenges. This work of conscious spirit-embodiment takes place amidst everyday life in the modern world. For most spiritual seekers, gone are the days of old where one secluded himself from the outside world to contemplate his place within it. Today, spirituality becomes infused and integrated into an external material world that is changing rapidly. As we know, families come in all shapes and sizes. Family members cannot be forced to spiritually explore or broaden perspective if it is absolutely not their desire to do so. If this is the case with either a spouse or a child, I recommend slowly pursuing spiritual companionship with those in the family who *are* interested. Begin with a more common secular language, and then slowly expand your teachings to include new understandings. It's important to allow each family member to come to spiritual exploration on his own terms and in his own way. Each individual knows deep within when they are ready for self-discovery.

Expose family members as much as you can by inviting them to participate and providing opportunities to grow together in this way, but never forcing. As I have seen many times in my own family and in those families with whom I work in my spiritual support practice, initial non-interest often turns into acceptance and active participation as children and spouse (if applicable) sense the importance of better understanding who they are and how they fit into a larger life perspective. A spiritual shift in even one family member has a way of infusing and enhancing the core of a family.

I am grateful and honored to be sharing with readers my thoughts on family spirituality and consciousness. The seeds of this book have been incubating inside of me for years. In a sense, I've always known that they were there, but had no idea how, where, or when they would blossom into a full-blown book to be shared with the outside world. One day while out on a long walk, I felt a tug in my heart and a nudging from my spirit which informed me that the time had come to begin this most personal endeavor. What has flowed through me onto these pages has been guided by a Higher Source; the co-creation of *Soul to Soul Parenting* with the Universe has delighted me to my core.

Chapter 1

A Personal Spiritual Journey Towards
Becoming a Soul Nurturer

*W*e are all interconnected as human beings, and often the greatest leaps into our highest potential occur when we share with one another our stories. All of our human stories together create the consciousness of our planet. The more clarity and truth that we can see within our own story, the more we elevate the story of our species as a whole. I feel that understanding a person's life story always leads to a greater understanding of her thoughts and perceptions. Through reading pieces of my story, I hope that you track the evolution of my soul that has carried me towards conscious parenting.

Childhood: Asking Questions

The inspiration for my future career as a soul nurturer was cultivated at a very young age. I grew up in a safe and loving, yet highly social home, the second child of very young parents. Ours was a peaceful family mainly due to the fact that my parents are both peacekeepers by nature, not because there wasn't any angst or strife. Our family wasn't particularly artistic and certainly wasn't overly spiritual in any way, but one aspect of my childhood stands out more than any other and remains threaded throughout my life as an adult: an openness to discuss *all* aspects of life in a straightforward, nonjudgmental, and conscious way. In our home we discussed *everything*. Nothing was off limits. We didn't simply skim the surface of topics, but instead swam in deep waters together. Family discussions took place everywhere: at the dinner table, in the car, on the back patio, or at the beach. This openness throughout my childhood is one of my fondest feelings about my early family life and is a hallmark of my past that propelled me into my current work as a soul nurturer. I yearn for depth, decoding, and analysis of life. My home life was very good, but in many ways rather ordinary, except for this extraordinary quality of openness.

Outside of my home, attending an economically and racially diverse elementary school in the late 1970s and early 80s in Norfolk, Virginia, gave me my first conscious experiences of empathy. At a young age, I felt compassion for other students in the school whose lives were less fortunate than my own. As far back as first grade, I vividly remember looking into the eyes of my classmates and seeing extraordinary beauty and potential, even though many of them couldn't readily see this in themselves. I understood that all individuals simply desired to be seen and heard. My experiences at this school greatly shaped an all-inclusive, broad perspective that fostered in me a deep respect for different paths, individual viewpoints, and soul to soul interaction.

My home life was very good, but in many ways rather ordinary, except for this extraordinary quality of openness.

My family didn't introduce me to formal religion until I was about eight years old. It was then that I began attending Sunday school at an Episcopal church near our home, but God somehow had always been in the forefront of my thoughts since I could remember. I thought about God a lot. I remember talking to God and asking him for help. In church I was taught to think of God as someone outside of myself who lived up in heaven and would answer "yes, no, or maybe later" to my prayers. However, deep down, I always sensed that there was more, much more, to this picture.

I loved church and its sense of spiritual community, but I also longed for my own personal, intimate relationship with God. I now realize that I was also longing for a deeper relationship with my own soul. I was the type of child who always asked my parents the difficult questions. I simply desired to reach a deeper understanding of life. Just when they thought I was ready to fall asleep, I would say things like "Let's talk about

God" or "What happens when you die?" or "Do you think even bad people will go to heaven?" or "Why are there so many starving children in Africa?" I never tired of quizzing my parents on how life worked. I guess you could say that it was my passion. Maybe some of you have a child like this in your own family.

As a child, I never really found the answers that I was looking for and knew that the story was incomplete. But *overall,* I emerged from childhood with a strong faith in a loving God. There definitely was never a question in my mind that God did, in fact, exist, and that God was good, very, very good. Most importantly, I not only knew that I loved God, but I knew that God deeply loved me.

Independence: An Expanded Spiritual Perspective

At the age of nineteen, as I was beginning my sophomore year in college at DePauw University in Indiana, my seemingly easy family life abruptly ended when my parents separated, and two years later divorced. It came as a shock to me, although looking back, on some level I knew how different they actually were from one another. They'd married young and, even now were only forty years old. After sifting through the drama and the hurt, I could see quite clearly that the divorce was a life-changing and wonderful opportunity for all four of us to develop new perceptions of love and intimacy. While going through the divorce, my father, in particular, began to seek out a different way of looking at things. It was at this time that he was introduced to spiritual ideas that would eventually shift *my* life much more than his.

One of the most pivotal moments in my soul's journey was a direct result of the breakup of my parents' marriage. Over Thanksgiving break during my junior year in college, my father gave me my first outside-of-the-box spiritual books. One was *Living in the Light* by Shakti Gawain and the other was *The Bridge Across Forever* by Richard Bach. When I was younger, I remember that my mom had a book on her shelf titled *Out on a Limb* by Shirley MacLaine, and while that book had always intrigued me, these books from my father were my first real experience with personal spiritual development. Those gifts literally changed the course of my life.

For the first time, God was something that I could now see and feel within myself. I realized that I have a creative and powerful divine spark within me that reflects the essence of God.

For the first time, I began to get a glimpse of what it feels like to see myself as a beautiful, light-filled, individual expression of God. It was here that I was exposed to the idea that I emanate a field of energy. For the first time, God was something that I could now see and feel within myself. I realized that I have a creative and powerful divine spark within me that reflects the essence of God. The door opened for feelings of separation from God to disappear. I began to sense the possibility of Oneness with God. These books immediately led to several other books, all speaking a similar spiritual language and leading to a shift in my consciousness.

This transformation in me, specifically how I viewed my place in the world, felt like I was coming home to divine knowledge that my soul had known forever. Seeing the world through this new perspective literally left me breathless because the message resonated so deeply with the truth that lay within my own soul. Finally, at long last, I was stepping out on my own personal spiritual journey that would remain beautifully and uniquely mine. I realized that my soul had been longing for this moment my entire life.

Consciousness and spirituality have now been my passion for over twenty years. While in graduate school at DePaul University in Chicago, my passion for spiritual exploration bloomed. Yes, at night I went out on the town and on the weekends I attended Cubs games at Wrigley Field, but what I most remember about this period in my life was my secret spiritual pleasure. On the inside I lived and breathed a new paradigm: a growing awareness of my deep internal connection to All That Is was greatly reshaping my perceptions and life experiences.

I had never lived in a big city before where passions and interests could be pursued so readily and easily. This was before the days of the internet when proximity still mattered. I felt alive and exuberant just to be able to explore the inner workings of my heart and mind on the streets of Chicago. Urban living with its exotic sounds, sights, and smells awoke in me a sensuality that I had never known. I fell in love with the energy of the city. To me, a large city like Chicago reflects back to me the infinite possibility that exists within each one of us.

A spiritual awakening occurred in me during those early years living in Chicago. I read a book called *Living with Joy* by Sanaya Roman that catapulted me into a state of bliss. I remember walking through the city or down by the lakeshore and seeing my surroundings almost as if I had never seen them before. Clarity and crispness, a vibrant aliveness at the core of all things that I had never noticed before became apparent and natural. I began to walk along a different route each day and bless others with love in my heart and mind's eye.

I experienced more solitude during this time period than I've ever been privileged to experience before or since. I was unmarried with no children and blessed with very few obligations. I attended my education classes at night so I was on an opposite schedule during the week from my roommates. I was gifted many free hours to sit down by Lake Michigan or on a park bench and just be, and these were golden moments for me. They were perfect opportunities to delve into my growing awareness of self from the inside out. They were delightful invitations to play with Spirit. I got a glimpse of what life could be like if I moved beyond my obsession with the external world and moved *into* my passion for inner awareness.

I got a glimpse of what life could be like if I moved beyond my obsession with the external world and moved into my passion for inner awareness.

I remember so vividly my feelings when I entered my first metaphysical bookstore and browsed through all of the colorful books. It was a little store called Transitions in Lincoln Park near where I shared a brownstone with girlfriends from college. My favorite thing to do was to walk over to this esoteric bookstore and feel the peace and joy wash over me. I would gently touch each book and felt interior elation just being surrounded by all of this wonderful spiritual material.

I didn't have much money, but I had a fiery passion. I slowly began collecting spiritual books, and they became the most treasured part of my personal library. In fact, for years, spiritual books were the only books I was interested in reading. I simply couldn't get enough contemplation of the Divine. It made my heart sing with delight. It made my body tingle.

It opened my mind to the delightful magic of the Universe. I was amazed at what had lain right underneath the surface of my life. I'd always felt there was something else about life that I was missing; I sensed a magnificence that I couldn't quite put my finger on. And now, I was providing myself the perfect opportunity to explore it all from the *inside* out.

My spiritual exploration has led me to hundreds of books, many workshops, numerous spiritual study groups, and thankfully, to many beloved spiritual mentors and role models. It's been like a beautiful dance with the Universe, changing partners and steps along the way. This journey has been my passion, my hobby, and my innermost delight. I am endlessly amazed at all that continues to converge in my life to continue the evolution of this wondrous spiritual path. This journey places me square in the face of God. It elevates me to my version of heaven on earth. I know now that it is, and always has been, my soul expressing.

Recent Years: The Emergence of a Soul Nurturer

While I loved my time spent teaching elementary school in Evanston, Illinois, I knew deep in my heart that what I really wanted to teach these beautiful children, my students, was to become fully conscious of their divine heritage and to help them *apply* that knowing to all relationships and life situations. Obviously, I saw the importance of teaching language arts and math; it's just that it wasn't my passion in the same way as the other. Teaching spiritual consciousness simply lit a much brighter fire within me.

Specifically, I desired to teach children about their own divine, intimate, personal connection to All That Is through their soul. I wanted to teach them to see themselves, and all others, above all else, as spiritual beings and all that this entailed. For the period of time that I taught in the classroom, I tried to assist each child in making conscious choices, understanding the natural consequences to those choices, and seeing himself as unique, special, gifted, and beautiful, knowing that one day I would teach using a more spiritual framework. I realized there are many different paths to expanded consciousness. Self-love, forgiveness, tolerance, kindness, and authenticity can all be taught through a variety of means.

Over the past several years, it became quite clear to me that my true heart's desire was to share this journey with others. I realized that, first and foremost, it was time to really share, on a much deeper level than I ever had before, with my dear husband Jim and our three earthly angels, our children. I suddenly knew in my heart that it was up to *me* and up to my husband to share with our children everything that we could about life and our spiritual existence. It was up to us as parents to raise conscious awareness in our own family. I was certain that I didn't want my children to have to face a tragedy or a disaster in their lives before they discovered their full-blown, everlasting connection to Spirit through their own soul. I wanted to liberate them *now* to lead a spiritually conscious life and to utilize, share, and celebrate their divine essence.

I realized that it was up to us, not just an outside religion, to teach our own children about life and universal laws. It was up to us to be the spiritual leaders of our own family. For too long in our societies, human beings have allowed spiritual teaching and wisdom for our children to solely come from outside sources. While others may have a lot to offer our children in this area, so do we. In fact, we know our children better than anyone else. I realized with absolute certainty that I wanted to take my kids with me on this spiritual journey that made my life soar with passion and peace. It was a conscious choice to include my husband and our children on this intimate journey of faith. I didn't want my children to *wait* until they were adults to understand how this beautiful Universe operates for them. I didn't want them to wait until they were adults to utilize their God-given intuition to guide them naturally and smoothly through their life. I didn't want them to wait until they were adults to know that they are one with God, an integral part of All That Is.

> Who are you really deep down? What lights you up? What are your true passions? What feeds your fire? What fills your tank? What puts you in your zone? What takes you to your sweet spot? What are your gifts? What makes your eyes sparkle and your lips unknowingly curl into a smile? These are the questions that I wanted to uncover with my husband and children. These are the things that I desired to gently unfold during our time on earth together as a family. It was the inner aspect of each family member which I hoped to provide the time and space to nurture. I knew from experience that when you focus on the interior facets of your being, you find your spirit and your passion.

I knew that they had the capacity within them *now*, right now, to consciously live wholly (holy) as spirit-embodied.

We had always spoken of God and our soul being the essence of who we are, but now it was time to make it a thread that was woven throughout the fabric of our family's life and journey together. It was time to officially begin to speak the same spiritual language on a regular basis in our home. It was time to be fully conscious and purposeful in regard to all aspects of life and our own spiritual growth. We decided to step outside of the traditional box and allow our spirituality to thrive *all* the time in our lives, not just every now and then. It felt incredibly joyous and liberating to come to that decision knowing that our children, at the time ages four, seven, and eight, would begin their spiritual journeys, journeys towards a higher consciousness and understanding of life, hand in hand, side by side, and soul to soul with their parents within the safety and comfort of their own home.

I passionately believe that we are here to create our own heaven on earth. I passionately believe that we can experience the divine in *every* aspect of our lives. I passionately believe it all matters, it all counts, and that God is a current that runs through and between all things. We are divinely interconnected with each other and all of life. The Divine Source resides in everything and everything resides in the Divine Source.

I now officially call myself a *soul nurturer*. My primary role as a soul nurturer is to remind others that they are spirit-embodied. Along the way, I hope to inspire individuals and families to awaken to their own personal truths about how life works for *them*. For me soul nurturing is about helping others reconnect to their own divinity whereby they are able to perceive themselves in a new light. I invite human beings to awaken to the extraordinary truth of their divine heritage and assist them on the

Are you listening to your own divine guidance that is your birthright—the subtle, loving, intuitive, gentle wisdom that is the voice of your own soul? Are you teaching your children to do the same? Amidst the chaos of your hectic, busy life are you forging a relationship with the most important aspect of yourself, a relationship that will help you navigate the trials and triumphs of life? Are you taking the time to experience with your children the reality of God in everyday life? This is what it means to take spiritual ownership of your family: seeing each other as souls, each on her special journey, dancing moment to moment with the Divine.

wondrous and intimate journey of self-discovery that has led to a sense of purpose and peace in my own life.

I have learned through my experiences as a soul nurturer that my empathy and compassion for others and their life circumstances have been both my point of power and my nemesis. I now know that in order to do good things for others, I must also do good things for myself. I now know that in order for me to *feel* good things about others, I must *feel* good things about myself. While it always came quite naturally for me to give love and compassion to others, the balance of empathy with an impenetrable self-love and a continual striving to experience fully my own authenticity has been paramount to my growth as an individual, a parent, and a teacher.

I feel that my most needed role as a soul nurturer in our society today is nurturing and inspiring parents so that they can better nurture themselves and guide their own children to live authentic, empowered lives.

I feel that my most needed role as a soul nurturer in our society today is nurturing and inspiring parents so that they can better nurture themselves and guide their own children to live authentic, empowered lives. Too often as adults we fear judgment and criticism as we plant ourselves in our own authenticity and become more open about our heart's desires and true passions. Years ago I began to look at this inner fear more closely in my own life, and I realized that I had kept my spiritual path, my greatest treasure, mostly underground for all of my life except among one or two inner-circle friends and within various small spiritual groups. The vast majority of my friends and even family members had no idea that this love and connection to Spirit simmered quietly inside of me. I initially held an underlying fear of rejection by my peers and extended family surrounding my *coming out* as a soul nurturer.

During the period where the energy began to move steadily in the direction of my creating a career as a soul nurturer, I began to feel incredible support from the Universe. While that support had always been there, it was at this time that I started both paying attention to it and expecting it. I began to have mystical experiences, primarily while walking or driving in my car listening to music. I refer to these experiences as my *divine flow energy* moments. They are all very similar in nature. I simply begin thinking about something unexpected, and I feel intense clarity on the topic at hand. Suddenly, I become overwhelmed with a feeling of Oneness with the whole of humanity and All That Is. My entire body tingles from head to toe, especially very strongly all over my scalp and face. I feel an expansion in my chest area, a tunneling sensation in my ears, and a breathless feeling in my diaphragm. My eyes often fill with tears as the most joyous feelings of unconditional love and inner knowing envelop my entire being. It was during these moments that I first began to understand what a mystical experience felt like for *me*. Connection to Spirit through your own divine channels will feel different for each individual, but may share some of the same qualities. The message for me when these moments ended was *always* the same: You are loved beyond your wildest imagination. Do not fear. And live true to your glorious and unique potential.

I began to share openly and enthusiastically with my children and husband my delight for the often unseen, yet deeply felt aspects of life and wanted to share the fruits of this new paradigm with others.

The Roots of Soul to Soul Parenting

There are many different facets to my work as a soul nurturer. The work continues to evolve and expand as I evolve and expand. A deeply rewarding aspect of my soul nurturing work is speaking to audiences about family spirituality. The roots of my original talk on this topic were the initial framework for this book. I became especially interested in working with other parents on a spiritual level as I began to teach my own three children how to become more conscious of their divine, eternal nature. I began to share openly and enthusiastically with my children and husband my delight for the often unseen, yet deeply felt aspects of life and wanted to share the fruits of this new paradigm with others. Helping individuals first discover life-affirming attributes within themselves naturally begins to extend and meld in a very integrated and cohesive way with parenting their own children. While my work is certainly not limited to those with children, my dual passions of family and spirituality coexist on an important and joyous plane with one another.

Four days after I made the decision to claim my passion for consciousness and spirituality as my life's work, a dear friend of mine asked me if I would deliver a talk at her church for a women's forum. This friend had not known, in the conventional sense, the decision that I had just made, but on a soul level she knew that she would be a dominant force in jump-starting my new career. We'd been spiritual companions for several years, simply talking about spirituality in playgroups and at the park. She was always the friend who listened intently when I spoke of our true eternal nature and seemed to have a strong yearning to dive more deeply into these calm waters herself. As our friendship grew, the spiritual connection that we shared became our greatest bond. Yes, we still talked about schools, recipes, jeans, and hair, but when the conversation turned to more esoteric topics, we could feel the energy shift. We were like magnets to each other, inviting our souls to partake in a meaningful spiritual exchange.

So it was a total surprise and not a surprise at all when this same friend gave me a most profound and intuitive gift packaged as my first speaking opportunity to share my spiritual perspective with other women. I was extremely nervous at even the thought of standing up in front of others and sharing my most intimate thoughts on expanding spiritual consciousness within the family, and I wasn't at all sure what I would offer my listeners in my talk, but I knew for certain that I would tell my friend yes.

I had about six weeks to create a business as a soul nurturer and prepare a talk on family spirituality that reflected my spiritual beliefs and shared what we were doing in our own family to teach our children about God. Yet the task never seemed overwhelming to me. At that time, I had young children at home during the day, but I knew this was a calling too deep within me to ignore. I also knew from the synchronicity of it all that I was receiving an unprecedented amount of help from the spiritual realm. I could feel it. For one of the first times in my life, I allowed my creativity to flow forth from me like a waterfall, with no resistance whatsoever.

My ideas came at all times and from everywhere. A stack of scrap papers grew and grew on my bedside table as my thoughts began to take shape. I remember folding laundry down in the basement when, all of a sudden, my family would see me running up the stairs yet again, with a fresh idea for my talk to write down on one of my little scraps. Or I would be out walking on a beautiful fall day, and in it would flow, just the right section, sentence, or thought for my lecture.

One day on a walk it came to me that my business would be called *Dancin' in the Light* as I feel that to dance in our *own* light is really our soul's deepest desire. I hired a graphic designer friend to help me create little journals to hand out to attendees. I came up with an idea for a business card, and an artistic friend executed it beautifully. The butterfly, our family symbol that reminds us of Spirit, became my business logo. Bright yellow paper would be used for all of my handouts and fliers, as it has always represented consciousness and light to me.

It still amazes me the ease with which I was able to launch my career as a soul nurturer. The Universe took care of every last detail. I simply asked for assistance and then received the gifts as they were bestowed upon me. This was a truly magical six weeks in my life. I was in an open state of allowing, and it was as if my soul had been patiently waiting for this opportunity for a very long time.

My first talk, which I have since delivered to many other audiences, was titled *How to Take Ownership of Your Family's Spirituality: 10 Steps for Raising a Conscious Family, Soul to Soul versus Role to Role*. When I give this talk to people, it feels like I stand before them and literally open up my heart as I share from a deep inner space that exists within me. This talk encompasses the two greatest passions and pleasures in my life, my family and my spirituality. The sharing of these two things with others has expanded my own awareness in a way that I didn't know was possible.

Through my experiences as a soul nurturer, I realize now, without a shadow of a doubt, that in helping to heal another, you ultimately heal yourself. As you gently hold another's hand, you gently hold your own hand. As you caress another's soul by sharing space in a time of need, you caress your own soul. And so it goes; as we reach out to other human beings, other spirits-embodied, we reach *into* ourselves. What results can be a depth of love towards the self and others, tenderness and compassion, the likes of which we've never known. This love, which could have remained only an intellectual concept before an expansion of the heart, can now explode outward to all of humanity in a sweep of grace, compassion, and forgiveness that was unimaginable in previous days. Healing can be mutual, simultaneous, and beautiful if we allow ourselves the opportunity to experience fully soul to soul moments with one another. It's amazing to me what we're capable of expressing to another human being when we allow love to flow freely through us. The capacity to love and be loved is our soul's greatest joy.

Integrate It into Your Own Family!

Parent Contemplations:

- What does spirituality mean to you? How does it differ (or not) from religion?

- Who or what has been your greatest spiritual influence?

- What life experiences/relationships have been catalysts for spiritual expansion?

- What kinds of self-exploration interest you today?

- Have you read any spiritual books that have stirred your soul? If so, what spiritual ideas resonated with you?

- Describe spiritual experiences where you have felt deeply connected to something greater than yourself or expanded feelings of compassion, oneness, and inner knowing. What do they feel like? When and where do they most often occur?

Chapter 2

Blaze a Spiritual Path for Your Own Family

So how do *you* blaze a conscious, spiritual trail for your family? What does a spiritually conscious family look like? How do you get started? What are the vehicles and universal themes involved with raising a spiritually conscious family? What tools are needed to create a more vibrant, open home?

In the coming pages, parents will discover everyday vehicles and nondenominational spiritual themes that they can utilize to begin creating a more spiritual and conscious family on a daily basis in their own home. The vehicles highlight the methods, and the themes share the family curriculum. They're meant as possibilities and examples for families as they move towards the unfolding of a more spiritually conscious perspective in their own unique way. I share my spiritual parenting methods and ideas so that other parents have a starting point from which to begin this most personal endeavor. This material helps to lay the groundwork for families to move into a beautiful place of spiritual companionship with one another. Families will become much more comfortable talking about life in an in-depth way. Family members will be encouraged to take the time to pay attention to, appreciate, acknowledge, and nurture their own soul, as well as the soul of others on a daily basis.

We fear that we don't know enough to teach our own children about God, matters of the soul, or the deeper aspects of life. But I feel strongly that we do know enough.

The soul—which has so many names and may be called spirit, divine spark, eternal essence, higher self, life force, core being, awareness, consciousness, or internal fire—is who we really are, even though the physical body and personality are what we typically show the world. I discuss the importance of seeing yourself, and all others, as souls first and as physical bodies and egos second, not the other way around. This one shift in perspective transforms all interactions with others. To allow your soul, not your ego, to be the compass that guides you through life changes everything. This book will help you create a family environment where you teach your children to view the world through this same perspective; where you assist your children in making the shift to seeing the world through the lens of their own soul.

As a parent, you'll model for your children what it means to exist as an intuitive, compassionate, and creative being. There will be no regrets that you didn't cover all of the important aspects of life that you wanted to discuss with your children. There will be no regrets that you didn't share your true self, your authentic self, your higher self with your children. Your children will come to know you, and you will come to know them on a *soul* level, one that transcends time and space.

My goal is not to overwhelm you with your already full parenting plates, but to empower you to broaden and enhance your family's spiritual life and lead the way for your children to become conscious of a larger life perspective than the physical senses alone allow. While we are all parents trying to do the best that we can in *all* areas of our children's lives, very few of us take the time to consciously and purposefully consider the evolution and expansion of our child's spiritual perspective beyond what others determine is best for our child. Ironically, I feel that many of us leave the area of our children's spiritual growth almost entirely up to others. Many of us don't even know exactly what our children learn from others about their true nature and place in this Universe. We fear that

The basis of this book is recognizing your personal, intimate direct divine connection with All That Is that is your birthright. This is accomplished by feeling your way versus only thinking your way. The time has come to listen to the voice of your own soul and to remind your children to listen to theirs. Your divine intuition, or inner guidance system, will take center stage in your life, steering you always towards your own true resonance and authenticity. Using this divine guidance will become the means by which the entire family begins to lead a more passionate and fulfilling life.

we don't know enough to teach our own children about God, matters of the soul, or the deeper aspects of life. But I feel strongly that we *do* know enough. If we allow an expanded perspective, we can experience life consciously in every moment of every day. If we allow an expanded perspective, we can feel a divine presence everywhere. If we allow an expanded perspective, we'll come to know an inner aspect of Self so beautiful, all-knowing, and loving that it will take our breath away. We need only to trust personal life experiences and intimate feelings and teach our children to do the same. We must attempt to break through thoughts of self-doubt and openly share our true feelings about *all* things.

The time has come to step into your own power and defy consensus thinking. The time has come to see others more clearly. The time has come to explore these all-important questions with one another: What do I truly love? What does my spirit choose? What is my soul's path up the mountaintop? How do I create my own heaven on earth? Where do my passions lie? How do I express my truth? An expanded spiritual awareness creates the freedom to fully express your spirit—the freedom to let your inner light shine *through* from the inside out, without fear and without apology. As you embrace the freedom to live true, you pave the way for your children to do the same. In this way, you change the world one individual and one family at a time. As many spiritual teachers have asked, "If not now, when? If not you, who? Where? How?"

It's not important that we *agree* on what or how to teach our children. The point is to have our own conversations about life and to share those with each other. This is only about awakening more deeply and fully into your own truth and then developing the means through which to share that truth with those you love. How it all evolves will be unique to each family. It's an intimate process that continually reworks and reshapes itself as you go, for each member of the family is constantly shifting and changing. All of the spiritual themes and vehicles through which they are taught will be used over and over again in numerous capacities as the family grows in both years and wisdom. Use your own language, and most importantly of all, *enjoy* the conscious expansion of life perspectives.

Integrate It into Your Own Family!

Parent Contemplations:

- How would you describe your family's current spiritual practices?

- What tools do you hope to gain from reading the vehicles laid out in this book?

- What does becoming the spiritual leader of your own family mean to you? What does it look like? How does it feel?

- Does your family currently have a religious home? How does it enhance your spirituality? What could it do better? What could you do better?

Part Two

••

*22 Soul to Soul
Parenting Vehicles
for Integrating
Spirituality into
Daily Family Life*

Chapter 3

22 Soul to Soul Parenting Vehicles
for Integrating Spirituality into Daily Family Life

··

*T*here are an infinite number of ways to expand consciousness and infuse spirituality into your family's daily life. Included in this chapter are twenty-two comprehensive vehicles that parents can reshape and use in any way that they choose to invite a new awareness into their family's life. The vehicles are what the parent uses to teach the family about the universal spiritual themes. These are the spiritual practices that families can adopt and adapt to both learn more about universal spiritual concepts *and* express their spirituality. Each one can be tailored to fit the desires and needs of *every* unique family structure. Vehicles can be used to explore spirituality of all shapes and sizes.

While major spiritual themes are provided later in this book, the material that's to be used while utilizing the vehicles is up to the parent and the family as a whole. Each vehicle is explained in detail with personal examples and applications. This part of the book begins the children's involvement in the process of awakening. Most of the vehicles invite parents to use aspects of life that already interest their children as they teach the universal themes. I encourage you to use these mediums.

We have created several Soul to Soul Parenting Vehicles that work for us, but I'm always on the lookout for new approaches. No matter which avenues you choose, the important thing is to make them uniquely yours. Every family is vastly different, on so many levels, that there is definitely not room for a one-package-fits-all mentality. Parents are encouraged to stay open, take risks, and have fun as they begin to lead the way and express themselves within a more spiritually conscious mindset while also encouraging their children to do the same.

Soul to Soul
Parenting Vehicle

1

The Weekly Family Discussion

Beginning at a young age, you provide the space and the opportunity to reveal aspects of one's soul. This becomes your own family conversation about life and your place in it.

A weekly family discussion, which is much more than simply a family meeting, is a treasured vehicle through which we teach spiritual themes in our family. In a family discussion, you're consciously exploring spiritual concepts together and relating them to your relationships and life experiences. It creates the atmosphere and the means for consistently peeling back all of the outer layers and discussing aspects of life in greater depth. Beginning at a young age, you provide the space and the opportunity to reveal aspects of one's soul. This becomes your own family conversation about life and your place in it. As for the details of exactly how it should all unfold, allow your inner voice to be your guide.

We have our family discussion once a week on Sundays, usually in the late morning. Depending on the age of the children and the topic, discussions may last five minutes or forty-five minutes. There's no time limit. Remain open to what arises. Be willing to take the time to sit together and share for as long as it feels right. The older the children, the more in-depth the family discussions will become. All of the spiritual themes mentioned later in this book can be tailored to suit the age of any child. The family discussions evolve to be a more complex and sophisticated exploration of life as the family evolves. This is where your parental intuition gets put to great use. You know better than anyone else what is appropriate to explore with your children. You become the spiritual leader of your own family.

I always have a topic in mind; *anything* that's occurred to me throughout the week that I'd like to discuss. All family members may add to or introduce topics, and you simply allow the discussion to flow where it may. We often revisit the same topics over and over again. You'll find that the same spiritual themes often arise hidden in different life scenarios. Bridging these gaps is a beautiful aspect of the family discussion.

We sit together, usually in our living room, but we've gathered on a dock in Wisconsin, on a blanket at the beach, at a restaurant, in the car, on special rocks by Lake Michigan, and on our back deck, among many other places. We've gathered just about everywhere you can imagine. Like Spirit itself, the family discussion is fluid and flexible so it's not a rigid thing to add to your "to do" list. It's just a way to be together in a more quiet and still way than we usually allow ourselves in the modern world. It's a safe, designated place to swim in deeper waters together.

I document in a special family spiritual journal the date and the topic discussed with highlights of what was shared. I relish the fact that through the years we'll have documented a small part of our spiritual journey together in this way. I also keep ideas for future discussions in the back of the journal as they come to me throughout the week. I have found that topics arise quite easily. We're simply consciously discussing our life experiences and sharing our feelings about them, while relating them to universal spiritual themes. In the family discussion milieu, we nurture each other's souls; we get to know each other's spirits.

That having been said, I do feel that the consistency of a weekly family discussion has been extremely beneficial and important to our family, especially in the beginning when we were first venturing into this new territory together.

The family discussion is about sharing feelings and opening perspectives. It's an intimate dialoguing between family members.

All of the spiritual themes shared in the second portion of this book represent aspects of our family discussions. These themes form the basis of the spiritual beliefs that we're choosing to share and celebrate as a family. The family discussion is the primary means through which these themes are first introduced to the family as a whole. Shared life experiences then exemplify the relevance of these themes in our daily lives. My hope is to give you a wide array of ideas for family discussions in the spiritual theme section where you'll also be able to see just how individual these discussions are to each family. The family discussion is about sharing feelings and opening perspectives. It's an intimate dialoguing between family members.

I view the family discussion as a forum through the years for *any* type of topic. It is my belief that everything is holy, everything is divine, and it all counts. I foresee down the road our discussing financial responsibility, sexuality, holistic medicine, classic literature, and much, much more during our family discussions. The possibilities are truly endless. It continually amazes me the ideas that come to me for family discussion topics. Nothing is off limits. Life provides the best curriculum that you could ever ask for. Be open to whatever idea comes to you, no matter how odd or "out there" it may seem. Trust yourself. Encourage all family members to do the same thing. Utilize books, poetry, movies, songs, relationships, vacations, and *all* life experiences as the perfect material for your family discussion topics. Creating a curriculum is not difficult. Pay attention to your life and the ideas will flow. The important aspect of this is that you trust your own inner voice to lead you as you take this most beautiful step with your family.

Keep in mind that some family discussions go beautifully and other family discussions do not. I always expect the best, but don't take it personally if and when the enthusiasm is not what I had hoped for. Sometimes you'll be met with resistance of one kind or another, as with all things with children. Every now and then, my son starts rolling around on the floor, ready to get back to playing. At other times, one of my daughters may seem preoccupied or uninterested. This is not about perfection in *any* way. I feel that one of the most important aspects of the family discussion actually lies in the fact that you are willing to "go there" together at all.

While sharing your views with your children, always let them know that this is how *your* soul interprets the world. Leave room for their spirit to share and expand on ideas as they carve their paths up the moun-

At the end of each spiritual theme chapter are book selections, as well as an extensive book list at the end of this book, which may assist you with this endeavor. Read a passage from a spiritual book that's fed your soul and discuss it each week. Share a picture book with the whole family that depicts a spiritual concept that you embrace and want to teach. Utilize an inspirational message that came to you via email as material for a family discussion topic. The Activities section offered at the end of each spiritual theme chapter provides several activities related to each theme and can be utilized during a family discussion to engage your children in their own conscious spiritual evolution. Use the activities as a starting point for creating your own imaginative ways to teach your children a more in-depth way of viewing life.

taintop, continually receiving information and listening to the voice of their own soul. It is so important that we allow our children to awaken to their *own* truth and not simply awaken to *our* truth. Of course, we assist them and help clarify many things, but ultimately they must lead their lives from a place of deep inner knowing of what is true for *them*. Permission and the tools to spiritually detect, dissect, decipher, and decode our physical reality is one of the greatest gifts that you can give to your children. The consciousness and love that is then able to permeate all areas of life is nothing short of magnificent. (For family discussion topic ideas, I invite you to visit my website: www.soultosoulparenting.com.)

Soul to Soul
Parenting Vehicle

2

Visual Cues

We use numerous visual cues around our house to help us remember our divine essence and connection to All That Is. We use aspects of the spiritual themes that we've explored during our family discussions. Visual cues serve the purpose of invoking in the individual a particular feeling. These visual cues are especially important in the beginning stages of expansion when a new spiritual perspective is taking shape and rooting itself into the family's belief system. We call our visual cues *Soul to Soul Reminders*.

The Soul to Soul Reminders in our kitchen are perhaps the most numerous and noticeable visual cues in our house. These always receive many comments from people who enter our home because they are so visible. Above my desk on two highly used cabinets in our kitchen, sit spiritual reminders. These divine blurbs help our family to remember our spirit and our divine connection on a daily basis. This is yet another way to be on the same page and to express your family's spirituality. The messages change periodically when the spirit moves us. Currently, *Remember All Is Well, Take a Conscious Breath, Like Attracts Like, I Am Deeply Loved, Transcend All Doubt, I Accept the Present Moment, Non-Judgment Opens a New Door, Express Gratitude and Appreciation,* and *Speak Truth with Love and Compassion* are but a few of the Soul to Soul Reminders displayed in our kitchen.

The Soul to Soul Reminders idea came to me as an adaptation as I've always been the type to post inspirational quotes around my living area. In our first condominium, I taped spiritual ideas onto my closet door, and in our first house, the side of our refrigerator was covered. In the past, these little reminders were always on display for my own personal benefit, but on this morning I woke up and realized that this method of daily remembering would also be great for the whole family.

Soul to Soul Reminders are a quirky expression of our family spirituality, and we absolutely love it. It announces our consciousness back to us on a daily basis. It's fun to see what's displayed on kitchen cabinets and in other parts of our house. The kitchen is a very tempting place for visual cues because it's such a high-traffic area. This room has proven to be a very beneficial place in the house to recap our family's spiritual journey as a reminder of from where we've come and where we are headed.

It must be noted, however, that Soul to Soul Reminders could be placed anywhere in your home. You may choose to purchase a big bulletin board and place it in a hallway or in the den. The door to the pantry or a basement wall might be a great place for a dry-erase board with spiritual themes. It certainly isn't limited to the kitchen. Right now we have over thirty messages posted around our home. Bathroom mirrors (ours says *I Love Myself!*), desktops, bedside tables, and dressers are all wonderful personal places to display a visual cue.

Soul to Soul Reminders are subtle, golden nuggets of wisdom. Each day brings several encounters with spiritual truths that we've discussed as a family. They make our spirituality a daily contemplation and help us to live consciously. Soul to Soul Reminders are not overly wordy, just a brief blurb to home-run the point. I use bright yellow as a visual cue for many things, and Soul to Soul Reminders are no exception. The yellow represents awakening to your light, thereby lightening your earthly load. It reminds us that we are spirit-embodied.

All of these cues throughout our home encourage family members to remember their soul. Until a spiritual perspective becomes the lens through which one views the world *all* the time, Soul to Soul Reminders can be an important means of shifting one's mindset to include a divine presence that connects us all. Even after one has shifted organically on a cellular level to seeing the world through the eyes of one's own soul, bright, simple visual reminders mirror your spiritual beliefs back to you on a daily basis. They announce your spiritual beliefs to the Universe and give others back to themselves, as well. I have found visual cues to be an important part of our awakening process. Even if they're not all actually read every single day, the subconscious mind knows that they're there, and it sends the message out into the Universe that Spirit matters to us as a family, and we are wide-awake and listening.

Soul to Soul
Parenting Vehicle

3

The Spirit Mobile

Much has been written about the car being a wonderful place to talk to your children. It turns out that the car is a great "vehicle" in which to express your family's spirituality, and in more ways than one. Communicate, listen, exchange energy, and generally see what comes up. Similar to the family dinner, the car should be utilized as a daily check-in center. It's a great place to get a pulse on the family's emotional vibe.

Our *Spirit Mobile*, our family minivan, is also used to promote Spirit in a couple of other important ways. Our family came up with ideas and voted to get SPIRIT on our license plate six years ago. Besides the license plate on the outside (I mean, talk about visual cues!), we have a COEXIST bumper sticker representing the symbols for seven of the world's major

A few minutes of quiet often can provide the energetic juice needed to get through the rest of the day.

religions. On the inside of the car, we've used fun, colored bubble letters to remind us of a few things while we're on the road. The first word is *Trust* displayed prominently across the steering wheel, and the other word is *Joy,* which sits on our glove compartment. Our funky little Spirit Mobile really works for us.

Sometimes, instead of communicating in the Spirit Mobile, we take the opportunity while riding in the car to get totally quiet. We may put classical music on or just have silence. In the hustle and bustle of the day, ten minutes of no talking can be a wonderful time to tune into one's soul; the opportunity to just be while staring out the window and resting the mind is very important to your spiritual nature. Carving out time for this type of stillness can prove difficult in our hectic family lives, but the rewards are well worth it. A few minutes of quiet often can provide the energetic juice needed to get through the rest of the day. I recommend letting your children know exactly what you are doing. Speak the language. Impress on them the importance of quieting the mind and getting still. You'll probably find that they welcome the opportunity to decompress. Even if it's just for eight minutes on the way to a music lesson, it truly can rejuvenate the soul.

On the other hand, sometimes the inside of the Spirit Mobile is neither chatty nor quiet. Instead the windows are open, the music is cranked, and we're all singing at the top of our lungs and busting out some upper-body dance moves. We're giddy and letting it all hang out. We use our *loud* voices in the car. Of course, we've discovered that this can do wonders for the spirit, too!

The movement of the car rolling down the road can be extremely peaceful if you relax into it instead of just rushing from place to place. The sights can touch your heart if you allow yourself to really *see.* The music can stir your soul if you allow yourself to really *hear.*

Here's another aspect of our Spirit Mobile, and it's my favorite. We had a wonderful family discussion one Sunday defining our Spirit Mobile as a symbol for each of us leaving our home and going out into the larger world to nurture other souls. We spoke of this being an integral part of

I find myself alone in my car a lot throughout my day. I've found that these times have become sacred "Annie" time. They can either be filled with more of the same: talking on the phone, mentally running through my "to do" list, allowing my mind to run crazy in many directions or they can be something different. My travels around town are now perfect opportunities for me to connect with my divine source. I often listen to music, clear my mind, and consciously open my heart, allowing myself to be receptive to spiritual guidance. I always keep paper and pen handy in my car because it is here where I often receive divine inspiration. I'm prepared to pull over and jot down new insights. Since I am focused on driving, my thoughts are able to flow more freely without the judgment and censorship that can occur at other times. Learn to allow that flow. Receive the answers as they come and acknowledge them with appreciation and gratitude when they do. Every individual must take full responsibility for remaining awake throughout her day. Recognize where and when your wakefulness is most prevalent and utilize those moments. Teach your children to do the same. Learning to attune oneself to the divine energy at hand is an art that can be learned by all; an art most definitely not saved for but a precious few.

our family mission. We understand that when we are full, we have the capacity to greatly impact the lives of others with small, everyday gestures of kindness. As we enter the outside world each day, we try to remember to ask ourselves, "Who will we nurture today? Will it be the friend in need? Will it be the produce man at the grocery store? Will it be a total stranger?" Teach your children to see themselves as soul nurturers each time they venture out in the family Spirit Mobile. Allow your children to bear witness to how you nurture other souls throughout your day.

Do you really see the waitress serving up your food? Do you recognize and acknowledge her in your heart as a sacred being? What about the person taking your money in the tollbooth? Do you look him in the eye and smile, consciously seeing him as a beautiful spirit? The individual, under his physical coverings, is actually a divine spark taking your quarter. Finally, what about the workers at McDonald's? Do you see them as souls? Do you see them as angels in disguise? The attitudes and the personalities really don't matter. *All* of these individuals with whom you have contact on a daily basis may or may not remember who they truly are, but you must allow yourself to truly recognize, if even for a moment, their utter perfection and beauty as part of the divine whole. It is simply a choice. It is a choice in how you perceive others and yourself. Human beings deeply desire to be consciously seen and heard, and doing so is almost always the most loving way you can assist another.

Ask yourself and your children how you can spread love each day. Contemplate how many souls you're *willing* to really see and nurture as you move around town both in and out of your Spirit Mobile. Most of all, remain fully awake to the Divine Presence that infuses and surrounds you, and enjoy the ride.

Soul to Soul
Parenting Vehicle
4

Sacred Spaces and Places

Creating spaces and places for sacred contemplation is another vital means of bringing spirituality into your daily family life. These remind you that you are a spiritual being having a human experience; they remind you to remain conscious of a larger perspective. They may be inside of your home or someplace in the outside world. It doesn't matter where they are or what they are; it only matters that they hold a special meaning to *you*. We utilize this vehicle of remembering both as individuals and as a family.

In our family, our sacred spaces and places are everywhere. While we see all spaces and places as sacred, certain ones speak to us in a calming, reflective kind of way. These are areas where divine inspiration seems to reach us more directly due to the receptivity and openness they activate within us. Begin to get a feel for which spaces and places, in and out of your home, assist you in getting quiet and still. What spaces make you feel joyful, peaceful, and relaxed? Where do you feel close to God?

Our family has designated several places as specifically sacred to us. In our hometown, we feel that the Wilmette beach, the rocks down at Northwestern University in Evanston on the shores of Lake Michigan, certain parks, our own backyard, and the annex of our master bedroom are easily accessible and particularly good places to hold our family discussions. They evoke in us an appreciation of our spiritual nature. Out of town, our beloved Lake Aidenn in northern Wisconsin is a tremendously spiritual place for the entire family. We go there every summer and experience high-quality family time wrapped in the arms of Mother Earth. We would never limit ourselves to only these sacred spots, but they are special places where we contemplate the divine together.

In the annex of our master bedroom, we've created our own altar with things that are special to our spirits. This is not a place of worship, but instead an expression of gratitude offered up to All That Is. The contents of this altar change as the spirit moves us. We display things that are special to each of our souls. Our altar is covered with a beautiful lace runner that belonged to my paternal grandparents. It had been stored away for years, and thankfully, was found one day while I was cleaning out an old cupboard shortly after we had created our altar. The minute I saw it, I knew that it was perfect for this sacred space in our home.

It's never too soon to teach a child how to get in touch with her own soul on a daily basis.

Right now we have an interesting array of items on our altar, each representing something special and soulful to a family member. Crosses, angel coins, a special heart-shaped rock, a Lego flower, a homemade glass bowl, butterflies, sea glass in a jar, baseball cards, a soccer ball, a state championship medal, horses, a picture of the moon, a photo of the ocean, eagles, a Shrinkydink guitar, a candle, all seven of the chakra colors, homemade tissue-paper flowers in a hand-painted vase, and a praying yogi, among other things, are currently being displayed on our altar. Each member of the family is free to add or take away according to whatever is speaking to him at any given time.

We have pens and paper available in our little sacred corner, as well as classical music available to play. It is a quiet place where family members are free to meditate, journal, read, or just be. It's comforting to have at least one place designated in your home for reflection and contemplation. In our modern world, I feel that it's vitally important to provide the space for ourselves and our children to get quiet and be still. As so many spiritual masters have taught us through the years, if you do

Clearing away the superfluous creates space for a deeper connection to your soul.

not go within, you go without. We want our children to reap the tremendous benefits of this universal wisdom at a young age. It's never too soon to teach a child how to get in touch with her own soul on a daily basis.

Besides choosing sacred spaces and places for contemplation, all spaces and places offer us a certain vibration, so all surroundings are extremely important to your spiritual well-being. I am very sensitive to the way a space or place makes me feel. I am in and out of restaurants, businesses, social gatherings, meetings, and any other place or event quickly if I don't feel good vibes when I enter the door. We can choose the surroundings that are right for us. It is an internal feeling of alignment leading to our preferences and decisions regarding space.

It's important to tune into your internal compass in all areas of life, including where you choose to live, work, and spend your free time. Speak openly with your children about allowing your spirit to lead you in all decisions. They will undoubtedly emulate this as they begin to make many more decisions of their own. Use the language as a family rather than just feeling these things and keeping them locked within your own heart.

For me, less is always more when it comes to feeling good in a space. The older I've gotten, the less clutter I can handle in my life. I like clean, uncluttered spaces in which to live and work. Nor do I like too many commitments on my calendar. An overabundance of stuff and an overscheduled life make me feel detached from my soul. It often actually makes me feel jittery and nauseous. In order for me to tap into my intuition, I know that I must live in an

I've created a personal altar on the two windowsills above the kitchen sink. Like many parents, I spend quite a bit of time there. It brings me tremendous joy to look at things that touch my spirit. It is a special and sacred space that is totally personal to me. While others may walk into the kitchen, notice it, and perhaps be touched by it, this altar was created especially for me. This is a space that celebrates my soul. I love knowing that my spirit shines a little more brightly as I stand before my own personal altar and mindfully make dinner or wash my dishes. Encourage your children to create personal altars in spaces that speak to them.

orderly, simple, clear space. For the most part, my spirit *also* really appreciates a calm, but spirited environment. This means one that is not chaotic or frenetic, but rather enthusiastic and joyful.

Clearing away the superfluous creates space for a deeper connection to your soul. An excess of stuff, whether it be physical things or social commitments, takes too much of your precious energy. It leaves no time to do anything except simply wade through your day. I suggest going through every inch of your living space and really cleaning house. Do this several times a year. Help your children do the same thing with their personal items and spaces. Make way for the extraordinary to enter your life by first clearing a well-lit path. Of course, there may be others out there who find inspiration amidst lots of things and in a more chaotic atmosphere. That is fine for them. Either way, it's incredibly important that we listen to our spirit which will always let us know which environment is best for us at any given time.

When I began to know, in no uncertai terms, that soul nurturing would become my career, I realized that there was some work to be done in m home to gently push me along. I still had boxes of teaching materials from my early years as an elementary school educator. I decided one day that it was time to clear my path physically, mentally, and emotionally make room for the seeds of my new career, which had been waiting my whole life to blossom.

I laboriously and lovingly went throug all that I had collected as an elementary school teacher. Besides a few special mementos and unique class writing projects, I cleared out all of my old teaching boxes. Many of the usable items, such as posters and books, I took over to the teachers' lounge at my children's elementary school and left them with a sign that read, "Please take and enjoy!" Within hours, I felt lighter and more focused as a new career began to take shape more fully in my heart and soul. It's important to keep things moving. Everything in the Universe is in constant motion. Everything is fluid. Choose to participate in the divine flo of life rather than resist it.

Color is another important aspect of what makes a space or place feel right to you. Our family prefers neutral earth tones. These colors make us feel relaxed and peaceful. They allow us to feel at ease in our own home. Many of my friends like more colorful hues. Their palettes are clearly different from ours. While I appreciate their vibrant reds and blues when I'm in their homes, I know that those colors wouldn't be right for my soul in my home. Learn to tap into your feelings regarding your surroundings. Listen to your body for clues. If something doesn't feel right for you, seek to change it in any way that you can by first getting quiet and seeing what ideas flow to you that could invoke change. Sometimes even small changes can do wonders to alter the feel of a space or place.

Soul to Soul
Parenting Vehicle

5

Spiritual Signs

The family spiritual sign is another vehicle through which one can explore spiritual themes as a family. This is a sign that every family member recognizes as the Divine Presence at work. Spiritual signs offer up great feelings of love and joy and are almost always very subtle and unobtrusive. Spiritual signs remind you that you *are* Spirit, and that you're an integral part of the divine whole infusing and surrounding all things. The questions become: Are you listening? Are you noticing? Are you grateful?

I always look for signs when I'm waiting for answers because it is magical and fun. You can only see, hear, and feel signs when you are fully present in each moment; to be worried about the future or reliving the past is a sure way to miss these precious gifts from Spirit. These wonderful gems usually come in the form of truth and insight and are liter-ally being showered upon you throughout your day, if only you wake up to their meaning. Give yourself permission to communicate with God in this way. Open the threshold of your heart and mind and begin to receive these ethereal gifts.

Give yourself permission to communicate with God in this way.

Our family spiritual sign is the butterfly. We collect them, and all five of us know the butterfly as an intimate and personal reminder of Spirit—the Spirit that is around us all the time. When we first wanted to acknowledge our family's spiritual sign, we weren't exactly sure what it was that spoke directly to our family. We came up with ideas, but nothing *felt* quite right. Then, after a week or so, we were driving to Indianapolis on the way to visit my family, and the car was totally quiet. We were about halfway into our trip, and everyone was in that connected, relaxed state just staring out the windows. I was sitting in the front passenger seat and had just finished writing down some thoughts in my Intuitive-

Gratitude Journal when suddenly we passed a big semi-truck with the word CATERPILLAR written in large letters on its sidewall. Ping! It hit me square in the solar plexus: the butterfly. Now *that* felt right. I got my divine flow energy feeling and knew without a doubt that this was our family's luminescent sign of Spirit.

I shared my discovery with the family, and we all laughed in delight. Of course! We have always noticed beautiful butterflies, and even more surprisingly, we already had them everywhere in our home. My middle daughter Piper had made a beautiful butterfly out of wire mesh and pipe cleaners that very week which was now hanging in our kitchen. Aidenn, our oldest daughter, had also just recently created a butterfly out of tissue paper that was now hanging on the wall in our pantry. Continuing to mentally scan our home, I realized that there was also a homemade stained-glass butterfly in the upstairs family bathroom, and Piper had only a few weeks ago received a chair for her birthday with butterflies all over it. Looking down on my lap, I noticed that the very bookmark I was using, which was given to me on Mother's Day one week before and had been made by Aidenn, had three butterflies and the words *I love you, Mom* on it. Finally, that very morning before we left on our trip, my little boy Pete and I had been on a walk around the block while the girls were at school, when all of a sudden, Pete tugged on my shirt and said, "Mommy, Mommy, look at that cool butterfly! She's pretty." Indeed, I looked up and there she was: a beautiful butterfly that seemed to dance around our heads for several minutes.

The signs were everywhere. The answer we had sought for a week was right there. We hadn't been *noticing* what gleamed right under our noses. We felt appreciation that the Universe had answered our request to discover our special family sign of Spirit.

A spiritual sign can take any form that one wishes. It reminds you to feel appreciation and gratitude for life. It's a form of *symbolic sight* reminding you to remember that something beautiful and real, yet unseen to the naked eye, is at work in all aspects of your life. For example, if I'm walking down the street and notice a butterfly, it is an immediate reminder for me to take a breath and remember who I really am—an eternal being connected to All That Is. Signs invoke in us a *feeling* of love and an acknowledgement that there's more to every moment than meets the eye.

The butterfly is a visual cue in our family's daily life. We have them everywhere, not in an overdone way, but simply as subtle soul reminders. We have one on our refrigerator and altar, and beautiful little ones on both the inside and outside of our Spirit Mobile. Specifically for us, the butterfly represents the transformation and shifting that's always occurring in all of life; Spirit at work. It's a reminder that life is very fluid. Life is constantly moving and changing, encouraging us to move with it and go with the flow rather than resist its call for change. In this way, the Universe is limitless and infinite. The butterfly serves us by reminding us to dance gracefully with what is so, knowing that all moments offer an opportunity for profound transformation and evolution.

Not only are signs a great reminder to love and trust, but they're also quite fun. They become an inside family joke of sorts. For example, if we walk into a store looking for napkins for the upcoming barbecue, we always get the ones with the butterflies on them. The whole family knows this without question. It becomes a family collection item whereby there is a unified sense of well-being, very similar to the totem poles used by Native Americans.

Of course, you're not limited to having just one spiritual sign. God is never limited to anything. Seek what speaks to your heart and sings to your soul. There may be a number of symbols on the earthly plane that do so. For me, the eagle is another spiritual sign. Whenever I have the pleasure of witnessing an eagle soar through the sky during our stays in Wisconsin, it fills my entire being with unbelievable delight and an inner knowing that this Universe is benevolent and good.

So what will *your* family's spiritual sign be? What will be your family's personal reminder that *everything is divine,* and that nothing is left out of the Divine Presence? What will be your family's personal reminder to feel gratitude and appreciation for all of life? What will be your family's reminder to lead a conscious life? I promise you that once it comes to you, you will begin to see your personal sign from God everywhere, even in the most random places. That's Spirit at work!

You'll notice that once a deep inner knowing that *everything* and *everyone* in life is truly divine integrates completely into your awareness, spiritual signs are no longer as specific. In the early stages of spiritual awakening, they are extremely powerful and important reminders to acknowledge the divinity in life. As one shifts into a steady state of gratitude and appreciation, he recognizes God in *all* things. So a cardinal, a butterfly, a baseball, a coyote, a rainy day—it really doesn't matter, for there is an impenetrable understanding that a divine presence infuses and surrounds all things.

Soul to Soul
Parenting Vehicle

Family rituals fill your life with grace.

Family Rituals

Creating your own family rituals provides another artery for the infusion of spirituality into your family's life experience. This means doing a few little things on a daily basis to really develop your own family's spiritual traditions. This becomes the common thread that creates your everyday spiritual practice. Family rituals fill your life with grace. It is here that your spirituality becomes fully embedded into your family life. It becomes no longer a separate entity, but simply who you are as a family. Your spiritual language becomes your native tongue, so to speak.

For example, I wrote a new grace for our family that we now say each night before sharing a meal together. The other grace was fine, and one that I had used since childhood, but it no longer held much meaning for any of us. Our kids just quickly stated the grace without really understanding what it meant. Now we have our own grace that represents more fully our spiritual beliefs. If this grace eventually becomes too common, then we'll write another one. We're always open to changing our spiritual practices because Spirit is not stagnant. We are divine ever-changing beings who are integral parts of the divine flow of life, and we *consciously* choose for our spirituality to represent this universal truth.

Reading prayers authored by others can also create freshness to family rituals. We may take turns reading a new prayer for one month, allowing time to absorb and integrate the prayer into our consciousness. Our children greatly enjoy participating in the reading and express excitement when we change course in this way. We recognize the new prayer as a fresh perspective.

We now end our grace with *Namaste*, a Hindu salutation meaning *The God in me sees the God in you*. In other words, *I recognize and honor your spirit*. This ending feels right for us *for now*. Namaste reflects back to us the soul to soul recognition that's been a large part of our spiritual work together as a family over the past several years. With this new ending to our grace, we are reminded, over and over again, to see one another as sacred and holy, each of us on his own journey dancing with the Divine. Our intention is for that to become the natural way in which we perceive the world. The nightly reminder of who we *really* are has helped us tremendously in that area of our spiritual growth.

Really the only question when it comes to family rituals is what feels right for *your* family. Think about it and change things if you are so moved. It's our responsibility as the spiritual leaders of our own families to become aware of what is working to bring us closer to God and what is not. It's extremely important to be open to seeking change and trying new things. You'll find that your family is spiritually energized by each shift.

I'd like to repeat here that, as is true for all suggested vehicles, this isn't meant to create added stress and pressure to your life. Do we eat dinner together and say our prayer every single night? Of course not. We too live in a busy world with meetings, sports practices, and music lessons. This is about keeping things fresh and opening the doors to go there with each other

A client recently decided to forego their usual family grace, which they felt was being recited without any particular attention, and sing *That's the Glory of Love* before dinner. Her three boys and husband have enthusiastically joined in. Their intention is to remain aware of the energy behind the words and change things as they go. They now ask three questions every night during dinner: What was the best part of your day? What was the most challenging aspect of your day? What is something kind that you can say about another member of our family?

when you *can*. No pressure, just a strong desire to create a spiritually active home life.

Another family ritual that we utilize is a loving reminder to walk in conscious awareness from me to each child before he or she ventures out into the larger world for school, sports practices, music lessons, or sleepovers. I remind them of their divine heritage. I use reminders of things that we've covered in our family discussions. I use our personal spiritual language. Our children have come to expect and relish these daily spiritual reminders. In fact, if I forget this little ritual, they remind me to send them off with a special message. I let my soul lead me in this area. These are not preplanned messages; I simply pass on whatever loving message pops into my head before I say farewell.

My Daily Spiritual Reminders

Expect the best today! My beloved teacher Sonia Choquette reflected this wisdom to me years ago. Absolutely, positively, expect the best. I want my children to take this literally. Train your mind to dismiss negative thoughts before they become embedded in your consciousness. The importance of optimism as an attracting force in life can be taught readily through your own words and actions. For young children to understand at an early age that thoughts are powerful threads of energy that greatly affect physical reality is an enormous step towards leading a spiritual life. Thoughts are creative in nature and should be monitored at all times. Awareness of thoughts, words, and deeds defines conscious living. "Expect the best today!" reminds children to be positive and expect the best that the Universe has to offer that day. They're reminded to take responsibility for the energy that they are offering the world.

Be open to the many surprises of your day! Be open to all possibilities, opportunities, and invitations that come your way. You never know how the answers you seek may enter your reality. My children understand that this means be flexible, trust the Universe, and listen to the voice of your own soul. Even though things may not go as planned, as they so often do not, know beyond all doubt that there is always another opportunity waiting in the wings to be acknowledged, appreciated, and embraced by you.

Ask for help! My children know that this means talk to God throughout the day. Talk to your soul. Talk to others. Tell the Universe what you want through your thoughts, words, and deeds. Know that you are never alone. In other words, keep the lines of communication with the spiritual realm continually open. The veil is thin. Help is always readily available. Know that you are loved, guided, and assisted in every moment of every day. The ultimate truth is that we are one with God, one with the spiritual realm, and one with all fellow human beings, and this connectedness provides us with an unlimited accessibility to assistance.

Share! This simple reminder is one that I use quite often with my children, reminding them to share not only materially, but emotionally as well. Share your energy, time, talents, love, compassion, kindness, and light with others. Choose to be generous of spirit easily and readily. Generosity of spirit immediately connects you more consciously to your own soul. A positive energy exchange between two people wakes you both up to your higher selves.

"Share" is such a small word that carries such enormous meaning. Teach your children how to share on all possible levels.

Remember your spirit today! This reminder helps them to remember the reality of who they really are. This is a reminder that they are in this world, but not of it. I remind them to let their spirit shine brightly without fear or apologies. Coming from a place of Spirit on a regular basis takes practice until it becomes an utterly natural way to view yourself and others. You can help your children make this shift by referring to their spirit, and yours, as often as you can.

Be forgiving! Yes, there are many things that come up which are upsetting and disappointing, but it is never beneficial, in any way, to hold onto negative energy. We teach our children that holding grudges ultimately closes their heart rather than expands it, and that this closing affects their health, both mentally and physically, not to mention greatly affecting the outcomes of their heart's desires. The message of all spiritual masters has been one of forgiveness. Clearly, the path that leads to forgiveness is the least arduous one to follow. We recognize that forgiveness may take a little time. It may take some effort to get your emotions turned back around. That's okay! We simply feel that forgiveness takes as much practice as any sport. If you can help your children learn how to forgive the small things that happen day in and day out, then down the road, it will make the bigger things that arise in life that much easier to overcome.

Express gratitude and appreciation! We feel that we cannot place enough importance on this in our family. Being grateful and appreciative of what's currently in your reality changes everything. Gratitude and appreciation are powerful manifestation tools that will change your life. Teaching your children to make gratitude and appreciation the lens through which they view the world delivers an incredible gift to them.

Love yourself today! No matter what comes into your experience, love yourself for being you. We must first honor ourselves if we are ever able to honor another. Sometimes it's far easier to treat someone else with more respect and devotion than we give to ourselves. Teach your children to treat themselves well, both internally and externally. It's okay to love yourself and to express that in any way that feels right for you. When you are filled with joy, love, and empowerment, your offerings to others will be of a much higher quality.

Be loose and flexible today! Relax and go with the divine flow of life. You live in a continuous stream of well-being whether you are conscious of it or not. It's always your choice to swim upstream against the current or swim easily downstream with the natural flow of life. Life is ever-changing and fluid; leading a spiritual life means being loose and flexible. Rigidity and the need to control outer conditions dampen your connection with the divine flow of life that is your birthright. Encourage your children to trust Spirit, trust life, and go with the natural energetic flow of the Universe.

As the spiritual leader of your own family, take the time to discover what spiritual rituals speak to you and your family. Take the time to determine what has meaning to you and yours. Listen to your inner voice and heed its call. There are thousands of spiritual traditions that you could choose to share with your children each day. Speak the same spiritual language every day. Over time, just like with anything else done on a regular basis, you will marvel at the organic shift that has taken place.

Soul to Soul
Parenting Vehicle
#7

The Intuitive-Gratitude Journal

Another wonderful way to integrate the Divine into your daily life is through keeping an Intuitive-Gratitude Journal. I refer to this as *The Voice of My Soul*. Some people may view the intuitive journal and gratitude journal as separate entities, but I've found the combination of the two to be most beneficial to me. All of my entries express gratitude and appreciation for *what is so* in one form or another. Currently I'm the only member of my family who writes in a journal throughout the day, but all of our children have a personal journal or a notebook of some kind in which to record their most personal thoughts and intimate feelings.

The Intuitive-Gratitude Journal is the place to record what comes through from your spirit. What are you *feeling*? Write down the intuitive hits, the spiritual guidance, the creative ideas, the insights into your life, and the tingly all-knowing moments that grace you with truth and understanding. Take note of the epiphany while out on that walk, the "aha" moment that hits you while folding the laundry, the information received during that "chance" meeting with a friend, the phone call that comes through with the *exact* answer you were looking for, the shift in perspective that occurred due to the movie you just watched, the creative idea that comes to you while lying in bed, the gut feeling that you get when you first meet someone, the hunch on a business deal, the first fleeting thought that comes to you in any situation, the synchronicities and divine winks that occur as gifts throughout your day. *All* of this counts! This is your soul co-creating with the Universe to guide you through your life. Notice it. Record it. Most importantly, be thankful for it. This is a place where I write out my heartfelt gratitude for all of the guidance coming through. It is here where I continually thank God for these divine gifts.

I keep a large notebook with dated entries going at all times, and I often carry it along with me outside the house. I also keep notepads and pens by my bed, in my car, in my coat pockets on long walks, and in the front satchel of my bike on rides. Once you start recording, you'll be amazed at how your soul is gently guiding you throughout your day. Recording breeds acknowledgement and appreciation, announcing to the Universe your intention to utilize the gifts offered. Keeping a journal like this one gets you into the practice of expecting and being grateful for spiritual guidance throughout your day. Each time you recognize the Universe at work, you open yourself up to a greater receptivity to receive more. Plan on hearing the voice of your soul each day—and you will.

Each time you recognize the Universe at work, you open yourself up to a greater receptivity to receive more. Plan on hearing the voice of your soul each day— and you will.

When my teacher Sonia Choquette first introduced me to the concept of keeping an intuitive journal going at all times, I was fascinated, but wasn't sure it was something that I could keep up in my daily life. I had kept a gratitude journal before, but this added a whole new component to that concept. Years later, as well as many, many full notebooks later, I realize just how much this practice cemented my belief that I was indeed an intuitive, spiritual being. Once you begin to pay attention to what is actually flowing to and through you each day in the form of sudden insights, synchronicities, and connections with others, it's impossible to ever go back to seeing the world in a less multidimensional way. I always tell my clients that this is one of the surest and fastest ways to jump-start your new perspective as a divine being connected to All That Is.

I find journaling very relaxing, rewarding, *and* fun. Writing brief snippets of consciousness throughout your day maintains a connection to your soul. When you take the time to write for longer periods, allowing for a full stream of consciousness to emerge, it can be a meditative act inviting a serene sense of well-being. I look forward to whenever I can rest for a few moments and record the voice of my soul. Much clarity, direction, and sense of purpose have been derived from journaling. This practice continually assists me with my inner work as I seek to uncover resistant threads in my energetic output. When you're in the flow of writing, you can often enter a place where you are "out of your head" which clears the space for your soul to come forth. Allow your pen to move freely across the paper without censoring your thoughts. This free-flowing stream of consciousness can offer tremendous insight into your life patterns. The result is a greater intimacy with Self. The love, appreciation, and acceptance flowing from this expanded intimacy can be life-altering. Writing opens the gateway to a grander perspective of you.

Soul to Soul
Parenting Vehicle
8

Imagination

The imagination is to be absolutely cherished as a sacred vehicle opening you to the nonphysical realm. Imagination is the gateway into your own divinity. It represents so much more than most people ever realize and should be utilized on a daily basis to allow God into your everyday reality. Imagination is the starting point for your creativity to manifest on the earth plane. Everything that is now visible to the naked eye first existed within the imagination. Bless imagination as it shows up within you. Encourage imagination in your children. Let your imagination soar and carry you to a place of spacious creativity.

It is in your imagination where you converse with God, and it is up to you, and only you, to trust what you're receiving.

When I was a young child, somehow I came to hold the erroneous belief that imagination was to be equated with being artistic. I'd imagine the most wonderful visions in my mind's eye, but then when it came time to put it on paper, so to speak, I would feel dreadfully inferior. Time and time again, I can remember walking into the classroom with my dream in hand, and upon surveying the other children's work, would instantly feel that my project was less than and not as good. In college, this feeling intensified when I was forced to share a self-portrait in my beginning painting class and received a poor grade. I've never been the most skillful artist in terms of drawing and painting, but that has nothing to do with the depths of my imagination. For years, I resisted my imagination, and I even came to distrust some of my creative ideas and was reluctant to share my ideas with others, thinking that I wasn't as creative as they were.

I have since come to realize that we all express our imagination in different ways. Shutting off your imagination shuts off your direct access to the unseen realm of Spirit. Techniques such as guided imagery and channeling have assisted me in regaining confidence in my own brilliant imagination. I am no longer resistant to my imagination, choosing instead to allow it to flow through me. I now choose purposefully to stretch myself in this way. Imagination is the home of your intuition. It is where the voice of your soul resides. It is in your imagination where you converse with God, and it is up to you, and only you, to trust what you're receiving.

I encourage all parents to help keep their children's imaginations activated. Explain to them that this is how they'll connect to the voice of their soul. Drawing, painting, writing, and many other acts are all creative endeavors that you can utilize to bring imagination forth, but they are not, in and of themselves, imaginative. It is your soul that houses this God-given gift, and then puts it into your mind. Learn to protect your imagination from self-doubt by expanding your ideas about what imagination truly is. Your imagination is infinite in its depth and scope, mirroring the Universe in which you live. Be highly conscious of what comes to you through your imagination and act on things that *feel* right to you deep in your soul, and teach your children to do the same.

Soul to Soul
Parenting Vehicle

#9

Meditation

To me, meditation is simply relaxing, breathing deeply, getting quiet, being still, and clearing away the endless mind chatter so that I can better hear the voice of my own soul. This voice is the subtle, pure, loving, gentle voice that often has a very difficult time getting through all of the loud mental debris, but which steers me always towards my true path. Sitting quietly for as little as ten minutes a day, without nonstop thought, can do wonders for your connection to the Divine. My thoughts don't always completely disappear, but I allow them to float by without attachment to them as something personal to me. I get out of my own way and let my spirit lead the slow, beautiful dance leading to greater intimacy with my own soul. The purpose of any spiritual practice is to become more intimate with your own soul and consciously connect with All That Is. Meditation is no different.

In the busy, loud world that now houses our modern-day existence, most of us rarely, if ever, sit in the void and do nothing. So much of what we value has to do with our accomplishments and productivity. This inclination to continually strive to achieve and succeed certainly doesn't exist solely in the workplace. Oftentimes, our own homes, the nests that are supposed to shield us somewhat from outside stresses, have become the busiest, loudest places of all. Doing nothing is almost taboo in our culture. Consider the possibility that downtime or doing nothing is actually *soul time,* and feel the shift in internal assessment that a pause in your day is indeed valuable. When do you access your deepest space? How do you activate the voice of your soul? Where do you feel an undeniable and unbreakable connection to All That Is? How do you allow feelings of infinite love and gratitude to bloom?

The answer to all of these questions is really rather simple and has been taught to us by all of the masters who have walked among us on this earth. You must take the time each and every day to go within. Going within and connecting to your inner being changes everything. It is in this quiet space that you come to know your true self. It is here where feelings of Oneness with God are born. Going within gives you back to yourself in a way that the outer world never can. It is here where you meet your soul.

I have found that meditating every day in one form or another is essential to my well-being. It's always such a relief to rest my mind. I meditate *everywhere!* While I may sit formally in the big comfy chair up in my bedroom with my eyes closed, I'm just as likely to sit on the lounge chair in my backyard for twenty minutes and pet my dog while basking in the sun. While I may choose to sit on the couch in my living room and stare at the beautiful oak tree outside of my window, I'm just as likely to walk down to Lake Michigan and sit on a bench and stare at the water. I'm open to *all* meditative experiences and view them as beautiful, purposeful pauses in my day.

Meditation is something that can integrate easily into your family's spiritual practice and provide your children with a gift for life.

Along with the sedentary meditative experiences mentioned above, I enjoy what I call an *active* meditation. Any type of physical activity is very meditative for me: a long walk, a bike ride, or dancing. These three forms of physical movement greatly quiet my mind and nurture my soul. They're all activities that I can do on my own, whenever I choose. In fact, while I love when the opportunity to dance presents itself anywhere and anytime in my life, I typically dance in this context alone in the annex of my bedroom. In the middle of the day when the mood strikes, I absolutely love turning on my music and allowing my body to move and flow in unison with musical vibration. What exhilarating freedom from my mind this gives me. Through all of these active endeavors, I root myself to the earth and connect to the spiritual realm at the same time. Exercise that you enjoy can free you from the ceaseless chatter of your mind and absolutely counts as an active meditation; a rejuvenation for your soul.

I've found that my meditation practice is uniquely and beautifully mine. As I say over and over again regarding all aspects of soul work, *nothing* has to look only one way. Like all spiritual practices, meditation is personal. Trust *your* meditative experiences. Let meditation look *your* way. Remain open; I cannot stress this enough. You will *know* where and when quiet and stillness come most easily for you. While I have taken formal meditation classes proving beneficial to my overall mediation practice, I've come to the conclusion that there is not one way to meditate, and meditation certainly doesn't have to be a big deal. Simply slow things down. Quiet the inner noise of your mind long enough to hear the beautiful voice of your soul. Lose yourself

A client of mine loves to get into bed at least fifteen minutes before her husband so that she can lie in the quiet dark of her bedroom and connect with her spirit. Another client chooses to meditate for ten minutes in bed before rising each morning. Make it a top priority to seek small slots of time in your day that work for you. Once you make it a priority, it becomes a treasured and all-important part of your day. It is in the quiet space where you open yourself to divine guidance that invites clear consciousness where creation resides at its best. The time spent meditating is not time on task lost. Meditation enhances all aspects of living an intentional life aligned with an internal creative power that far surpasses the power and creativity of the mind alone.

every day deep within yourself. Feel the ecstasy and bliss that come from being alone, totally alone, with you. For periods of time throughout your day, learn to release the worries, concerns, and judgments that clutter your mind and create a barrier to your own soul.

We have many family discussions on meditation so that our children understand the purpose for getting quiet and being still. Sometimes we end our family discussion with quiet meditation. An easy way for children to learn to meditate is to count four breaths in, hold four counts, and then release breath four counts out. Initially, the parent can help by repeating the counting in a slow, steady voice. You can also teach children to focus on their breath, a specific word such as *love* or *peace*, or on their favorite color. Too, looking directly at a specific object or the flame of a candle for ten minutes can be a wonderful starting point for the family as you begin a meditation practice together. Modeling a personal meditation practice on a regular basis for your children will greatly serve their understanding of the importance of quiet inner time devoted to their soul. Meditation is something that can integrate easily into your family's spiritual practice and provide your children with a gift for life.

Soul to Soul
Parenting Vehicle

#10

Conscious Breath

Conscious Breath is simply focusing attention on several deep breaths, bringing about an instantaneous reconnection with one's soul.

While very much related to meditation in our minds, I feel that Conscious Breath deserves its own section as an all-important contribution to an ever-expanding family spirituality. Yoga has greatly enhanced our understanding of the value of Conscious Breath. Conscious breathing only takes seconds and can be done throughout one's day to realign with the divine flow of life. Conscious Breath is simply focusing attention on several deep breaths, bringing about an instantaneous reconnection with one's soul. Placing focus on breath creates an automatic stillness in the mind, allowing for a space in which your awareness can once again reflect your undeniable, mystical connection to All That Is.

Teaching conscious breathing to children is a rather easy task, for breathing is something that we already do unconsciously twenty-four hours a day. Nobody needs to learn how to breathe; he just needs to train himself to be conscious of it. Conscious breathing becomes a tool for peace and calm in the mind, a most wonderful gift to give your children. Explain to children that they are breathing in love and peace, and breathing out worry and fear with each divine breath. Explain to them that each and every breath connects their soul to All That Is and reflects their own sacredness and divine nature.

I suggest first explaining Conscious Breath to your children and then practicing it together often. Also, frequently remind children to utilize this technique on a regular basis, especially when they are feeling over-whelmed or stressed. Invite them to consciously breathe anytime they are facing a difficult situation *before* they try to solve things using their mind. This is a spiritual practice which takes such little time, but which deems huge results. The more we consciously breathe, the more powerfully we feel the infinite and eternal awareness that lies in our deepest space.

Soul to Soul
Parenting Vehicle
11

Prayer Boxes, Vision Boards, and Blessing Bowls

To consciously realize and appreciate all that occurs in life for our benefit is truly magnificent for a family to behold together.

There are many ways to create *physically* in your home a specific means of communicating with the Divine Presence. Prayer boxes, vision boards, and blessing bowls are but a few which promote familial spiritual interaction on a regular basis. They each provide an opportunity to outwardly and inwardly ask God for assistance. They enliven our heart's desires, our prayers, and our gratitude to a more tangible level. These spiritual vehicles also incorporate family sharing in a beautiful way. Just one or all of these methods may be utilized to enhance a feeling of daily remembering in the home.

We created a prayer box for our family altar. One Saturday we went to an art-supply store and bought a special box and art materials and came home and decorated our prayer box together. We created a wonderful little box for our family's prayers. This is a place where one can write down a special prayer, put it into the box, and place the prayer into God's hands. Every few months we go through the box together during a family discussion and see which prayers have been answered. You will be absolutely amazed at the different ways in which prayers have been answered in each person's life. To consciously realize and appreciate all that occurs in life for our benefit is truly magnificent for a family to behold together.

The prayer box provides the opportunity for children to listen to the voice of their soul and dialogue with God. Just recently we read aloud the prayers in our prayer box and discovered that our middle child had written a prayer about each member of our family and tucked them deep inside. Each prayer thanked God for that family member by highlighting what that individual offers to not only our family, but to the world at large. Her insight into each of our gifts was astounding. She ended each prayer asking for a round of applause for that person, creating a truly memorable family discussion for the whole family.

Remember, the prayer box, like all other spiritual practices in the home, isn't a rigid thing to add to your "to do" list. It's never been made into a big deal in our house; it's just something personal and beautiful that we share. Sometimes our prayer box is overflowing with prayers, and we share all of the prayers as our family discussion that week and then start over. At other times, it remains empty until someone is moved to write down another prayer. We may decide to write prayers at the end of a family discussion. The Universe is fluid and flexible. It is not coercive and demanding, and it certainly isn't rigid. The prayer box is simply a joyful way to pray and share one's prayers with others.

Vision boards have become an extremely popular means of utilizing the Law of Attraction to create your heart's desire. We discussed the validity of vision boarding during a family discussion and then created our own vision boards on two cloth-covered bulletin boards. One is a family vision board, integrating all of our dreams as a whole, and the other is my own personal vision board representing my growth and empowerment. Our vision boards are located near the back door and in full view each time we enter our home from that direction.

Anything can be placed on a vision board. The idea is to envision your dreams, to consciously express your dreams using words and pictures, and to live your dreams in your everyday reality so as to manifest it into existence. *All* possibilities already exist within the divine presence that is this Universe. It's a matter of you creating enough sustainable energy *around* the possibility to pull it into your current reality. It is a matter of you matching your energetic vibration, created by your emotions and internal beliefs, with the energetic vibration of your desires. All of the masters who have ever walked this planet have understood this truth. Vision boards are an easy way to begin seeing yourself as a powerful co-creator who is driving the bus that is your life within the most adoring, loving, and creative Universe imaginable.

Our family utilized magazines, newspapers, fliers, cereal boxes, photos, and our own creative writings and drawings to create our vision boards. Once you get started, it's amazing what will catch your eye as a symbol for your current journey and future path. You begin to view yourself from an expanded vantage point while opening up to a vast new array of possibilities. In and of themselves, vision boards won't *magically* do anything; but they can be *activated* by your creative power and vision and serve as a continual reminder that you are all-powerful and worthy co-creators with God. Allow yourselves to become extraordinarily inspired and joyful while creating your vision boards. While creating ours, I felt Spirit with us, enthusiastically guiding us to live wider and love ourselves deeper.

Blessing bowls can be used in the same way. They provide the opportunity to offer physical, mental, and emotional energy towards what you desire to create in your life. Simply find a big, beautiful bowl that feels right for your family and begin. Write down the ways in which you desire to be blessed by Spirit and place them into the bowl. Acknowledge the ways that you are *already* blessed by Spirit and also place those into the bowl. Set the blessing bowl in an area of your home that's highly visible so that all family members can be reminded each day to *count their blessings,* so to speak. Activate this bowl through your touch. Pass it around in a family circle during a family discussion, blessing and acknowledging it as a sacred piece within your family. Ask God to utilize this bowl to communicate with your family. The blessing bowl, just like the prayer box and vision board, can be a beautiful portal to the unseen realm. Allow God to enter your reality in as many ways as possible. God is always there, for we are a part of God; it's just that we often don't recognize this as we move through our day in tune only with our personality.

The most important aspect of all three of these techniques is gratitude. We write our prayers and heart's desires with the strong feeling that we are already blessed beyond measure. There's a level of belief, deep within us, that the Universe has already answered us. In other words, it is the inner belief that we live in a divine, loving, all-knowing, creative, ever-expanding, limitless, infinite Universe that enables us to co-create with it. Prayer boxes, vision boards, and blessing bowls, in and of themselves, have no power. It is your energy, your faith, and your creative force that travels through them and announces your desire to manifest your dreams.

> The more readily you imagine your desires through touch, sight, hearing, and smell, the more easily they manifest into your current reality. Use these tools as a family-wide connection to God. Let the Universe know, beyond a shadow of a doubt, that all family members are ready, willing, and able to receive, consciously and gratefully, what the Universe has to offer.

Soul to Soul
Parenting Vehicle
 # 12

Music

Music has always been such a tremendous gift in my life, and I've found that it can be a *fantastic* way to connect to your soul. Many of us know this intuitively, if not consciously, and this is why so many of us enjoy music in our lives on a daily basis. I love this quote from the movie *August Rush*: "Music is the harmonic vibration that connects all living things." This description of music gave me my divine flow energy feeling because I feel that truth deeply within my own soul. Much has been written about the transcendental quality which music evokes in human beings. It's a wonderful way to infuse spirituality into family life.

I grew up in a family that listened to all different genres of music together on a regular basis. When it was time to clean the house on a

Saturday morning, the music went on to make it more joyful. Car trips evoke fond memories of both singing along together to favorite tunes *and* sitting quietly with my own thoughts as I felt a vibration that touched my heart and stirred my soul. Today much of my divine inspiration and intuitive knowledge come to me while listening to music. Long walks and private times in my car or home listening to music have proven to be most beneficial to my spirit.

In our family discussions, both planned and spontaneous, music *and* dancing play a major role. We often discover God together right there in the words of a great song on the radio. We feel moved, and we share those feelings. Music can be a daily way to connect with your children, for most children regularly listen to and enjoy music. Songwriters are poets, and they provide wonderful fodder for deeper conversation with each other. It continues to amaze me that the exact words that I needed to hear to reconnect me to my own soul to find answers and feel joy often come to me, without any effort, through music. Begin to listen more carefully to what it is you might need to hear. Lyrics and/or the vibration of music can be gifts from God coming to you at just the right time.

I believe in music so much as a portal to the nonphysical realm that I often utilize it in workshops. I invite participants to close their eyes and breathe in as they allow their soul to slow-dance with God in their own

We've based many family discussions on music. One discussion in particular that stands out in my mind was a tribute to the 1970s Stephanie Mills song *I Never Knew Love Like This Before*. For some reason, this song always touches my soul. During this particular family discussion, we decided to sit together quietly in our living room and play this song through twice. Each of us sat with eyes closed and really listened to the words and felt the cascading music. Afterwards, each person shared how that song made him feel. My husband shared that he felt tremendous unconditional love for all of us, his precious family. He never knew that he could love four other human beings so much. Our children shared their thoughts on love and how this song made them feel as well. Then I shared that it had finally hit me why this song moves me so much. Until spiritually awakening, I never knew that God could love me this much. This song opens me to receiving love—a love that I now feel from the Universe each and every day, changing my life. It has expanded my capacity to love myself, and all others, more fully. This old song from the disco era helped us to uncover deeper feelings and truths that lay within us, exemplifying one of the infinite number of ways to connect more intimately with your own soul.

unique way. It's an amazing spiritual tool to use with the whole family. Invite your children to share songs that touch *their* soul during family discussions. We encourage our children to move through their day knowing that God is *always* speaking to them in *all* ways. Are they listening? Are we as parents listening?

Soul to Soul
Parenting Vehicle

13

> *Movies provide wonderful openings for lively family discussions.*

Movies

Like many families, we enjoy watching movies together on a fairly regular basis. Knowing that God can be found everywhere, I always look for universal life messages while watching movies. They can be excellent jump-starts for family discussions, and children are usually very interested in analyzing a movie together as a family. Pay attention to the many spiritual themes that come to light as you enjoy films.

After watching *Forrest Gump* together one Friday night, I knew that we would discuss aspects of this movie at our next family discussion. Forrest Gump, as a character, is all about soul to soul. He doesn't care about your physical appearance or your status in society. He treats everyone with the same respect. He sees others as human beings, plain and simple, without layers of judgment or superficial validations. Forrest Gump *really* sees others as valid and worthy, and his life reflects right back to him his naturally expanded perspective. It is his *lack* of reliance on his mind and ego that enables him to see clearly. Our children thoroughly enjoyed this discussion and were able to discern many ways that Forrest modeled spiritual attributes that we would all do well to emulate. There are many protagonists and themes in high-quality movies today that may also embody some of the spiritual qualities and themes that you're currently discussing with your children.

Movies provide wonderful openings for lively family discussions. Our family recently saw the blockbuster movie *Avatar*. We remained transfixed throughout the entire film as the realization that this movie speaks our spiritual language overcame us. The poignant, yet larger-than-life message emphasizing the energetic connectedness among all living creatures captivated us. We left the theater feeling awe at the infinite potential a movie like this has to reach the world at large to inspire and teach oneness.

Soul to Soul
Parenting Vehicle

14

Books

I simply cannot say enough about how much books in general, but specifically spiritual books, have changed my perspective and my life. I have a collection of well over 200 spiritual books that are truly my most prized possessions. They have come to represent my spiritual journey over the past twenty years.

When we first moved to our current house, I was very busy with our three young children and didn't have any time to read my beloved books. For many months, they were kept in boxes down in the basement. I was focusing on more earthly endeavors such as changing diapers and getting dinner on the table at a decent hour. But one day, after we'd been in our new home for almost nine months, I knew in my soul that it was time to bring those books back into the light of day. I remember feeling total joy and peace as I carried the boxes upstairs and lovingly placed each book on the bookshelf by my desk. It was on that very day that I knew the time had come to pursue my spiritual journey with gusto once again. My books were back, and I was ready to fly.

I've often said to my husband that if anything should ever happen to me, the only thing that I care about passing along to our children is my collection of spiritual books. In having those, along with my Intuitive-Gratitude Journals, they would most accurately have a written memory of who I was and what woke me up to the glory of All That Is.

Books offer an unprecedented opportunity to assist you in carving out your own path up the mountaintop to God.

I have always simply wanted my children to have an open door into the unseen, yet deeply felt aspects of life if they should so choose to explore it. I know that my greatest gift to my children will always be having provided them the opportunity and the encouragement to embark on a spiritual journey and walk consciously as spirit-embodied on the physical plane.

I encourage you to utilize the many wonderful spiritual books for both children and adults that are available today. I encourage you to use *all* books in every single genre if they speak to your soul. It is no longer my perspective that we live in a time of only one book and only one master. Today, as has always been, we are being invited to become masters *ourselves* and emulate the Christ Consciousness and Buddha Within, the divine presence *within* us that masters consciously embody. There's a wealth of knowledge to be found in modern literature as to how this can be achieved. Share these books with your family. Read whole books or passages aloud together. Read novels that explore universal life themes by interweaving them into the plot and characterizations. Books offer an unprecedented opportunity to assist you in carving out your *own* path up the mountaintop to God.

Most homes have books that can be used for more than just the joy of individual reading. Even if family members are reading their own solitary books, family discussions can be a time when each person brings her book and shares one theme running through it relating in some way to an expanded understanding of life.

We recently read aloud together a chapter book by Jerry Spinelli called *Star Girl*. It was an absolute joy. We kept Star Girl's authenticity and light with us throughout each week as we waited to see what would evolve next in the book. Star Girl, the protagonist who shares her spirit openly and freely with others, still comes up sometimes when one of us has really given herself permission to elevate her joy to new heights. These moments are now "Star Girl" moments for us, reminding us to live true to our unique potential, preferences, and passions.

Soul to Soul
Parenting Vehicle

#15

Art

All forms of art can be used to connect children consciously to their spiritual nature. Explain to children what happens as they allow their spirit to express itself freely while engaging in artistic endeavors. Encourage freedom from rigidity and perfection as your children allow their own imaginations to soar. Provide the space and the opportunity for unlimited artistic expression. Art enables many children, and adults alike, to feel deeply connected to their soul.

Art enables many children, and adults alike, to feel deeply connected to their soul.

I suggest not only plentiful opportunities for all art forms in your home, but also using art activities to enhance or be the main focus of family discussions. Young children can oftentimes more easily express their deeper understandings by creating a picture. In a young family, talking may be kept to a minimum while drawing feelings and interpretations of spiritual themes works best. Of course, individuals of all ages can participate, too, enjoying the space and the time to express their soul in this way.

Family mosaics can be created on large boards added to at the end of a family discussion. Each tile can represent the theme for that week, with individual family members taking turns being the artist. Active journaling can also be incorporated as a means of expressing individual and/or family spirituality. An active journal utilizes freeform writing, drawing, collages, lyrics, poetry, and so much more to artistically express aspects of one's spirit. Each family member can keep his own active journal or a larger active journal can be kept where individuals can contribute after family discussions or at any time throughout the week.

All artistic expressions including music, movies, books, dance, opera, art, symphony, and stage are wonderful avenues through which to evoke in a family its spiritual nature. Explore these offerings together in a myriad of ways. There are no limits as to what can be discovered and explored when opening one's self up to artistic expression. Art has connected human beings more deeply to their inner space since

> Working with clay is extremely relaxing and grounding, and can be done while holding a family discussion to keep everyone involved and actively engaged. The whole family sitting around the kitchen table, moving clay around in their hands while sharing thoughts and insights about life is an extremely peaceful way to hold a family discussion.

the beginning of time. Begin to learn what art forms speak in a soulful way to you, and then share your insights and findings with your family as you help them assess what forms of art speak intimately to their soul.

Soul to Soul
Parenting Vehicle
#16

Role-play assists children in accepting that their truth is not necessarily the truth of another.

Role-Play

Role-play can be an excellent way to teach spiritual themes to children. We utilize role-play spontaneously in our family as an important tool to use while teaching children about the role that relationships play in our ever-evolving spiritual expansion. Relationships provide daily, hourly opportunities to spiritually evolve. When analyzed and discussed, you can often see the larger aspect of different roles in any given situation. For this reason, differences in perception and perspective are a frequent discussion in our home. We act out another's point of view in the hopes that we'll gain insight as to his perceptions and intentions, thereby leading us to a deeper, more purposeful understanding of life experiences shared with that individual.

Teaching your children to put themselves in another's shoes always opens the door for soul expression and growth. A conscious family understands that you each view the physical world through your own lens and that this lens determines to a large extent how you individually perceive the world. Role-play assists children in accepting that their truth is not necessarily the truth of another.

Your children will learn about relationships, different life perspectives, tolerance, joy, forgiveness, and many other spiritual themes through role-play. It's proven to be an extremely effective and expansive tool in our family. We greatly enjoy this time spent together often including much laughter and fun.

Soul to Soul
Parenting Vehicle

17

Make-Her-Day Moments

This wonderful family spiritual game started one morning at a family restaurant in Eagle River, Wisconsin. It was a cold winter morning in February, and the five of us were sharing a delightful, leisurely breakfast together. We were all filled with joy and peace that morning (no squabbling over who sat where) and feeling extremely grateful, and we began to speak openly of our many blessings. All of a sudden, out of nowhere, upon seeing our waitress move around the restaurant, I started quietly chanting, "Make her day! Make her day!" The family giggled and then joined me. I explained that I really wanted to tip our adorable, friendly waitress double what she'd be expecting. We all agreed, and we again began to quietly chant to ourselves, "Make her day! Make her day!" The meal ended, and we left a 40 percent tip on the table and quietly left the restaurant. We laughed and felt absolutely elated as we rode away in our car.

With Make-Her-Day Moments, you consciously choose to extend yourself to another.

It became clear that this was the beginning of something dear to our family.

When the feeling overtakes one of us, we know that it's time to join in and partake in something good for another soul. It could be paying the person's toll in the car behind us, letting someone move ahead of us in the grocery store line, or offering to help a neighbor carry bags into her house. So far our gestures have been "small," but we know that size is not what matters here. With Make-Her-Day Moments, you consciously choose to extend yourself to another. It's the joyous dance of consciousness uplifting all individuals involved. A camaraderie and revelry envelops your family, infusing all with love and laughter; and hopefully, touches others in meaningful ways, too.

Soul to Soul
Parenting Vehicle

#18

Crank Up the Joy

> We always have the capacity within us to reach deep inside for more joy.

Crank up the joy has become a mantra in our family. It captures our desire to live a spirited life together in a spiritual way. Those words are an instant reminder to all family members to step out of ego and into spirit. No matter what is occurring in the external world, one always has the option to breathe deeply, appreciate life, and crank up the joy, even if it's just a little bit. We always have the capacity within us to reach deep inside for more joy.

Resisting joy can be an easy pattern to fall into, especially with those whom we share the daily tasks of living. We often feel that we have so much to accomplish in our daily lives that we actually forget how to be joyful. We've found that *Crank up the joy* is the perfect reminder to embrace life in whatever form it's being reflected back to us in a more open, relaxed, and joyful way. After all, when has feeling more joy ever been a negative experience?

Through your example, teach your children to seek out more reasons to feel joyful each day. Loosen up and allow true joy to well up from within and infuse your relationships and life experiences. Feeling and expressing joy are imperative to your overall well-being, and joy is often contagious. As spiritual leaders of your family, it's important to be a role model for every aspect of the spiritual journey being shared, and joy is no exception. Sing while you make dinner, dance as you leave a great movie, join your children on the swings at the park, hum while folding laundry, laugh out loud at the silly aspects of life more frequently, give bear hugs, spontaneously change your plans, or simply smile a lot more often throughout your day. The more felt and expressed joy the better!

Soul to Soul
Parenting Vehicle

19

Speak the Language

Speaking the same spiritual language is one of the surest and fastest ways to expand spiritual awareness in your home. Like anything else, you must release what you're currently holding in your hand to reach for something higher. Let the words and ideas that arise from the family discussions become your new language. Seek to weave the spiritual themes into daily conversation. Explore life experiences that come your way in a more spiritual context. Search for the deeper spiritual meanings behind life circumstances. View relationships with others as your greatest teachers. Be open to the underlying opportunities for growth with each disappointment. Look for new beginnings in the folds of failure. Discuss making the higher choice in any given situation.

As you begin to see the world from a more spiritual perspective, *speak* this perspective, too. Share with one another the epiphanies, the vibes, the gut feelings, and the divine flow energy moments. Consciously analyze choices, beliefs, and perspectives in an open forum of truth. Decide together whether or not your current paradigm serves your soul or your ego. Speak truth in a language that you all understand rather than deny, stuff down, or hide from what's showing up in your shared reality.

Speaking the same spiritual language on a daily basis in your home amplifies the realization that you are all integral parts of a divine whole.

Our family refers to universal life themes in our everyday conversations. Our spiritual beliefs are infused into every aspect of our lives. No matter what we're discussing, we acknowledge that there's a much broader perspective available to us if we are only willing to look at it. We understand that there's always much more to every experience than what meets the eye. We give ourselves permission to draw support and insight from the unseen realm.

Changing the way you speak to one another to a way that more accurately reflects the core beliefs of who you *really* are changes everything. It is what makes the spiritual transformation within a family real. Your actions stem from your words, which stem from your thoughts, which stem from your beliefs. Speaking the same spiritual language on a daily basis in your home amplifies the realization that you are all integral parts of a divine whole. Conscious use of a more soul-based language in your home clearly articulates your spirituality and helps to make it the family's own.

Soul to Soul
Parenting Vehicle

#20

Show Your Spirit

Dance, sing, play, and swing with your children. Get silly together. Be *giddy* with one another. Call your spirit up! Open the gateway for your spirit to fully express itself. Come out with your real self. Live true. Let your children *see* the artist in you, the dancer in you, the gardener in you, the empathizer in you, the fire starter in you, the Broadway star in you, the best friend in you, the teacher in you, the nature lover in you, the

> *Open the gateway for your spirit to fully express itself.*

entrepreneur in you, the student in you, the minister in you, the healer in you, and the lover of life in you. Allow them to get to know your true self, your authentic self, and your higher self. This is your soul expressing itself. Show your children your spirit. If not now, when?

Showing your spirit liberates your children, as they get older, to show theirs. It frees them to live their lives as flowing, playful, creative, beautiful spirits. Be a role model in this area. Live life full-out without fear of what others think of you. Become comfortable in your own skin. Dance in the light together *now*. Crank up the music while cleaning up the house together now. Show each other your best dance moves now. Enjoy your favorite foods together now. Smile and laugh *a lot* now. Live a spirited life together as much as possible!

Soul to Soul
Parenting Vehicle

#21

Intimacy

It was Dante who said, "Hell is proximity without intimacy." When I first contemplated his words, it struck me how absolutely true they are. I can think of almost nothing sadder than being in a marital or familial relationship where one truly desires emotional and physical intimacy, but where none exists. To be proximally close to another human being, but share no sense of connectedness, is extremely painful to the soul. Spiritual beings long for connectedness with others of like kind.

As the spiritual leader of your own family, promoting and exemplifying intimacy within the family is an important calling. Being with others in your family in intimate ways allows God to move through you and touch the other individual. Share openly with one another. Touch one another in loving ways. Look deep into another's eyes. Express gratitude for another's very existence. Participate fully in another's life. Really see another's soul essence. Make soul to soul connection a top priority in your family.

After visiting a close friend and her family for a week, I came home realizing fully, for the first time, how differently we all live in regard to levels of intimacy in our relationships, especially relationships within our own family. My friend and I had spent the week engaging in many deep talks about our marriages, friendships, and children. I realized that we each expect and allow specific levels of intimacy in our lives. What seems "normal" for one individual may seem quite lonely for another. Every relationship that we create has the potential to be supremely intimate, mildly intimate, or not intimate at all. I feel that it is important to become increasingly attuned to your own personal desire for intimacy.

Encourage your children to embrace intimacy in their relationships with themselves, with you, and with others.

This involves analyzing relationships and really examining your capacity for intimacy within each one. Allowing deeper levels of intimacy in your relationships with others beckons you to live more intimately with Spirit, and ultimately, with yourself. Encourage your children to embrace intimacy in their relationships with themselves, with you, and with others.

Soul to Soul
Parenting Vehicle

#22

Nature

Nature is so vast and so important to your spiritual awareness that it can serve as an external bridge to your internal world. Nature is both a vehicle and a spiritual theme in that there is no greater outward expression of God than nature itself. The easiest and fastest way to access your inner feelings about God while being fully awake and present in your physical world is to explore and deeply experience nature.

Our time on earth is exquisite in its natural beauty and wonder. As a family, utilize what lies before and around you to access your own divinity.

No matter where you live, the natural wonders of your physical world are apparent and available for you to perceive in new ways. You interact with nature all the time, but the question is whether or not you do so consciously, with a deep acknowledgement of its relationship to you. As you observe nature in a highly present state, on some level you understand that you are observing God. You sense an underlying, unseen connection between human beings, nature, and All That Is. This connection is absolutely undeniable to an open heart and a receiving soul.

In early times, it was much easier for human beings to connect with nature because its beauty and magic could not be missed; we were connected with the rhythms and cycles of nature due to our living conditions. As our surroundings have become more artificial, we must realize that the essence of nature rests within us and can be felt at all times no matter where we stand. We can derive power from walking barefoot outside *or* by understanding the internal threads of the Universe that exist within all living things.

Our time on earth is exquisite in its natural beauty and wonder. As a family, utilize what lies before and around you to access your own divinity. Nature exists as the primary external window to perceive the truth of your own identity. Cherish every aspect of nature that touches your life. Appreciate the surroundings and creatures with which you *chose* to inhabit this planet at this point in time. Really pay attention to the current of life coursing through all living things; feel the life force in each and every one. Notice your connection to your physical surroundings and bask in the grace, beauty, energy, and life experiences that they provide.

Go outside with your family and engage your five senses in physical, earthly contact as often as possible. Touch, smell, see, taste, and hear nature as it calls to you. As you interact with nature on the physical plane and relax into its arms, begin to listen to the voice of your soul. What lies in the deeper folds of the interaction? Where does your coexistence with nature meet underneath and mesh as one? Allow your inner senses full, open access to the garden. As you feel peace and harmony with nature, you allow the seeds of peace and harmony to cultivate in your very own soul. Encourage your children to join you and teach them to acknowledge and appreciate the divinity of all living things in the natural world.

Every flower, every tree, every squirrel, every deer, every blade of grass, every snowflake, every platypus, every mountain, every pond, every sunrise, every butterfly, every acorn, every raindrop, every season, every birth, and every death hold within them the moment of your blessed awakening. They all reflect back to you your own miraculous, glorious true state of being. Nature is the largest, most wide-open gateway to the spiritual realm that exists in this space/time dimension in which we live.

Summary of 22 Soul to Soul Parenting Vehicles

These vehicles represent a family's methods for inviting a higher consciousness into their life together. The spiritual practices that become integrated into your lives will always be wonderfully and uniquely your own. Every family is a divine matrix in and of itself meant to evolve spiritually in its own special way. It is an organic process that slowly develops over a period of years. *Feel* on a soul level what works for you and yours. Hold hands and gracefully take a leap of faith together into the unseen, yet deeply felt and absolutely knowable realm of Spirit. Remember that it is your relationships with other human beings, specifically within your family, that are meant to be your greatest teachers and act as the best possible vehicle for exploring your spiritual nature. Create a new spirituality that exists to be expressed solely through your beloved family. Use what interests your children in the physical world to weave a greater spiritual consciousness into all that they do.

Integrate It into Your Own Family!

Parent Contemplations:

- Make notes about each vehicle. Which vehicles are you currently utilizing? Which most excite you? Which feel like the best fit for your family? Why?

- Which ideas offered feel like the easiest to implement into your daily family life?

- Introduce each vehicle during family discussions. Listen to input from your children. Which ones would they like to explore and implement as a family? Why?

- How can you adapt or enhance the vehicles to make them your own? Are there any new ideas that you can add to the offered vehicles?

Part Three

....

Soul to Soul Parenting
Spiritual Themes

Soul to Soul
Parenting
S p i r i t u a l   T h e m e s

....

This section introduces the reader to the core curriculum of this book: the prospect of threading large, universal spiritual themes throughout the family structure so that all family members can contemplate life experiences from a spiritual perspective. Each theme can represent a dynamic and integral strand of the family's spirituality and can be related to a variety of relationships and life experiences. Parents are encouraged to tap into their own intuitive wisdom to decide how the vehicles detailed in the previous chapter and these spiritual themes will be incorporated to best meet the spiritual needs of their own family.

You'll see that the themes merge with one another in a beautiful way, as they interrelate with one another on many different levels. They're meant to broaden perspectives so that life can be viewed from multiple angles, allowing the interconnectedness of all things to be felt and observed. One can explore as far and wide as she desires with each of these themes. There are no limits. There are an infinite number of ways that they can be explained, explored, expanded, and shared. There's no one *right* way to open up to a shared family spiritual practice, only what feels right to those having the courage to contemplate life at this depth at any given time.

The themes aren't presented according to an order in which they should be introduced. These themes are shared simply as a presentation of the spiritual ideas that have been included in our family's spiritual practice and should be seen as *possibilities* that can be utilized in any way that one chooses. Whether or not each theme is a perfect fit for your family's evolving spirituality is not an issue. Some themes will clearly speak to you and call you lovingly towards them, and others will not.

Either way, the family spiritual practice expands and grows. Identifying spiritual concepts that *don't* feel right is just as important as identifying those that do.

I encourage parents to utilize the suggested activities, books, movies, and songs if desired. Trust yourself to know what, when, where, and how they will best serve you and your family. Use what stirs your soul, touches your spirit, and delights you. It is always the *feeling* that captures the soul and inspires. Soul to Soul messages come in many, many packages.

Sharing spiritual themes with your family is simply experiencing life together, consciously.

It's about being awake to what resides inside of you, and then taking the time to share your truth with the ones you love.

All family members are encouraged to awaken from auto-pilot and view life from a more expansive lens rather than from merely an ego-centered perspective.

•••••••••••••

Chapter 4

Soul to Soul Parenting *Spiritual Theme*
Soul to Soul Versus Role to Role

*W*hen I first heard these words while participating in a workshop, I immediately *felt* the meaning. Isn't this what we all truly desire—to be fully seen, heard, and acknowledged; to be accepted and loved to our core. It is the deepest, most pure part of us that we really want the world to know and accept without judgment, even if many of us are too afraid to allow it. We all intuitively know that the most meaningful relationships in our lives are the ones in which we allow our inner selves to emerge and engage with the other in an intimately carved out space.

Teaching your children to see individuals from a Soul to Soul perspective is probably the most important and far-reaching spiritual wisdom that you can give your children. Everything else stems from this expanded view of humanity. The Soul to Soul perspective is a spiritual leap which will transform your life. Soul to Soul is a shift in perception that forever alters the lens through which you see the world. This perspective invites you to fully acknowledge another's validity, no matter what you may think of the human identity they're currently expressing. It encourages you to see and hear *beyond* appearances and words. Humanity takes on a whole new meaning due to this one change of vision and heart.

Shift your perceptive gears so that your soul, and the soul of another, is your first consideration in all relationships and life situations. *I see you, and you are a beloved and integral part of this Universe* becomes a felt vibration emanating directly from you to all others.

The essence of who you *really* are is a most beautiful, divine, loving, eternal, intuitive, creative, unlimited, formless spirit. You are actually a soul made of God's divine essence. You are literally a magnificent, mind-blowing, vibrating field of energy. As I sit in wonderment observing human beings, I can *see* that. Most importantly, I can *feel* it. Remind your children of who they *really* are every chance you get. Create a family where the normal mode of interaction is Soul to Soul, not Role to Role.

When you see *all* others as souls first, in *every* interaction, the nature of the interaction totally shifts. It immediately becomes more loving, nurturing, understanding, compassionate, forgiving, joyful, and authentic. From this perspective, it can be no other way. You create relationships that are truly conscious and real, where the energy exchange between two individuals has a higher potential to be positively charged.

Soul to Soul is your natural way of interacting, whether you recognize this consciously or not. In the nonphysical realm, this is the only way; for there is no physical body; there is no ego. It's only Soul to Soul. On a deep level within, most of us understand that there is much more to human beings than meets the eye. Jesus, Buddha, Mother Theresa, Gandhi, the Dalai Lama, Martin Luther King, and many, many others perceived the world from a Soul to Soul perspective, as they consciously understood the truth of our collective divinity. There are many wonderful teachers walking among us today, speaking in modern terms, giving us this same message again and again, hoping and praying that we will finally heed its call. The shift is simply a choice in making the Soul to Soul perspective no longer an outer religious concept, but an inner spiritual experience that becomes your everyday reality.

The Soul to Soul perspective is not a sort of, kind of, for one hour on Sundays type of thing. Practice it daily. Put Soul to Soul reminders on

> It's not really parent to child...it's Soul to Soul!
>
> It's not really teacher to student...it's Soul to Soul!
>
> It's not really grocery store cashier to customer...it's Soul to Soul!
>
> It's not really doctor to patient...it's Soul to Soul!
>
> It's not really lawn care worker to client...it's Soul to Soul!
>
> It's not really neighbor to neighbor...it's Soul to Soul!

your bathroom mirror, on your steering wheel, on your desk, and on your bedside table. Place these reminders in highly visible spots throughout your day until they are no longer needed. Take the time to really *see* people. *Feel* their presence. Feel their magnificence and divinity. Make it utterly natural to view yourself and all others from this perspective. Begin to look inside of another individual rather than simply viewing them from a surface perspective. Begin to recognize your own soul essence first, and then recognize this same essence in others. Always look for the soul in every interaction.

I had my first conscious Soul to Soul experience while walking alone listening to music on a beautiful spring day. From the outset of the walk, I felt very connected to my soul, feeling extremely grateful for my blessed life and connected to All That Is. About thirty minutes into the walk, I happened to look over at a lawn care worker maintaining someone's lawn. As I observed him at work, an overwhelming sense of Oneness, my divine flow energy feeling, overcame me. My heart beat faster; I felt breathless; my whole body tingled; I was unable to form words, and I began to cry softly. I felt deep love for this other human being who appeared to be quite different from me in earthly terms. I knew in that moment that he and I were simply different aspects of the same whole; that we each reflected different aspects of divinity. I knew in that moment that we were made up of the exact same sacred essence. I knew in that moment, without a doubt, that God flowed through him, flowed through me, and connected us both in the space in-between. I felt, in my own body, the universal hologram existing in all living things. I experienced a knowing that I am in all things and all things are in me. In that moment, I felt the truth that separation from God and separation from all living things are but an illusion.

That moment was truly magical for me, and it represents the beginning of my Soul to Soul shift. Time stood still and space evaporated as I experienced my core truth. I now recognize this as a mystical experience. These divine flow energy moments of truth and Oneness that always create in me the same feelings of breathlessness, tingling body, accelerated cellular vibration, and tears of joy have gifted me with the most acute feelings of ecstasy I have ever known. Actually, looking back, these physical signs of deep Soul to Soul recognition have occurred throughout my life, but I never understood their spiritual meaning. I understand now who I really am so can therefore, more readily and easily see this universal truth in others. Once the shift from Role to Role to Soul to Soul has been activated completely, your energetic vibration accelerates to such a state more and more frequently and for prolonged periods. It is simply who you are and how you view the world. It becomes your natural state of being and no longer feels paranormal. Everything, and I mean everything, looks different from this perspective.

Keep in mind that Soul to Soul is not about baring your soul to everyone you meet. It's not about placing the needs of others before your own. This perspective is not about having no boundaries or becoming a doormat. In fact, it requires you to speak your truth, but in a different way. This shift in reality is about consciously, in your heart, recognizing others as spirit-embodied.

Initially, for weeks I *practiced* seeing other individuals as souls. On my desk at home, I kept track of one full month where I made this new way of viewing all individuals an ingrained aspect of my reality. I would sit in my car in the preschool pick-up line, sit on a bench at the park, or walk through the grocery store and view *every* individual who walked past me as a divine soul. When practiced enough, "ordinary" human beings begin to appear differently to you; they become extraordinary extensions of All That Is.

One of our first official family discussions was based on a children's spiritual book called *Little Soul and the Sun*. We'd read it to our children many times before, but this time, we read aloud together with a new energy, knowing beforehand that we would analyze it together as our family discussion on this particular day.

Little Soul and the Sun by Neale Donald Walsch, best-selling author of the *Conversation with God* books, is a beautiful story about remembering who you truly are and forgiveness. The central message is the belief that God has sent nothing but angels. In other words, we are all angels in disguise.

To recap briefly this wonderful story, a beautiful soul has a conversation with God in the nonphysical realm. The soul is expressing a strong desire to come to earth and experience, physically, as spirit-embodied, what she knows to be true in heaven. The soul finally decides that she specifically wants to experience forgiveness. Excitedly she looks around for someone to join her on this wonderful earthly adventure, but quickly realizes that there is actually no one to forgive, for all she can see for miles and miles are other beautiful souls just like her.

Suddenly a beautiful soul who has been listening to this conversation with God appears and says that he will assist her in her desire to *feel* forgiveness in physical form. He assures her that he will come to earth at the same time and create something for her to forgive. He will provide her the opportunity to be forgiving so that she can expand and evolve with this experience and knowing. She thanks him profusely, for this is her greatest desire—to experience in a physical body, on a physical plane, all she knows to be true in the spiritual realm. For a second she wonders why he would do such a thing for her, but then remembers that he unconditionally loves her and is willing to do anything to support her growth and evolution.

So these two souls excitedly get themselves ready to venture to earth. Just before joining with their physical bodies, however, the soul who has agreed to do the "unforgivable" says, "There is one thing though. Promise me that when I enter your life on earth and do that not so nice thing to you so that you may experience what it feels like to be forgiving, you will look deep into my eyes and remember me. Most likely, I will have been in my physical body for so long and will be so caught up in earthly endeavors and perspectives that I will have forgotten who I *really* am. I will be living the dream behind my physical mask, and I will need someone to come along and lovingly wake me up." She reassures him that she could never, ever forget his eternal, loving, divine essence, and off they go to experience life on earth in order to expand their eternal consciousness.

This book is a powerful presentation pointing us towards an expanded view of relationships and life experiences. I often refer to this material when sharing the Soul to Soul perspective with others.

Little Soul and the Sun speaks our family's spiritual language, but it might not speak yours. I encourage you to search for children's spiritual books that do speak to your family. There are many wonderful nondenominational books out there for children that beautifully express, in subtle ways, this idea of Soul to Soul interaction. For younger children, you could collect several books that stir your soul and read them, over and over again, as your family discussion. There are many children's movies teaching this concept as well. Watch them together and discuss the Soul to Soul aspect of each movie. These early family experiences lay the groundwork to move easily into more in-depth discussions as the children grow older.

Soul to Soul interaction manifests as beautiful insights, compassion, tolerance, and a deeper understanding of humanity as a whole by allowing a greater capacity to see another beyond his physical mask. It's so simple, yet remains a revolutionary perspective that can open the door in today's world for a grace and compassion towards self and others that has rarely been realized in the history of the human race.

Integrate It into Your Own Family!

Parent Contemplations:

- In what ways do you see yourself as a soul nurturer? How do you currently support others in meaningful ways?

- How do you encourage your children to nurture other souls?

- How will adopting a Soul to Soul perspective enrich relationships and enhance life experiences for all family members?

- How can you remind each other on a daily basis to see others as souls rather than as simply roles?

Activities:

- Together as a family, create an ongoing list of ways that you can help others in your community. Research options and add to the growing list; perhaps something you read about in the local paper or a social service opportunity arrives in a school bulletin. Be willing to take risks and try new avenues of service to others. Devise a plan to enact some type of community outreach at least a few times a year. You could volunteer at a soup kitchen, or assist an elderly neighbor. These are just a few examples.

- I learned the "I Am That" game from author Neale Donald Walsch. When you leave the house and experience your physical surroundings, say silently to yourself, "I am that, too!" This game acknowledges the unity and expansiveness underlying our relationship to all things that can be deeply felt and perceived on a daily basis. This can also be done as a family while sitting in a circle simply naming different things in the physical experience.

- The Mirror Game: As a family, decide on a soul attribute (love, joy, generosity, encouragement, forgiveness, enthusiasm, laughter) that you agree to share with the world on a particular outing. Attend the outing with the soul attribute in mind and consciously offer it to the world through your interactions with others. Observe, discuss, and record how it was mirrored back to you after the outing. You may also choose an attribute for exploration over the course of a whole day or week. Ceremoniously, post the attribute in a highly visible place in your home. This game teaches children to *be the source* for what appears in their life. More joy begets more joy.

- Small Change: Purposefully keep small change in your pockets to offer anywhere needed in the external world. Offer the extra money with both the desire to help another with no strings attached *and* with a total belief that you have much money to give. This activity is powerful on two levels: it demonstrates generosity of spirit *and* an extension of personal prosperity. Your recipients could be a homeless person, a Salvation Army kettle, or someone behind you in the grocery line. (Adapted from *The Hope: A Guide to Sacred Activism* by Andrew Harvey.)

- As a family, create a list of individuals who you know who may need assistance or a word of encouragement. Commit to contacting one per week or one per month via mail, phone, or email. Make a conscious decision to recognize not only why the person may be in need of a soul to soul interaction, but also identify that person's soul attributes in some way. Discuss all aspects of each choice, including the reason for choosing this particular individual and how to best make contact. (Adapted from *The Hope* by Andrew Harvey.)

- As a family, practice seeing others as souls rather than roles for thirty days. At a family discussion, talk about the power of training yourself to acknowledge the largest view possible of fellow human beings who are actually angels in disguise. Make a simple, highly visible chart together and keep track each night by marking off the day.

Books:
Picture: *Little Soul and the Sun* (Neale Donald Walsch)
Chapter: *Bridge to Terabithia* (Katherine Paterson)
Adult: *Journey of Souls* (Michael Newton)

Movies:
Forrest Gump (1994)
Radio (2003)

Songs:
Smile (Uncle Kracker)
Celebrate Me Home (Kenny Loggins)

Chapter 5

Soul to Soul Parenting *Spiritual Theme*
The Physical Body, A Sacred Vessel

A physical body is a gift from God like no other.

The physical body is a beautiful, sacred vessel designed to house your soul and allow you to exist in a physical world, providing access to the divine, universal wisdom that infuses and surrounds all human beings. Every cell in your body is aligned with your soul's truth even *before* you have allowed that truth into your conscious mind. Every cell in your body holds your soul's history and future. Your cells hold the secret of your divine heritage. The physical body is a tool to be used by you in a myriad of ways during a single lifetime. Most importantly, your body should be intimately loved, acknowledged, and appreciated as you would love, acknowledge, and appreciate your own child. A physical body is a gift from God like no other. Each tiny part of your body is an integral and all-important aspect of the whole system. This relationship of the human body to all of its parts mirrors an individual soul's relationship to God. It is this magnificent system, your physical body, which is currently a home to your soul.

For young children, utilize their fascination with the physical body to instill a strong appreciation for their beloved vessel and to view it as a sacred instrument; and therefore, not abuse it, care for it, and be aware to notice changes in it. Help children understand that they're meant to be active participants in the care and healing of their own body. It is helpful to acknowledge frequently all of the different body parts and their important functions. Encourage children to touch and talk to their body. At a young age, invite children to *listen* to their body and recognize what their body is telling them. This profound respect and acknowledgement of the body cannot begin soon enough.

It is extremely important to begin teaching children as early as possible to allow what they are feeling in their emotional landscape to be fully expressed. Emotion is essentially energy in motion and must move through the body freely and release when complete. Through the years if you continually deny, stuff down, or resist certain emotional patterns, they'll become blocked in different areas of the body related to that particular emotional blockage. Without emotional release, enabling the free flow of emotional energy once again, disease (dis-ease) will indeed show itself within your physical form. Once manifested, you can choose to look more closely at root level emotional causes for the ailment or not. Inner work is always a personal choice.

I have discovered from personal experience that the body, when connected *consciously* to the mind and the spirit, has tremendous healing capabilities. Of course, this is what many masters have told us for centuries, but you must give *yourself* the opportunity to get to know your own body on a deep level before healing work can begin. From an early age, I sensed that there was much more to healing than modern medicine alone. My mother was very open to alternative healing practices and readily looked to them as another path to vitality and health.

Recently, I experienced a beautiful inner body meditation. As I focused on, and moved through, all seven chakras and their related body parts, I acknowledged them, caressed them, and lovingly cared for them in my mind's eye. I felt my body tingle all over as it basked in the gratitude that I was freely giving every corner of my beautiful vessel. This meditation reminded me of the sacred and creative healing powers of my own body. I left this meditation with a deep inner realization that not even one breath should ever be taken for granted.

At the age of twelve, I developed a "problem" with warts on my hands. Warts are caused by a virus that can be difficult to overcome with medicines, and after months of struggling to rid myself of these unattractive warts, my mother took me to a hypnotherapist. I remember feeling excited about getting to the heart of the matter with my minor, yet bothersome, health woe. Something inside of me knew that this was going to address the root cause of the issue rather than continue to simply scratch the surface of the chronic problem. The hypnotherapist taught me a wonderful method of visualization to use in conjunction with my body each night before I fell asleep. This was something that proved to be right up my alley as I enjoyed relaxing with my body in this way. The warts began to disappear within days and were totally gone in less than a month.

Healing the warts was wonderful, but really the least important part of this whole experience for me. The real benefit of this experience came as an awakening to the belief that I can participate, in a powerful way, in the healing of my own body. From this experience, I opened myself up to healing modalities that exist outside the realm of modern, allopathic medicine, seeing myself as an active participant in my own healing. Since that early experience, I consciously choose to go deeper within my emotional patterns and belief systems to explore dis-ease in my body.

While I respect and utilize modern medicine when called for, I readily utilize my own healing capabilities, as well as enlist holistic healing methods during times of imbalance in my body and mind. I view all physical ailments as an *invitation* to intimately connect with my body and emotional state in a deep and profound way. Seen in this light, the aches and pains can be perceived as a gift—an opportunity to expand self-awareness.

> The understanding that I, as a creative, eternal, spiritual being can look within to initiate the healing process has been one of the greatest insights of my life.

For many years, I have been blessed to work with numerous gifted healers. These relationships are ones that I consciously sought out as minor physical ailments arose in my body. One in particular has been my integrative health doctor for over fifteen years. I discovered him at the age of twenty-three while suffering from lower back pain that had been unassisted for years using traditional medicine. With his more eastern approach to medicine, he's been a tremendous blessing in my life. When I visit him with any type of health issue, my entire being is taken into account at all times. With his gentle guidance, it ultimately becomes *my* work to dive into the deep emotional waters of my life and connect with the beliefs that are blocking the free flow of energy in my body. The understanding that *I*, as a creative, eternal, spiritual being can look within to initiate the healing process has been one of the greatest insights of my life. I am deeply grateful to all of the healers with whom I have worked for their thoughtful contributions to my total health and overall well-being.

Soon after I birthed my second daughter Piper, sixteen months after having given birth to my first child, I developed horrible eczema on both of my lower legs. At night I would fall into terrible "itching fests" that created scaly patches on my shins. I went to five dermatologists and used numerous tubes of skin creams before I realized that my body was really trying to tell me something, and I wasn't listening. It turns out, on a subconscious level, I was holding a belief that I'd been unwilling to look at, and my body was literally screaming at me to wake up and pay attention. I ended up at a hypnotherapist for the second time in my life, and after a three-hour session, uncovered exactly what was behind the eczema.

Essentially, I was stuck in an internal place of angst, feeling that I'd given up my teaching career too soon at a time when I was just beginning to blossom and stand on my two feet (hence, issues with the lower legs). Subconsciously, I felt that I had cut my legs off, so to speak, and was now dependent on my husband, as I had been once on my parents, for monetary support. My husband didn't make me feel this way, but it was a belief embedded deep within me just the same. I also discovered during that session that my recent preoccupation with the physical realm led me to totally neglect my spirit. My passion for this aspect of my life had become completely submerged for several months, as I once again birthed a child and laid down roots for years of homemaking and caring for children.

That night after the visit with the hypnotherapist, I took a long, luxurious bath. During this bath I realized that I was doing in my life *exactly* what I had intended to create all along. I chose to be a young mother and have my children close together. I wanted to be a stay-at-home mom and relish each fleeting moment of my children's lives. I had not diverted from my path; this *was* my path. It was a beautiful turn in my path designed and created by me. This epiphany eased my body, mind, and spirit back into beautiful alignment with one another. My life energy could again resume its natural, easy, vibrant flow without any blocking belief patterns. The eczema was totally gone in three days, and my body, thankfully, resumed its normal state of health.

Healing can only take place if you acknowledge inner beliefs that sabotage your body and work to remove them. Interestingly, I have since found that simply acknowledging deeply lodged "hidden" beliefs such as these goes a long way towards healing them, and often is the only thing that needs to be done. The body will usually *kick in* and take care of the rest once it realizes that the light of awareness has reached its mark.

Pay attention to what your beautiful body is trying to tell you and teach your children to do the same. In doing so, the mind-body-spirit connection will lead you to your next perfect evolutionary step in your never-ending expansion.

I always, always look *within* first in an attempt to acknowledge the root emotional cause of the ailment. If it's laryngitis, I seek to acknowledge what it is that I really want to say. If an eye twitch shows up in my body, I look to acknowledge what it is that I am unwilling to really see. There have been numerous books written on this topic; perhaps most noteworthy is Louise Hay's *You Can Heal Your Life*. The care of a human body is a personal and intimate process where one looks for the deeper meanings behind those tugs and pulls and then listens for the answers. Doctors and healers are wonderful assets to your healthcare, but ultimately, they can only do so much. Your body is designed to lead you to an expanded awareness of what it means to live in divine flow with All That Is. Pay attention to what your beautiful body is trying to tell you and teach your children to do the same. In doing so, the mind-body-spirit connection will lead you to your next perfect evolutionary step in your never-ending expansion.

I deliberately do not choose to offer my perspective on dis-ease in the body to anyone who is currently facing a life-threatening disease in her physical body, unless she invites the conversation. In these situations, I simply feel compassion, offer support, and hold space for another with tenderness as she grows in her own way from her experience. Everyone must begin to see himself as a soul who co-creates physical reality on some level in his own time. You must always allow others the freedom to perceive their life experiences in a way that feels right to them.

In teaching your own children, however, it's important to encourage them to regard their physical body in a conscious way. Help them become aware that what they eat and drink greatly affects the health of their sacred vessel by encouraging conscious eating habits. It is always a choice as to what you consume as fuel for your own body. Assist your children in protecting their body by encouraging conscious sports participation and recreation. Explain and exemplify the importance of exercise, rest, and hydration, as well as proper versus improper touching by another. It is always a choice to do the best that you can to protect your body from unnecessary harm. Finally, teach your children how to consciously care for the overall well-being of *every* aspect of their own body. Children should cherish their own body and never be ashamed of it. Make the caring and protection of the body a conscious and often discussed aspect of daily family life.

Your body is organically wired to allow mystical experiences to unfold within you. It is where you can actually feel your magnificent divinity; it is the vehicle through which you experience in the physical realm All That Is flowing through you.

A large part of listening to the voice of your own soul is listening to your body. Begin to feel divine guidance through your body. It is your earthly means of receiving spiritual instruction from your soul and the spiritual realm. You are a channel of divine wisdom, and your body fully recognizes this. It understands that part of its job is to transport information to you. Your body is in constant communication with your soul. Your *vibes*—energetic vibrations that you can feel, both *good* and *bad*—speak to you through your body. One of my teachers refers to this as a red light/green light navigational system, a true gift from your body. Teach your children to listen to and feel the crucial signs from their body that keep them swimming easily in the divine flow of life. You must get to know your body's specific signals and come to understand what every signal means to you. Your body speaks truth, even when your mind wants to deny and resist that truth, and as we now know, what you resist persists; your body always sees to that.

Your body is in constant communication with your soul.

I place great importance on what my body is attempting to tell me in any given situation. It can be very subtle, but a red light/green light signal can usually be felt if looked for carefully. Look to how you *feel* in all circumstances, not to how you *think* you should feel. My red light bodily signals might include a headache, an upset stomach, lethargy, minor ailments, a lower-back ache, a drained feeling, full-blown fatigue, depression, or a closed throat. I check in with these "bad" vibes and seek to protect myself in any way that I can. This could mean changing my plans, crossing my arms, leaving a situation, or simply saying "No." I base my decisions on my feelings and direction from my body. I know that my body is letting me know, in no uncertain terms, that I need to become aware of what is going on around me. It's reminding me that it is time to listen to the voice of my soul and heed its call.

Your beloved body can teach you so much if only you take the time to listen to its great wisdom.

On the other hand, green light signals from my body are very different. They may feel like exuberance, a burst of energy, tingly sensations that move over my body in waves, flutterings in my stomach, goosebumps, enthusiasm, a contracting in my diaphragm area which creates a wonderful sensation of breathlessness, tears of joy, warmth all over my body, an unstoppable smile, a pulsating expansion in my heart area, wakefulness, a feeling of ecstasy, a feeling of Oneness, or an inner sense of peace and calm. Green light signals often are accompanied by joy and a deep feeling of connection to All That Is. When I feel these sensations in my body, I know without a doubt, without a moment's hesitation, that I am on the path designated by my soul. I'm in the right place at the right time and flowing freely in alignment with my eternal soul. Basically, I become consciously aware that the Universe has my back.

Obviously, I enjoy the green light signals from my body more than the red, but I bless them *both* as gifts. I rely on them consistently throughout my day to show me the way that is best for me at any given time. The green light signals from my body may even lead me to walk down a more arduous path, one that is filled with important and necessary life lessons for me at this stage in my life. I trust my body's accuracy explicitly and deeply appreciate the relationship that we share with one another. I view my physical body as a spiritual companion that helps me move ever closer to my soul purpose. Teach your children to get into the habit of constantly checking in with their body for divine guidance, as they would have a compass in the distant past.

Your beloved body can teach you so much if only you take the time to listen to its great wisdom. Help your children make conscious choices in regard to their own body and continually remind them to consciously utilize their body to interpret life experiences. Instill in your children the importance of viewing themselves as spirit-embodied so that they may reap the rewards of their divine heritage.

Integrate It into Your Own Family!

Parent Contemplations:
- In what ways do you regularly show respect and appreciation for your body?

- How do you encourage your children to care for and protect their body?

- How do you feel about integrative medicine/holistic healthcare? Which alternative healing modalities appeal to you? Why?

- In what ways do you actively participate in your own healing?

- Describe what the mind/body/spirit connection means for you.

- Do you regularly receive messages from your soul through your body?

- Do you recognize your unique red light/green light navigational system? Describe what it offers you.

Activities:
- Name at least five activities that your physical body really enjoys. How often do you allow yourself to enjoy your physical body in this way? Examine how you can shift priorities to create more opportunities to engage in physical activity that you love.

Take one activity from each person's list and make a plan to experience it together. While doing so, encourage your children to appreciate the physical life experience and all that it offers (biking, gardening, etc.).

- Food/Rest/Downtime/Exercise: Make a chart to see how conscious you are in each area. Name at least one thing that you do well in each area, and at least one thing that you could improve on in each area. Help your children to assess the importance and purpose of each area to their overall well-being. Offer ideas and opportunities for each.

- Red Light/Green Light Activity: Create a large human body with posterboard overlaid with a stoplight in the torso area using construction paper. Hang somewhere in your house to remind the family to listen to their body for intuitive guidance. Young children can actually point to how they are feeling about situations and relationships to become more conscious in everyday life experiences. A red light means to wait and assess further; a yellow light symbolizes to proceed with caution while looking at more closely and analyzing; and a green light represents a resounding yes. This activity encourages children to always check in with their bodies for inner guidance.

- Recall a situation or experience that gave you bad vibes. How did it feel? Where did it express in your body? Recall a situation or experience that gave you good vibes. How did it feel? Where did it express in your body? Do this activity fairly regularly so that children begin to recognize and trust their vibes.

- Are there negative energies that you regularly tune into? Examples might be a violent video game, the tragic stories in the news, spending too much time with a gossipy friend. Name three positive energies that you regularly tune into. Examples might be a daily inspirational email message, a morning hug from someone you love, a healthy fruit smoothie. Assess regularly the choices, priorities, and focus of your days and weeks. Assist children in taking small steps at a time to consciously make life-enhancing changes to their routines.

Books:

Picture: *Incredible You!* (Wayne Dyer)
Chapter: *Tuck Everlasting* (Natalie Babbitt)
Adult: *You Can Heal Your Life* (Louise Hay)

Movies:

Delivering Milo (2001)
Iron Will (1994)

Songs:

Thing of Beauty (Hothouse Flowers)
Sunshine on My Shoulders (John Denver)
Dancin' in the Moonlight (The Hit Crew)

Chapter 6

Oneness *and* Individuation

*W*hen you uncover the central, underlying message in all of the world's major religious traditions, it basically comes down to one word: *oneness*. This was our first official family discussion topic many years ago, and it is now a belief that has become infused into our everyday life. Oneness is a vantage point through which we view all relationships and life situations. While this seems like a simple message, it is a spiritual concept that can be difficult to teach children and adults alike, much less have it be something that resides in the forefront of daily living.

The spiritual truth of Oneness reflecting our divine origins has the potential to reshape the future of our world.

The idea that all living things are made of the same divine essence, although they may not appear to be similar in their physicality, can be taught to children through close observation of their natural world. That we are part of a holographic universe wherein we are individual aspects of the same, divine whole is perhaps the greatest paradox that exists in the Universe and is most easily explained to children using a variety of analogies. The tree/leaf and hand/thumb analogies are two very basic examples of this concept. The leaf can be viewed individually or as an integral aspect of the whole tree. The same can be perceived in looking at the hand and the thumb; different when looked at singularly, but the same when viewed from a broader perspective. A deep understanding that we are individual aspects of the same, divine whole cannot be understood in the mind alone. One must feel it in her deepest space. It is an inner knowing that exists in your eternal soul and once uncovered offers a spiritual sustenance and understanding that the mind simply cannot comprehend. Oneness *and* Individuation is, indeed, the greatest of all paradoxes. How can we be both one and separate at the same time? Quantum physics is getting closer and closer to being able to explain this divine paradox mathematically, but a true understanding of this dichotomy can only be found in your true essence, your soul.

Briefly, and in very elementary terms, as I understand it, the Universe is holographic; all aspects of the whole exist in every individuated part of the whole. Everything perceived as matter and form in the physical world carries within it the all-encompassing, total energy that exists everywhere. For this reason, the Universal Hologram becomes part of every living thing that exists in the entire Universe. *All things are in me, and I am in all things* denotes the wholeness and oneness that spiritual masters have referred to since the beginning of time. In other words, we are delineations, localized creative energy aspects, of the Divine Whole.

It is my belief that even an *awareness* of this truth is enough to forge a life of compassion and empathy towards your fellow man. As this beautiful divine paradox becomes embedded in your belief system, it becomes most useful to you on a daily basis. An understanding of this divine dichotomy changes the way in which you view, not only yourself and loved ones, but also humanity as a whole. The spiritual truth of Oneness reflecting our divine origins has the potential to reshape the future of our world.

You must do your best to understand the seemingly incomprehensible by feeling it in your heart and soul. I suggest first teaching this concept to children in very simple terms, using animals and nature, and then building on this concept together as children grow older and spiritual concepts have evolved to a higher level of understanding within your family. Children can explore this far-reaching dichotomy over and over

> One day while standing in the check-out line at the grocery store, I began observing very closely the bagger bagging my groceries. All of a sudden, he looked up at me and in his eyes I could see the whole Universe there. As I watched him, I began to feel the universal life force that was him. I sensed trees, the sky, oceans, and flowers in his essence. I sensed the whole of humanity in his essence. My divine flow energy feeling came over me as time stood still. I felt the presence of God. It was everywhere; in him, in me, and throughout the whole store. In that moment, I knew in my deepest space the truth of the Universal Holograph.

We explain to our children that what you do to another you are actually doing to yourself, because metaphysically speaking, you actually are the other, not in a singular way, but in an all-encompassing way.

again through life experiences consciously discussed within this framework as a family.

We teach our children that we are individual expressions of God, beautiful, unique aspects of God as a whole. We explain that we are divine, integral parts of a magnificent totality. We explain that we are all made up of the same Divine Essence. We explain to our children that all of the heart-centered masters who have walked this earth have delivered this very message in their own way. When Jesus said, "Love thy neighbor as thyself," he meant that literally, not just because it was the loving, nice, neighborly thing to do. Similarly, the familiar and oft-used adage known as the Golden Rule—*Do unto others as you would have them do unto you*—also exemplifies Oneness. We explain to our children that what you do to another you are actually doing to yourself, because metaphysically speaking, you actually *are* the other, not in a singular way, but in an all-encompassing way.

One way we talk about Oneness is through an ocean/wave analogy. We designate God as the vast and diverse ocean. Each wave represents an individual soul, unique and beautiful, as it crests into shore in its own way. Each wave is made of the exact same water that is the ocean; but each wave also is an individual expression of the ocean, with its own power to create and transform the beautiful shells into sand. Again, we see a perfect example of the possibility for individuation *and* wholeness to exist at the same time.

This analogy was taught to me by my spiritual mentors and is a great way to explain to children, in simple terms, the far-reaching concept of Oneness. First, we have our children imagine the biggest, grandest birthday cake ever. We call it the Universe's birthday cake. On this cake, there are trillions of beautiful candles aglow with individual flames. The individual flames are all made of the same fire and come from the same source. Each flame represents an individual soul and the whole cake represents God. You see different aspects of the cake depending on your point of view. When you look at the cake from close up, you recognize all of its individual parts, but when you look at the birthday cake as a whole from a slightly different perspective, like say from above, you see a much different picture. From the expanded perspective, you can see the one powerful light that emanates from the cake. This all-encompassing glow, which is the one true light shining so brightly from the cake, is God; and we, as the individual flames, are each an essential, unique part of the overall glow, that is the Creator.

I recently received an email detailing another great way to explain this divine paradox of Oneness/Individuation. A rabbi talks about God being a long rope. He says that we are the individual knots in this divine rope, and when we die, our knot simply unties and we easily transition back into our natural state of oneness with the rope. Of course, we are never separate from the rope, but as a knot in the rope, we perceive ourselves in that way. When you see God as a beautiful, infinite rope that twists and turns connecting all of life, the transition from birth to death to rebirth, knotting to unknotting to knotting once again, appears gentle and natural.

My husband and I were chatting about Oneness over coffee one Sunday morning, when he offered a wonderful way to explain this concept to children and adults alike. He suggested using the artist Seurat's pointillism as a visual way to perceive Oneness, and I thought it was a terrific idea. Using this model, each little dot represents a soul, a divine individual expression of God. It's not until you step back and view the entire painting that you can then perceive the whole beautiful, intricate painting which represents God. As we talked, it became apparent that there are so many things in life sharing this dichotomy. Individual letters are an integral part of the whole word. Each individual cell is an integral part of the whole body. All of life seems to be connected in one way or another; it simply depends on how you look at it. How you perceive and subsequently translate life always comes down to your personal perspective. Are you willing to look at life from a broader, more expansive perspective or are you determined to see only a smaller, narrower view of reality? Like with everything else, we all have a choice as to how we perceive the world.

Finally, the diamond, a precious stone so beautiful in its multifaceted nature, offers yet another wonderful metaphor for the Oneness/Individuation model. The diamond, as a representation of God, holds infinite facets and angles, each of which is an innate part of the whole. If a diamond is cut into a smaller piece, it remains a multifaceted diamond with the same components and essence. The same is true of the interrelationship between an individuated aspect of the divine whole and the divine whole in its totality.

The question of Oneness versus Individuation comes up all the time in the different workshops that I teach. For so many people, there's an inner sensing that understanding this truth opens you to a whole new world, and that sensing is actually very accurate. This core concept, when fully integrated into your reality, propels you forth into a major shift in consciousness, altering your entire perspective of life as you know it.

Seeing God Everywhere

Seeing God Everywhere is another very practical way to teach children about their overall connectedness to All That Is. I love this topic because it can be used to assist all ages in deepening their understanding of ultimate reality. One of my favorite things to do is to sit quietly and carefully look, *really look*, at everything before me, and see God. And we certainly don't have to stop with *seeing* God; how about *hearing* and *feeling* God everywhere, too. This is such a great topic for younger children and one that can be talked about each and every day. A sense of being connected to God through all of nature is a beautiful starting point for children as they begin to see themselves as unique, integral parts of the Divine Whole.

A sense of being connected to God through all of nature is a beautiful starting point for children as they begin to see themselves as unique, integral parts of the Divine Whole.

God can be seen in all shapes and forms. We encourage our children to have an unlimited and infinite perception of God. You may see God in the purple flower on the way to school or in the colorful fall leaves. Then again, you may hear God in the song on the radio or in the rain falling on the roof. You never know, you may feel God in the new, unexpected best friend or while reading a great book all snuggly in bed. Of course, God may show up as a bright idea or on the family bike ride on a beautiful day. Your job is to be awake and conscious as you walk through the moments of your own life. We explain to our children that God isn't a distant male figure somewhere *out there*, but rather a gentle, loving, absolute presence *in here*, as we point to each of our hearts. We share with our children that God is here, there, *and* in the space in between. Our God runs through everything and connects us to all things. In our family, God cannot be confined, enclosed, or limited in *any* way.

We never want our children to feel that they have to keep God in a neat and tidy package. We feel that it is the opening of that package to allow for limitless expressions of self that leads one to God. From a young age, we hope to encourage our children to see, hear, and feel God everywhere, at all times, even in the midst of the not so nice aspects of life. When I pray to God each morning, I thank God for the ups and the downs, the blessings and the curses, the good and the bad. I see glimpses of God in all of it. I experience God in all of it. I am grateful for all of it, for it is the beautiful tapestry of my life.

Speak, speak, and speak to your children of your perceptions and experiences of God. Sharing them openly will bring God into the light of *their* reality so that they, too, may be liberated to experience God always, in all ways.

Integrate It into Your Own Family!

Parent Contemplations:
- Do you feel that human beings are part of a greater whole? Do you sense an underlying divine essence in all things? If so, describe.

- Create other examples/analogies that depict the Oneness *and* Individuation Divine Paradox.

- How can an understanding of the Divine Paradox change the way in which you perceive and interpret life experiences? How can you help your children utilize this understanding daily?

Activities:
- Fill a large pitcher with water. Use different colored, shaped, and sized glasses to represent the soul of each member of your family. Pour the water (All That Is) into each glass and observe quietly. Then pour the water back into the pitcher. Notice and discuss

that the essence of the water does not change, only the containers (outer forms) change. Invite each child to lead the activity and explain each part.

- Bake a cake together as a family. Place each ingredient on the counter and identify before carefully pouring into a large bowl. Add lots of fun ingredients such as chocolate chips, gummy bears, and nuts, as the cake does not have to actually be consumed. Mix the ingredients together and bake. Acknowledge the whole cake for several minutes before slicing. Note that when you slice the cake into many different sized pieces, the same ingredients exist in each piece of cake no matter what the size or shape. The ingredients can never be taken out of the whole cake once mixed together. A great example of the Divine Holograph. (Adapted from *Nurturing Spirituality in Children* by Peggy Jenkins.)

- Find a shoelace. First view it as a straight line with no knots (All That Is). Create several loose knots along the shoelace (individu-ated souls). Then unknot the shoelace to return to wholeness once again. This can be repeated with different size knots or using other items such as a rope. The essence of the shoelace, its continuity, does not change; only its form changes.

- Expanded Perspective Exercise: This can be done using anything in life, moving from the narrowest, localized perception of some-thing all the way outward to All That Is. As an example, begin perceiving your thumbnail, your thumb, your hand, your arm, your whole body, everyone in your family, your house, your street, your neighborhood, your town, your state, your country, the entire planet, the solar system, and outward. Teach children that all are the same essence and actually *one*, depending on how you look at it. You can also start with the vein of a leaf, the leaf, the tree, the backyard, etc. Rising slowly up into the sky on an airplane, perspective changes in each moment. You may draw concentric circles moving outward for each growing perception as a great visual.

Books:

Picture: *Becoming Me* (Martin Boroson), *Maddie's Moonbeam Garden* (Karen Nowicki), *Zoom* (Istvan Banyai)
Chapter: *Because of Winn Dixie* (Kate DiCamillo)
Adult: All *Conversation with God* books (Neale Donald Walsch)

Movies:
Patch Adams (1998)
Music of the Heart (1999)

Songs:
Angel (Sarah McLachlan)
Halo (Beyonce)
One Love (Bob Marley)

Chapter 7

Soul to Soul Parenting *Spiritual Theme*
Connectedness *and* Boundaries

As you begin to recognize your essential Oneness with All That Is as your spiritual reality, on the physical plane you experience the truth that you have incarnated into a separate physical body with your own soul purpose and agenda. While you are always connected to another in your divine essence, you will not always *feel* connected and experience harmony with all individuals. This is more than okay, and that's why as a human being, you must incorporate boundaries into your day-to-day living space. It is imperative that you learn to protect yourself from another's ego energies emanating from an unconscious mind and creating discord in your harmonic state of being. It's not necessary to shield yourself from the spirit of another, which is an aspect of the divine whole, but it *may* be necessary to shield yourself from another's localized version of "I" which is their ego. As a parent you must teach your children the beauty of connectedness coupled with the need to create boundaries and protect themselves from unhealthy relationships and situations. A heightened awareness of how you *feel* in all circumstances, as well as a greater intimacy with the voice of your own soul will assist you in remaining conscious and awake as you assess all aspects of your surroundings. What it means to remain conscious and awake in regard to your own energy field as you move through your day should be discussed and modeled within your family daily.

Connectedness and Boundaries offer us yet another invitation to explore a divine paradox. Yes, we are all eternally connected to Total Consciousness through our own soul, but boundaries do indeed exist on the physical plane so that we may do the work that we came here to do, root to Mother Earth, and emanate our own unique, vibrant energy to the world at large. In other words, it does not behoove you to merge with energies that are not in harmony with your own. It does not behoove you to take on another's energy that may be detrimental to your own. While diversity among individuals and circumstances is a purposeful aspect of the physical world, your unique energy field is to be protected, loved, respected, and cherished at every turn. It is imperative that you factor yourself in at all times, especially when you are in service to another.

Boundaries can be particularly difficult for some women to create as they tend to have a strong desire to nurture others, and in nurturing others, it is very easy to lose oneself. In my own life, I've struggled tremendously with this particular divine paradox. My empathy towards others has at times been overwhelming for me. I have

Oneness does not mean sameness; we are one in essence, but not in form.

desired to do their work *for* them instead of empowering them to do their work themselves. I have often learned the hard way that loving others doesn't mean sacrificing me. I used to feel that loving another meant carrying her load, holding her suffering, and merging with her pain. I now understand that holding the space for her to experience all that she came to earth to experience is enough. That *is* loving her.

My compassion is no longer showered upon everyone else in the world but me. I've finally accepted the fact that boundaries are a necessary and loving means of protecting my own energy. Yes, I am ultimately one with all living things, but in a physical sense, right here right now, I'm very much my own special entity; I am an individuated aspect of the whole. Factoring *me* in no longer feels selfish and is viewed as a loving act of self-preservation. I choose to fulfill my soul's path by remaining true to my chosen incarnation. Oneness does not mean sameness; we are one in essence, but not in form.

As you and your children become more open and conscious to the multidimensional aspects of life, you also become more sensitive to your surroundings. Awareness of psychic debris entering your energy field becomes quite apparent as you learn to feel subtle shifts in your body and in your energetic vibration. While this is occurring to *all* people *all*

The best means that I've found to maintain a high energetic vibration is to end my need to people-please in order to receive external validation from others and liberate myself to live true to my own unique soul path.

the time as we engage with others in the physical world, once you're conscious of the energy exchanges actually taking place with every interaction, it becomes possible to protect yourself from undesirable energy which can greatly affect your health and state of mind, not to mention the vitality of your spirit.

Many teachers have explained to me different ways in which to protect myself from negative energy. One instructed me to imagine myself surrounded on all sides, top to bottom, with a silver sphere threaded with gold and infused with light. I use this imagery often as I head out into my day, knowing that I'm nurturing myself in the most loving possible way which will greatly assist me as I nurture others who cross my path. Another teacher recommended that I mentally create a pyramid around myself infused with liquid gold. Start under your feet and then move upward, surrounding your entire body with it as you go. The imaginary result is a golden pyramid of light that surrounds your body and your energy field. *All* of my spiritual teachers have spoken of protecting yourself with white light. Whatever visions are most appealing to you should be the ones that you use. I encourage you to try a few out and see what feels the most protective to your spirit.

I've found that simply crossing my arms and holding them around my midsection serves as a protective shield against unwanted energy that may be emanating from an individual or a particular situation. Saying no, leaving the space in question, withdrawing from toxic relationships and situations are all means of not only protecting ourselves, but most importantly,

In a recent channeling class taught by my gifted teacher Sharyl Noday, we did a wonderful guided meditation where we explored this aspect of staying grounded in your own energy in a universally expansive way. We closed our eyes and imagined a strong, vital, illuminated silver cord running from the bottoms of our feet straight into the core of Mother Earth. We then imagined this cord running through our entire body and out the crown of our head where it grew to be so long that it connected to a star. We were invited to feel the power and strength in remaining totally grounded to the physical plane, and at the same time, fully open to our expansiveness as Spirit. It was an absolutely beautiful divine dichotomy to feel within my total being.

SOUL TO SOUL PARENTING   105

actions exemplifying self-love. We must be attuned to our vulnerability to the energy that surrounds us. While we desire to remain open to all that the Universe has to offer, we must also understand the power of the energetic connections that incorporate us into the web of life. We want our connective cords to be clean, clear, and positive, not muddied, dense, and draining. The best means that I've found to maintain a high energetic vibration is to end my need to people-please in order to receive external validation from others and liberate myself to live true to my own unique soul path.

Begin to feel what type of energy your children possess. Chances are they will each exhibit a very distinct vibe.

My middle child Piper is extremely ethereal and intuitive. She feels the psychic energy around her at all times, and we celebrate her uniqueness in this way. The flip side of her wide-open energy field is that she has a more difficult time staying grounded than my other two children. While they are also open to Spirit, their feet are more firmly rooted to earth. They are anchored to earth in a tangible way; you can feel it in their presence. Piper's energy simply feels different.

Her openness to the energy that surrounds her can also sometimes lead to situational sensitivities. When she was younger, she experienced separation anxiety and was much more comfortable in quiet, calm settings and socializing with others in one-on-one situations. While not able to place her fears into words at the time, we now have a much greater understanding of Piper's sensitivities. Being a wide-open receiver means that you are literally channeling the energy around you into your own nervous system. This download of continuous energy can be very difficult to integrate. As a result, Piper is an individual who needs a lot of solitude and downtime where she can relax and decompress. She now understands this about herself and consciously makes her life choices accordingly. Begin to feel what type of energy your children possess. Chances are they will each exhibit a very distinct vibe.

Explore how *you* personally relate to outside energies. Become sensitive to all situations and to all people. Monitor your choices so that every single choice reflects your strong desire to maintain well-being. Trust yourself as you consider which external vibrations are in harmony with *your* vibration, and choose accordingly. Self-loving choices versus detrimental choices are *always* the highest choice. When you remain in alignment with your core truth, you offer the world your highest potential. Understand that connectedness does not mean total immersion when it comes to oneness on the physical plane. Ground yourself to Mother Earth and feel her fire course through your veins. Create healthy boundaries and use them to ensure the well-being of your beautiful soul which is united on the deepest of levels with all things. Teach your children how to do the same thing by sharing protective measures with them. Become acutely aware of life as energy and live accordingly. Finally, always remember to *ask for help* if you need it! Model this for your children on a daily basis. You have more spiritual helpers waiting to assist you on your physical journey than you could ever imagine. You are cherished top to bottom, side to side, in and out, and through and through. Without question, invite Spirit to assist you in all endeavors, including your safety and protective measures. Honor yourself and All That Is by enlisting help. The joy felt will be mutual!

Integrate It into Your Own Family!

Parent Contemplations:

- What attributes of another enable you to feel highly connected to that individual?

- What do you feel, both emotionally and physically, when a relationship/situation resonates for you? How do you feel when something *doesn't* feel right?

- How do you protect yourself from negative energy?

- What aspects of nature enhance your feelings of connectedness to the world at large?

Activities:

- Collect lots of buttons and string. Create necklaces with many different types of buttons on one string. The buttons represent individual souls and the string represents All That Is. Notice the connection yet boundary created by each button. Acknowledge the beauty and uniqueness of each button coupled with the beauty of the whole necklace. (From *Nurturing Spirituality in Children* by Peggy Jenkins.)

- Describe different ways you can use your imagination to protect yourself from undesired energies; a sphere of white light or a golden pyramid are two possibilities. Reiterate the importance of conscious awareness of the energies that surround you. Empower your children through this exercise to utilize their knowledge and power to act and to choose. Ask your children to close their eyes and imagine what works for them. They can then draw on a sheet of paper what they imagined.

- Plan time together in nature as a family (time in the backyard, walks, parks, plant a small garden). Express your gratitude for all that you see. Use your physical senses to delight in your intimate connection with Mother Earth. Invite your children to spend as much time as possible simply enjoying nature in their own way both individually and as a family. Make it a priority to acknowledge your intricate connection with nature whenever possible.

Books:

Picture: *Where Does God Live?* (August Gold and Matthew Perlman)
Chapter: *Island of the Blue Dolphins* (Scott O'Dell)
Adult: *Everyday Grace* (Marianne Williamson)

Movies:

Avatar (2009)
The Blue Butterfly (2004)

Songs:

Keep It Loose, Keep It Tight (Amos Lee)

Have a Little Faith in Me (John Hiatt)

Chapter 8

Soul to Soul Parenting *Spiritual Theme*
Presence and Openness

*B*e here now. There's really no other way
to put it. Every single spiritual master who has ever
walked this planet has encouraged us to, above all
else, be fully awake to the present moment. Ram Dass
wrote an entire book called simply *Be Here Now.*
Eckhart Tolle wrote a profound book titled *The Power
of Now.* Being in the moment comes naturally to us as
children as we are still very much attuned to the no-
time aspect of the spiritual realm. As you grow older and become more
attached to form and your outer world, your ego strengthens and time
and space begin to rule your life. The ego, which is your false sense of
self based on a conception in your mind, begins to lead the way, and you
allow your true essence, your soul, to take a backseat. At this time you
typically begin to live life almost entirely in your head, relying on the past
or the future to make you happy.

> *Assist your
> children in seeing
> the connections
> and synchronicities
> that surround
> them, and then
> encourage them to
> act upon them.*

In truth, there is no past or future. Everything happens in the
glorious moment of Now. As an adult you must limit the endless mind
chatter from the ego that's continuously pestering you about past happen-
ings or future events, and become very much awake to the aliveness that's
occurring in the present moment. In the beginning this requires much
thought guiding, but it is very possible to retrain yourself to live in a
constant state of wakefulness. When this occurs, the ego subsides, the
spirit comes to life, and the present moment becomes your reality. The
fastest way to monitor your thoughts moment-to-moment and become

an active participant in the present is to *appreciate*. Pivot each thought into one of appreciation and pivot yourself into presence.

Help your children to pay attention to the world around them. There are no coincidences. There are no accidents. Every individual must learn to listen to the voice of her own soul to receive the answers that she seeks. Teaching children to stay awake in the outer world, while at the same time acutely tuned *in* to their interior world, creates balance in their lives. Assist your children in seeing the connections and synchronicities that surround them, and then encourage them to act upon them.

When you become fully present in life, you become totally open to life. This is called living in divine flow. You experience life as a part of you rather than as something you must resist or hold on to tightly. Living in divine flow creates spaciousness in your life: an expansion of self that is unparalleled in an ego-centered existence. In this way, you invite God in, for there is now room for Spirit to move freely through you. You become open to experiencing God, the free flow of divine life, in every moment of the day. Where do you see, hear, and feel God? When do you see, hear, and feel God? How do you see, hear, and feel God? The answers become everywhere and all the time and are felt through the energy of appreciation.

Allow to grow a deep understanding that the many seemingly invisible aspects of their day often have the greatest impact on their life and lead to a new appreciation that a co-creative force is continually working on their behalf for their highest good.

One of my favorite authors, Eckhart Tolle, in his latest book *A New Earth* says, "Nonresistance, nonjudgment, and nonattachment are the three aspects of true freedom and enlightenment." When you become fully present and open to life, these are the natural outcomes. There's no resistance to what is happening. To resist it would be to resist the divine flow of life, which you can only do within a suffering mind. There's no attachment to a certain outcome because to resist the actual outcome that shows up would be to resist the divine flow of life, which is only possible within a suffering mind. There is no judgment as to what is occurring.

Each morning before I rise out of bed, I thank God for assisting me in remaining fully present and totally open throughout my day. I pray, "Thank you, God, for assisting me in being open to joy, open to truth, and open to love. Thank you for assisting me in remaining present and awake in each moment of this beautiful, glorious day. Let us co-create together today and merge freely within the divine flow of life." I know that Spirit is with me, shining light through the cracks and crevices as my mind rests, and I experience life as an extension of me rather than as something happening to me.

*Accept what is so
right now, then
reach for the
highest thought or
choice that is
available to you,
waiting to lead
you into your next
moment of now.*

To judge it, you resist the divine flow of life, which you can only experience within a suffering mind. As you begin to diminish your ego, you realize that resistance, attachment, and judgment are simply products of your mind and have nothing to do with the inevitability of the present moment.

As all spiritual masters remind us, the first step in becoming one with a situation that seems "unseemly" is to *accept* it. Accept it just as it is. Become one with it. Then, from this place of peace, listen to the voice of your soul, and in that moment seek to expand it or change it. Be open to spiritual guidance. Ask for assistance. Be receptive to the seeds of change. Small acts are often invisible acts of courage and strength creating change. Divine flow is about staying in a place of receptivity and alignment with the Universe and all that it's offering to you in every moment of the day. Accept what is so *right now,* then reach for the highest thought or choice that is available to you, waiting to lead you into your next moment of now.

Several years ago, I went for a walk with a good friend who was utterly distraught because her brother's wife had just left him for another man. He was understandably devastated and depressed, and as his sister, my friend felt that the situation was absolutely bleak. The whole family believed that this was a tragedy of large proportions. There were children involved, and the situation was indeed going to be a painful process to endure.

As an outside observer. however, I could see that a larger force was at work here. I intuitively felt that on some level the marriage had probably been over for him as well, and that this woman, unknowingly, was offering my friend's brother the gift of a new beginning. I listened with compassion and empathy for her pain and her brother's pain, and at the same time, the voice of my soul quietly began speaking to me. I shared with her what I was feeling, which was to wait. I advised her to hold space for her brother's sorrow, but not to judge what was happening as good or bad. This was simply a twist in his expected story. What if this was a new beginning for her brother, one that on a soul level he had co-designed? I encouraged her to remain open and present and see this unexpected *bump* from a broader perspective. I encouraged her to trust the Universe and know that there was life work to be done here. I felt that the invitation to spiritually evolve for *all* involved had been extended. I encouraged my friend to accept the invitation with grace and move forward grounded firmly in the present moment.

Create the space for all possibilities through your commitment to nonresistance, nonattachment, and nonjudgment.

Fast-forward three years: her brother just married the love of his life and is happier than he's ever been. His children have adjusted beautifully to this next step on their life's journey, and his *new* life brings him tremendous joy. The cracks in his old life created just enough space for light to shine through. The end result was soul illumination, liberation, and expansion. Had my friend's brother remained closed, bitter, and resentful towards life, these things wouldn't have been possible and many opportunities for love, joy, and companionship would have been lost. If you remain mired in the muck of your past, access to Spirit is greatly diminished even though God continues to infuse and surround you. You simply cannot receive divine gifts in a closed state. The voice of your soul becomes drowned out by your hurt and defensive ego.

Oftentimes we expect relationships in our lives to continue on forever as determined by social parameters. It's my belief that we arrive at relationships with a deep, inner knowing of the work that we have agreed to accomplish together. Some relationships will exist in the lifetime category, and others will come and go. Your spirit always lets you know when the work in a relationship is complete. There is an interior knowing that emotional and spiritual growth intended with that individual has been achieved. This feeling signals that it's time to set yourself and the other person free to continue on his path in this incarnation's journey. Hopefully, this can be achieved in an honest and transparent way.

Create the space for all possibilities through your commitment to nonresistance, nonattachment, and nonjudgment. The famous Sufi poet Rumi teaches us, "Out beyond ideas of wrong-doing and right-doing, there is a field. I'll meet you there." The field of Presence and Openness is where the magic begins. There are infinite ways to perceive reality. You must ask yourself after contemplating the above story, should the wife be labeled villain and the husband victim? Is it possible that instead of blaming, the ex-husband

and ex-wife can step back from their story, bless one another, thank one another, and move forward knowing that their soul work together is now complete? From a larger perspective, can all relationships and life situations be viewed as catalysts for growth and change?

Although things are changing, most humans still want to play the "blame game" instead of taking responsibility for their own soul evolution. We allow societal norms and others to dictate our path, often leaving us feeling trapped in relationships, jobs, living locales, and overall situations that we no longer truly desire and that no longer serve our higher good. Living a life of quiet desperation, resisting what is true in your heart, literally drowns your spirit. What you lovingly and authentically do for yourself, you always do for another because when you come from a place of alignment with your inner core, the other can feel your spiritual honesty. I encourage others to remain open to the voice of their own soul and where it might lead them. While the process may prove to be painful and uncomfortable, there is *always* deeper meaning in the seeming madness.

> Your relationship with another is always ultimately about you, not them. How much love am I able to give and receive? How much truth am I willing to look at and accept? How much of my own divinity am I willing to share with the world? Begin to teach your children how to consciously perceive the deeper meanings in their relationships and life experiences, and you catapult them into a whole new world. Analyze, decode, and decipher the underlying, soul level aspects of physical reality together and shift perspective. Perception is everything. True change must first occur here before it can manifest in the external world.

It is my view that we will meet again in the spiritual realm those who caused us the most pain on earth and thank them for the opportunity to experience a life circumstance that invited us to grow *beyond* our believed capacity. Every person and situation that shows up in your life is an invitation to know and experience your soul *consciously*. This invitation puts you in the perfect position to expand and evolve.

Choose to Live Heaven on Earth!

It is your responsibility to live from Spirit. I've realized it is a conscious, personal choice to see the beauty and perfection that exists in each moment. You can choose to see God everywhere. You can choose to reach for the highest feeling and the highest thought in every moment.

You can choose to live within the earthly illusion of duality or as witnesses to it. We tell our children that creating heaven on earth is a choice that is totally up to them. It is simply a choice in how they choose to perceive the world. They create what will be their *internal experience* of life. No matter what's occurring in the external world, your internal peace or resistance to it is yours and yours alone.

See the Synchronicity and Act On It

This statement sits front and center as a Soul to Soul Reminder in our kitchen. The more you are in divine flow with life, the more frequent and high-quality the synchronicities that appear as guideposts in your life will be. Synchronicities, or divine winks as author Sera Beak calls them, appear in your life all the time as guidance from Spirit. Make yourself receptive to these miraculous gifts from God.

We encourage our children to pay attention to the world around them. Be aware of subtle shifts in your energy field. Be ready to act on the divine flow that comes into your life each day as the exact right person, place, thing, or idea that you need for your soul's evolution as it *magically* appears on your path. Many of us totally miss much of the divine guidance that comes to us through synchronicity. Be fully present and bless even seemingly unwanted occurrences, as on some level you attracted them, and you can choose to gain as much knowledge and expansion as you can from them.

Remember Small Acts of Grace

As author Caroline Myss reminds us, the small acts of grace actually carry the most power in the Universe. Every act is an act of self-definition that affects the Universe as a whole. Remember that many seemingly *invisible* things that you do throughout your day can greatly affect another in ways that remain unknown to you. You will rarely know the extent to how you touched another's life. Your very presence has the ability to shift another's day immeasurably.

The small things often hold the most power. Are you being warm, positive, compassionate, and forgiving? Does your generosity of spirit extend beyond simply monetary contributions, but also to your smile, your acknowledgement, your appreciation? Remind yourself to remain present enough to offer small acts of grace to the world throughout each day. They're perhaps your greatest contribution to peace on earth of which so many of us speak without much thought.

Tune In, Tap In, Turn On

I love this reminder of wakefulness that I learned from two of my favorite teachers, Esther and Jerry Hicks. In order to live a conscious life that mirrors the divine flow of the Universe, you must remain tuned in, tapped in, and turned on. You truly resemble a radio receiver in your vibrational, energetic makeup. So put up your antennae and walk through this world awake, so that you can see, hear, and feel divinity in all of its forms. God energy is truly everywhere!

Listen to the beautiful, subtle voice of your own soul and open yourself up in a way that can receive Spirit in all ways, at all times. Pierce the space of joy, appreciation, and oneness that resides deep inside of you. It is there, and it can be felt on a regular basis once uncovered in the folds of your consciousness. Turn up your dial and invite a higher vibrational frequency into your daily living. Be here now, basking in the divine flow of life and *all* that it brings. You might not understand *why* life is flowing in a certain direction. Know that it's *okay* not to know. In fact, it is more than okay because this signifies a surrendering to Spirit which is the hallmark of enlightened living. Practice acceptance and surrender *now* with the smaller difficulties so that life experiences requiring a grander capacity for surrender won't be such a hardship. The more tuned in, tapped in, and turned on you are, the easier this transition will be.

The present moment is where it's at. What else really matters? What else is there?

You'll have many unconscious moments throughout your day, until suddenly you realize that you don't have as many anymore. Begin to recognize when unconsciousness seeps into your mind through your ego, robbing you of the wakefulness that is your true identity. The first step to detaching from the ego is acknowledging that the ego is not who you really are; therefore, the thoughts coming from ego have nothing to do with the life experience that reflects the divine flow of life that is your birthright.

If you look closely at your life, you'll find countless examples where you have surrendered into the spaciousness of nonresistance, nonattachment, and nonjudgment, only to find that what occurred actually turned out to be for your higher good. It's with the intention of embedding this belief into the fabric of my life that I wrote the following Soul to Soul Reminder and put it on my bedside table: **I AM IN LOVE WITH THE PRESENT MOMENT!** The present moment is where it's at. What else really matters? What else is there?

Ask yourself these questions: How much goodness can I stand? How open to Spirit am I? How willing am I to trust my soul to hold the reins in my life? How much faith in God am I willing to allow myself? How wide will I let my heart expand? How much joy am I willing to feel? How much love and compassion am I willing to give? How responsible am I willing to be for the creations in my life? How free am I willing to become from the material trappings of the physical plane?

It often seems like we all have a limit. For example, I can open my heart *this* much before . . . boom! I feel I must close it down and shut it off, out of fear. Or I can feel *this* much joy before I begin to question, who am I to be this joyous? At times we might let ourselves feel it for a few seconds, but then our ego chimes in, and we're no longer present in that state of pure grace. Explore the self-sabotaging boundaries that you place on yourself, keeping you contained in a tight little box of conformity—the conformity of the ego existing only in your mind. Encourage your children to do the same. I invite you to *allow* yourself to become *lost* in Presence and fully open to the gifts of the Universe which are continually bestowed directly upon you.

The only limitations that we have are those that we place on ourselves. We are travelers by nature. We may choose to travel using a physical body, within the mind, or enraptured in dominion with the soul. The choices before us are always ours to make. There are no real barriers to truth, joy, and love. Even if there appear to be physical barriers, these can be transcended through interior means. So relax and freely sample all that life has to offer. Following your bliss is really the only way to give others permission to follow theirs.

I invite you to allow yourself to become lost in Presence and fully open to the gifts of the Universe which are continually bestowed directly upon you.

Integrate It into Your Own Family!

Parent Contemplations:
- Describe a typical weekday. Do you allow yourself to fully focus on the task at hand or do you usually multitask?

- Are you present in your daily life? Name specific areas where it's easy for you to remain present and areas where it is not.

- Do you perceive connections, synchronicities, and exchanges with others as spiritually meaningful or as mere coincidence?

- Do you expect spiritual signs that you are on the right track and living true? If so, cite examples.

Activities:
- The Balloon Release Exercise: Draw several balloons on a large piece of paper. Inside each balloon, write or draw an aspect of your life (thought, relationship, activity, object) that is no longer serving you; something that no longer makes you feel good/worthy/positive. Once completed, take a deep, conscious breath and imagine grabbing each one and releasing it up above your head to the Universe. When all have been released, say a brief prayer of acknowledgement and gratitude for the experiences and throw the paper away.

- Make a list of five things in your life that you're ready to clear away (old clothes, a weekly habit, an old story about yourself, etc.). Discuss and then devise plans of action. Take care of one item on your list right then and there. Hold each other accountable. Have fun with the lists; laugh and enjoy the cleansing process. Do this regularly as a family.

- Sit in a room together as a family and breathe deeply. Look around the room and observe all aspects of it. Notice colors, shapes, sounds, lighting, etc. Be fully present in that room while sitting quietly. Share your feelings of being fully in the moment. Share what your senses picked up on that they might normally miss.

Books:

Picture: *Stone Soup* (Jon Muth), *The Three Questions* (Jon Muth), *Milton's Secret* (Eckhart Tolle)
Chapter: *Jonathan Livingston Seagull* (Richard Bach)
Adult: *The Power of Now* (Eckhart Tolle)

Movies:

Dead Poets Society (1989)
The Pursuit of Happyness (2006)

Songs:

Your Life Is Now (John Mellencamp)
With Arms Wide Open (Creed)
Blue Sky (Allman Brothers)

Chapter 9

Soul to Soul Parenting *Spiritual Theme*

Cause and Effect, Natural Consequences, and Free Will

*W*e teach our children that cause and effect, natural consequences, and free will are very important aspects of *everything* that they think, say, and do. They're universal laws that we all must adhere to whether we consciously do so or not. As humans, we are energetic, vibrational beings who are infinitely more powerful than most people realize; since thoughts, words, and deeds are energy, it's important to be aware of what you're actually creating. Instead of talking about sin in our home, we choose to speak of natural consequences, both positive and negative. With every single action comes a consequence. It really is as simple as that.

> *All of life is a choice, and every single choice matters greatly because it has a natural consequence that determines future reality.*

All of life is a choice, and every single choice matters greatly because it has a natural consequence that determines future reality. The power of choice is our greatest creative tool. Every choice is either empowering, self-loving, and life-enhancing or the opposite. Every choice either leads us towards our highest potential or away from our grandest vision. Every choice either serves the soul or serves the ego. Children can learn at an early age that they are indeed co-creators with the Universe. As children begin to understand cause and effect, natural consequences, and free will, encouraging them to make the highest choices possible in their daily lives takes on a new meaning. We do not only speak to our children about external consequences such as those incurred when breaking the law or missing a homework assignment at school. We focus more on the internal natural consequences that affect who we are as spiritual beings. We teach our children that the consequences that lead to being out of alignment with your soul are actually more painful than any external consequence could ever be. You have the opportunity to create either heaven or hell right here on earth in your own life according to your perceptions, belief systems, and choices.

God gave us free will; free will is viewed by us as *one of our greatest human blessings,* not as original sin. It is by using your God-given free will that you're able to experience in a physical body the creative, eternal, and infinite aspects of your spirit in the realm of the relative. It is this experiential quality of your endeavor on earth which leads to no less than the evolution of your very soul. Without free will, you wouldn't be free to create in the image of the Creator. We encourage our

> Cause and effect, natural consequences, and free will are discussed frequently in our family, for it is our belief that when the internal aspects of these spiritual realities are fully understood, the external aspects are no longer an issue. Integrity is something that can only be felt on the deepest of levels.

children to utilize their free will knowing that while there are no *wrong* or *right* choices per se, there are very real natural consequences that emerge with every single choice. We're by no means a perfect family, but we choose to be accountable.

Jim and I take our roles as parents very seriously. We understand that we must guide our children and keep them safe. Of course, in their early ages, we didn't let them touch a hot stove because it was their free will to do so. When it was time for potty-training, we made the decision that there would be no more diapers in the house and didn't make it a choice each day of underwear or pull-ups. There are obviously many choices that children are simply too young to make on their own so, as parents, we act as their energetic vortex. As children grow older, intuitively we know as parents when to promote and encourage independence, but even at a young age children are fully capable of learning accountability for their choices. What I'm encouraging here is more about speaking the language of their divine heritage from the beginning. Let them know that you are in the role of parent and will guide and protect them, but that they in their own right were born with everything they'll ever need deep inside of them. So yes, you guide your children in all possible ways, but guiding children can be done in such a way that children know that they, eventually, really will be the ones steering their own ship. Children come to realize that human beings are energetic, vibrational entities who are infinitely more powerful than most people realize. They come to know that thoughts, words, and deeds are creative tools used in every moment of the day to manifest physical reality. This understanding of their creative, spiritual nature already exists deep within them and can be shaped at an early age with the language used in the home.

You are the source for what is created in your life. Choose wisely for you.

Making the Highest Choice

One day my daughter Piper brought home a book from the library by anthropologist Jane Goodall who did the amazing work with the chimpanzees in Africa. At this time, we were working with our children on cause and effect, natural consequences, and free will. I happened to notice this quote on the back of the book:

Every individual matters.
Every individual has a role to play.
Every individual makes a difference.

I decided that we would base our next family discussion on this quote as it so clearly spoke to those concepts. The quote led us to a wonderful discussion about choice. We talked about everything in life being a choice. We always have a choice and it simply comes down to what sort of difference do we want to make? There's always a choice: *To be loving, or not? To be joyful, or not? To be courageous, or not? To be kind, or not? To be authentic, or not? To be forgiving, or not? To be lighthearted, or not? To be compassionate, or not? To be truthful, or not? To be flexible, or not?* There is no right or wrong choice, but know and understand on a deep level that your choice *will* head you in a certain direction. All choices should be made as a direct result of the direction in which you currently desire to go. Some directions can lead to rockier, more arduous paths, whereas other directions lead you to well-lit, easier ones. You are the source for what is created in your life. Choose wisely for *you.*

We teach our children that masters who walk this earth, and I believe there are many walking among us today, *always* make the highest choice. We teach our children that they can, too. Each one of us is on the road to mastery. Many of us are still beginners, but we are capable and actually invited to emulate the masters who have walked among us. Mastery is not just meant for some, but meant for all. A master's grandest hope is that you choose to consciously engage your spirit in earthly existence and become a master yourself. The Universe never coerces you into making the highest choice for you; that decision can come only from within.

What Would Love Do Now?

I've had this question posted somewhere in my house for many, many years. It is a powerful question posed throughout the *Conversations with God* series by Neale Donald Walsch. When we take the time to ask ourselves this little question and then take the time to actually listen to the answer before we think, speak and act, our lives evolve much differently. Every person, condition, and circumstance offers you an invitation to give and receive love. Without exception, you can choose love if it's your greatest desire to do so. This simple question reminds you each and every day to even *consider* love as an option. I invite you to include love for yourself in this question. When you love yourself enough to live true to what resonates with your soul, you always provide others with your highest offerings.

Be the Change that You Wish to See in the World

This powerful, yet subtle quote by Gandhi can be found all over the world today. Step into a yoga studio or bookstore and you'll see it. Actually living this quote as the major tenet of your life, however, is much more difficult; but I believe it's where we are all headed. The realization that we must change if we desire our world to change is slowly, but surely entering into our belief systems. The more you begin to deeply understand that you're a spiritual being having a human experience, not the other way around, the more you accept the possibility that you have the capacity within you to create change in your world. You see that your

You see that your world is only a reflection of what you believe to be true within yourself. As your internal belief systems evolve, your experience of the outer world evolves in tandem.

world is only a reflection of what you believe to be true within yourself. As your internal belief systems evolve, your experience of the outer world evolves in tandem.

A good example from my own life where I truly began to understand Gandhi's words has to do with the environment. As a young child I was always concerned about the environment. My mother was a staunch environmentalist as far back as the 1970s, long before it became trendy. Several years ago I became an obsessive eco-friendly person, and my friends and family often teased me about it. I spoke fervently to others about my desire for a healthier planet. My husband Jim and I made choices in our life reflecting green ideals. We walked all over town, we bought a push mower, we stopped getting the Sunday paper with all of its fillers, we recycled everything that our town would accept, we used canvas bags at the grocery store, and we used an environmental long-distance phone and internet company where 100 percent of the profits supported environmental causes.

While I was doing all of these things, however, I also worried *a lot* about things like overpopulation, trash, and global warming. I focused on those things in a negative, unsettling, and anxious kind of way. These topics created within me much stress and discomfort. If I attended a Cubs baseball game at Wrigley Field in Chicago, for example, I had a difficult time being in the moment and enjoying the game because I focused on the tons of trash being created; outwardly I appeared to be at ease and having fun, but internally, I fretted over where it was all going to go.

Around this time, Jim and I decided that we deeply desired a third child, as our family did not yet *feel* complete. It was this decision to have a third child that led to an epiphany about Gandhi's words. I realized that while I'd tried many different ways of being *green*, there were other things I desired that were actually not very green at all. Slowly, I began to relax my judgmental thoughts about others' environmental choices and realized that the best thing I could do to help the environmental movement, at this point in my life, was to make sure that *my* choices matched *my* beliefs.

It occurred to me that some of my choices were in alignment with my beliefs and some were not. It became clear to me, for example, that while I was a strong advocate for population control, I personally was making the choice to have a third child. Could it be that I was claiming the rest of the world should limit themselves to one or two children, but I could have three? Also, at this time with a growing family, we decided that we *needed* a larger car. Could it be that the rest of the world should drive small, low-emission vehicles, but I could drive a minivan? Shortly thereafter, we made the decision to buy a new house. We felt that we *needed* a bigger house now that we were to be a family of five. Could it be that I thought the rest of the world should live in small eco-friendly houses without air conditioning, but I could own a larger house cooled with central air?

Through these realizations that literally shocked me back into a place of nonjudgment, I began to really examine my beliefs on the environment. It led me straight to Gandhi's truth. Real change occurs in this world when your beliefs are mirrored back to you in your choices. You must be the change that you desire to see in the world. This has been such an important teaching in my life and one that I really want my children to understand and integrate into their daily lives. Teach your children to examine their belief systems and their choices. Assist them in becoming reflective and aware individuals who make conscious choices that match their inner beliefs.

Now my environmental stance is one of gentle reflection and personal activism. I am the change that I wish to see in the world without concern or criticism for what others are choosing. I still use my canvas bags, but don't expect that to be right for everyone. Recycling is still a passion of mine and I definitely see a hybrid car in our near future, but I respect other's decisions to buy whatever car they choose. I will vote for candidates who espouse eco-friendly policies, but in the meantime, I will make my choices, not based on governmental mandates, but rather on an inner knowing that this is the right choice for me at this time. I now allow myself to be a totally relaxed, fun-loving Cubs fan who simply goes and enjoys the game, aware of choices that I can personally make to use less trash along the way.

The Law of Attraction

The concepts of cause and effect, natural consequences, and free will have become extremely important aspects of our daily family spirituality. Recently, they led us to teaching our children more formally about the Law of Attraction, the universal law that states *like attracts like*.

This law at its core refers to our being energetic, vibrational beings who are natural co-creators of our own reality. Through your vibration you energetically draw like experiences unto yourself. You are the creator of your own experience, and you are powerful beyond your wildest imagination. All human beings are made in likeness to the Creator in that they are creators themselves, co-creating on some level everything that occurs in their lives. It's what spiritual masters have been trying to tell us for centuries. The collective consciousness of the entire planet creates what we see in our world today. What this means to you on a daily basis is this: love attracts more love, joy attracts more joy, a strong desire for a buyer attracts a buyer, a strong desire to be more gregarious attracts a gregarious partner, and so on. In other words, you call forth what appears in your reality by attracting it.

Through your vibration you energetically draw like experiences unto yourself. You are the creator of your own experience, and you are powerful beyond your wildest imagination.

At its most basic metaphysical explanation, like attracts like so what you draw, literally draw, into your physical experience on earth is what you focus on, whether it be negative or positive. We are teaching our children to become very, very attuned to what they think, say, and do. We are teaching them to be conscious in every way. Energy grows

We teach our children that they are spiritual, beings who create their reality by attracting like energies through their vibration primarily via thought, word, and deed. We assist our children in utilizing their emotions as a definitive measure as to their energetic output and capacity for optimal creation. Their emotions will never fail to show them exactly where they are in their alignment with their soul. Many, many books have now been written on the Law of Attraction alone, so I will not go into the fullness of it in this text. I will simply explain the law here as we have explained it to our children. *Ask and It Is Given* by Esther and Jerry Hicks opened my eyes to this universal law as I had never understood it before. I highly recommend their numerous magnificent teachings on this subject. Not only is it the most in-depth teaching that I have ever come across on this subject, but they also offer many processes that can be utilized on a daily basis to assist you in becoming a conscious creator.

stronger and stronger with every thought, word, and deed towards a particular subject. Energy begins moving in a distinct direction, and the creative process that is your life is underway. The Universe is set up to assist you in always remaining aligned with your soul's purpose. You may choose to either resist or move gracefully with divine flow. It comes down to personal choice and free will.

At a young age it is important to teach children to move through this world wide-awake. Wakefulness is something that comes naturally to us as children, but quickly becomes lost as we grow older and become trapped in the endless drone of our mental chatter. It is our job as parents to first reawaken ourselves, and then to allow our children to remain in their natural state of wakefulness or gently guide them back to it if it's been lost along the way.

Basically, there are three simple steps to living in divine flow that we desire our children to understand and utilize on a daily basis in their lives. (They really *are* quite simple; it is the mind that makes them difficult.) The Law of Attraction can only be taught well and understood *after* the groundwork teachings of who your children are as spiritual beings has been laid first. The cart cannot be put before the horse in this case because the Law of Attraction would be rendered meaningless without this *knowing* firmly in place.

The first step in the Law of Attraction involves *asking* for what you desire. This step comes very naturally to you. You are asking the Universe for what you want all day long through your thoughts, words, and deeds, but the key here is to become very clear and conscious of what you're actually asking for. Essentially, you ask for what you focus on, whether you're conscious of it or not. Understand that thoughts, words, and deeds are forms of energy carrying their own vibration. You continually emanate a field of energy that mirrors your current thoughts, values, and beliefs. This is what you offer to the world moment-to-moment, and it greatly determines your state of being or energetic frequency. Thoughts are the weakest vibration and deeds are of a higher frequency, but they all recapitulate throughout the Universe and begin, on some level, to create what you will see in your future reality. It's very important to note here that it is the *intensity* of the thought or belief that matters most as far as how quickly something becomes physically manifested in your life, but *everything* affects your field and what you offer the world.

It's also extremely important to appreciate what you already have in your life because gratitude and appreciation are two of the highest and most powerful vibrations that exist in the Universe. Even if you don't particularly care for what you've created, it is still to be blessed because the contrast allows you to know yourself more deeply and understand better what you do desire to create and just may have been created on the soul level for that very purpose. So acknowledge and accept every single relationship and circumstance, and internally appreciate the process as a whole.

With this first step, help your children become aware, on a very basic level, that they are indeed captains of their own ship. It's important to monitor your thoughts and make them of a more positive nature whenever possible. It's during this stage where your heart's desires become known to the Universe and activated. Encourage

What you truly believe you will receive and what you receive is always a perfect vibrational match.

*I want a new house . . . BUT my true inner belief is that it's impossible because I have no money, I never get good deals, and my current house is too small and in a total state of disrepair.

*I want the perfect mate . . . BUT I'm lonely, my body is ugly, relationships never work out for me, and there are no good partners left out there anyway.

*I want good health . . . BUT my problems are chronic, I have no time to exercise, and I am unable to heal myself.

These examples make the important point that if you focus on the lack of something, then that's what you'll continue to receive because you get what you focus on. As I've heard many spiritual teachers say, *energy flows where the attention goes.* Turn all of the above BUTs into positive statements and give those cues to the Universe instead.

your children to envision their preferences by using creative visualization techniques. *Thinking big* is highly invited. Teach your children to have preferences, but *also* to hold space for all possibilities in their mind. Encourage them to utilize their majestic imagination. Invite them to live their dreams in their mind, as if they already exist. This first step of the Law of Attraction only *you* can accomplish for yourself. It is absolutely your job to ask for what you want out of life. No one else has the power to choose your future reality for you, but you.

The second step of the Law of Attraction doesn't actively involve you. This is the answering of what you have asked for. This is the Universe's job. It is in the realm of Spirit where the *hows*, the connections, the synchronicities, the orchestration of events, and the gifts are born. Once you have set the energy in motion, it's time to *let go and let God*. Be proactive, but patient and allow the Universe to perform and do its job. Relax, get out of the way, and let the spiritual realm do its part in setting up the perfect circumstances and conditions for your optimal growth and expansion.

> *Relax, get out of the way, and let the spiritual realm do its part in setting up the perfect circumstances and conditions for your optimal growth and expansion.*

This is what the masters are referring to when they speak of the importance of total faith. This is where you release and transcend all doubt and fear. *Know* that the Universe is converging beyond the realm of human comprehension to assist you with your creation. *Know* that you are never, ever alone. The spiritual realm is continuously providing assistance to *all* within the complex, unimaginably beautiful divine matrix in which we all exist. Your only work during the second step is to remain awake and proactively move towards your desires as you feel the impulse to do so. You must continue to pay attention to the voice of your soul in order to receive direction from the Universe and then remain confident and courageous enough to follow the inner guidance that comes through you.

Patience and trust are a large part of the second step. Do you trust that the Universe is grand enough, creative enough, and loving enough to support your heart's desires? This step is much easier for you when things appear to be going *well* and much more difficult when things appear to be going *badly*. Some may wonder whether or not the Universe would deliver an ego-based desire, but judging the depth and validity of your

---

Many of our preferences are, in actuality, quite wishy-washy, fluctuating between positive and negative expectations. Often, we then receive what appear to be wishy-washy answers. If you send a mixed message, you receive a mixed result. The Universe will continue to give you exactly what you give it. This is for your highest good because eventually, and it may take many, many lifetimes, you do become fully conscious and understand the depth of your own creative power as a spiritual being. It is with this realization that you can begin to deeply enjoy the fact that you are co-creating your own reality with every thought, word, deed, and belief because you know that you can always change things if you so desire. Even if things do not outwardly seem to change, your inner perception of them absolutely can.

desires is not the Universe's job. It is for you to determine whether or not you're ultimately fulfilled by what you ask for. It is your work on earth to choose whether or not to create from ego or spirit. Every choice and every creation will have its own natural consequences and learning posts.

The final step of the Law of Attraction is *your* work, and it has to do with placing yourself in a state of *allowing* and *receiving* the answers as they come to you from Spirit. You do this by relaxing and enjoying the journey. Open yourself up to the process of life. See, hear, and feel God everywhere. Flow with your own personal energy surges that match the ebb and flow of universal energy patterns. In other words, learn to ride the wave according to how you *feel*. Go with divine flow and remain in alignment with your deepest space. Are you able to recognize, notice, and acknowledge the gifts that are being given? Do you expect them to look only one way? Are you *open* to all possible outcomes? The answers come as gifts to us packaged in a variety of ways. They could come in the form of a synchronistic meeting, the next article that you read, a phone call, the words to a song on the radio, or as a powerful all-knowing feeling that sweeps through you.

The third step is where many of us have the most difficult time. It requires understanding your emotions and what they're telling you. They pinpoint exactly where you are in your capacity to receive and show you where your thinking and beliefs are holding you back from divine flow. As Esther and Jerry Hicks explain, it becomes a moment-to-moment process of accepting exactly where you are while simultaneously (and sometimes slowly) reaching for a slightly better feeling thought. On the most basic level, you train yourself to always move towards what makes you feel better in your deepest space. Every answer to every question can be found deep within in this way. The answers flow to us in so many different ways, but many of us remain blocked and locked in a state of resistance. We often dismiss outright anything that doesn't show up for us in the way that we expected, and our emotions reflect our resistance. It is here where we must release the need for a certain outcome and trust that what is given is for our highest good. The third step has everything to do with faith. There is an absolute knowing that on some level, whether on the conscious, subconscious, or soul level, we asked for and co-created this reality with Spirit.

When you are in alignment with your soul on a daily basis, you open up the gateway to be guided by Spirit, and the more easily you move through your day in divine flow with the current of love and well-being that many call God. Raising the frequency of your vibration is being fully and rapturously *open* to this current of life at all times, and in all situations. When practiced enough, you eventually know yourself so well that you can feel when you are in a

There's no right or wrong here, only a movement towards acceptance and consciousness, allowing you to utilize your own ebb and flow of energy.

high-vibration state of being and when you are not. You can literally feel joy, appreciation, love, and empowerment vibrating on a cellular level in an outward motion when you're in a high state of allowing. Likewise, you come to know without a doubt when you're vibrating in a slower and denser pattern of energy. There's no right or wrong here, only a movement towards acceptance and consciousness, allowing you to utilize your own ebb and flow of energy.

The collective consciousness of the planet is also creating much of what we see in our world. You must fully acknowledge that you are a part of that collective consciousness. You may not directly be creating large-scale events that are occurring in the world, but you must nonetheless feel enough responsibility to continuously look very closely at your own belief systems and choice patterns which are reflected in the world at large. The entire earth matrix interconnects us all in a complexity that remains almost incomprehensible to the human mind; and our earth matrix is just a miniscule aspect of the whole universal matrix. It is all-important that children understand their relationship to the divine whole. In order for the collective consciousness of the planet to shift, our young must become more self-aware and responsible for their part in creating change.

The Law of Attraction works in your life always, in all ways, both big and small. In fact, many of us apply it only to the enormous aspects of our lives, when really it's the small desires and choices that we make each day that often have the most influence on our life as a whole. To receive, you simply need to open yourself up to the open-ended, ever-expanding, never-ending process of life, *all* of life, not just what you perceive as *right* and *good*.

Whether on a conscious, subconscious, or soul level, begin to understand in your innermost space that you are in fact creating your life experiences. If you don't enjoy what you have created, bless it, appreciate it, accept it, and then seek to change it. Conscious living requires us to become acutely aware of what exactly we're offering *energetically* in each moment.

Individual responsibility, yet alone collective responsibility, is extremely difficult to wrap a human mind around unless it's a perspective encouraged at a young age. It comes down to both conscious awareness *and* faith. If you try to mathematically, analytically, or logically *figure* it all out, you won't be able to do so. Our greatest scientific minds have certainly moved closer to mapping out the *secrets* of the Universe in recent decades, but even they realize that each new discovery is simply the tip of the iceberg in the fullness of their understanding of the Universe entire. Grasping the concepts of *limitless* and *infinite* is almost impossible for the human mind to comprehend in our dualistic, relative, three-dimensional world. Thankfully, not fully understanding the physics of it all is more than okay because this leads to surrender, and surrender is the gateway to heaven—the heaven that exists within you. The mystery and the unknown aspects of life can be cherished and used to your benefit, as they carry a high vibration, an energetic frequency that can be harnessed by you to create an expanded faith which leads to a new world.

As you begin to consciously use the Law of Attraction in your own life, it's important to remember that your intentions must be of pure heart. Let the gentle wisdom that flows from your soul *exist* as the guiding force in what you choose to call forth into your reality. It's also important to understand that any and all contrast and variety that show up in your life are to be blessed. Contrast, in the form of challenges or opposition to what you're attracting, will always show up in varying degrees so that you may experience what it is that you have called forth. It's in the contrast that you get to *claim* your truth in a new way. Without the contrast, in the relative world you would have no way of experiencing and understanding the shift in perspective that's actually occurred. Remember that you cannot know tall without short, forgiveness without resentment, light without dark. The minute you begin to create a new idea or path, life will provide you with opportunities to begin experiencing your vision in the physical realm. See contrast for what it is and continue towards your goal knowing that God is by your side.

Relationships and life experiences offer children plenty of daily interaction with the concepts of variety and contrast. Provide them with the opportunity to explore more deeply and share their findings with you. Learning to expect and bless contrast and variety liberates your children to live true to their own preferences and choices. Choices become not a matter of right or wrong, but rather a matter of deep inner knowing of what resonates as true for your soul.

Even if we're unconsciously manifesting what we really don't want by continually focusing on it, God is always calling us home through thousands of symbols and signs that are unique to us. Your own soul is always offering you gentle wisdom no matter what vibrational pattern you seem to be stuck in at the moment. Even if you're mired in the muck of negative thoughts and self-doubt, your inner being is *always* right there, attempting to lead you to a higher thought, choice, and vibration. Even the creation of something in your life that you don't truly desire serves as a learning post towards something greater on your path. So yes, the Universe delivers to you what you call forth, without exception, but the highest vibration—God—is ever-present and always available to you because it resides within you. Everything that shows up in life is to be blessed, for even contrast has the capacity to lead us home.

> *Everything that shows up in life is to be blessed, for even contrast has the capacity to lead us home.*

Prayer

Another family discussion initiated in relationship to the Law of Attraction was how to pray. I realized that while we shared grace before dinner and sometimes shared prayers before bed, my husband and I had never consciously discussed with our children how we individually pray, when and why we pray, or the power of prayer. So we held a family discussion on prayer and its all-encompassing benefit to us as spirits-embodied living on the physical plane.

I shared with my family that I pray every morning before my feet hit the floor. I lie in bed having just awoken to a new day, and I thank God and my soul in advance for co-creating with me that day. I shared that I say only prayers of gratitude. These prayers of total, undeniable, magnificent gratitude bring me much peace and calm as I start my day. I pray as though everything has already been answered. I shared that I believe in transcending all doubt with my prayers. For example, if our family is leaving on a road trip at 5:00 pm, that morning, before I get out of bed, before the car has even been packed, I thank Spirit for delivering us to our destination safely, knowing that it has already happened. I pray for inner peace, expanded self-aware-ness, and the capacity to express my highest potential. I pray for acceptance of what is so, and the courage to seek change where desired. I pray for a moment-to-moment conscious inner knowing that I am part of the divine force that creates my world. I pray for receptivity to All That Is to permeate my entire being and manifest as my life lived. And I pray for others that they may come to experience their own unique expres-sions of divinity through the folds of their own life.

Invite God into your life through a daily conversation.

My morning prayers are a time of deep connection with my soul. As the early morning sunlight gently streams through my window, I experi-ence God through me. I consciously access the divine dominion. It is here where I place my spirit in the palm of Total Consciousness and express gratitude for each and every aspect of personal consciousness that is my own. This is a specific time in my day where I bear witness to my glorious internal connection to All That Is. I also pray at other times throughout my day, namely for a few minutes before I meditate. Find times to pray that work for you. Prayer is a deeply personal and intimate experience.

I shared with my family that I view my thoughts and intentions as prayers. I believe that we pray energetically with every thought, word, and deed. We discussed the importance of being very aware throughout each and every day as to where you focus your energy. We talked about the importance of positive thinking and reiterated our belief that *like attracts like* in our Universe. We discussed the importance of taking the time to envision your day and literally draw the experiences that you desire into your life through the power of prayer.

Prayer is a powerful means of reconnecting to your spirit and reigniting your undivided, unfiltered oneness with God. As with every-thing, there is no one right way to pray. Do what comes naturally to you.

Invite God into your life through a daily conversation. Prayers are an intimate, personal dialogue with the Creator. Thank God for co-creating with you in all of your life's work and play. Acknowledge the gift of life by dialoguing with God every single day. Encourage your children to do the same as they witness the power of prayer in your own life.

Understanding cause and effect, natural consequences, and free will takes children a long way towards understanding, on a very basic, metaphysical level, how the Universe operates and what it all means in regards to their daily life. We must encourage our children not to be afraid of their co-creative power with the Universe, but rather to understand it more deeply and to consciously use it to create a life they desire. As a spiritual being, the forces of this grand Universe cannot be denied. You exist within the divine matrix, and you are an integral part of it. The question becomes, do you choose to move through it consciously with grace and gentle wisdom, or not? Do you choose to help your children experience their eternal existence consciously, or not?

Integrate It into Your Own Family!

Parent Contemplations:

- How do you feel about the Law of Attraction? Is it something that you acknowledge and utilize in your own life? If so, cite several examples.

- How can you integrate true free will more fully into your choices?

- In what ways will state of being become a higher priority in your life? What can you do to raise your vibration on a daily basis?

Activities:

- Co-Creation Bracelets: Take two different colors of thread. One color represents the Universe entire and the other color represents *you*. The color representing you will have two threads because you have two jobs in the co-creative process. The Universe color will only have one thread because it has one job. The Universe thread should be placed in the center. Make a friendship bracelet representing your co-creative relationship with the Universe: steps one and three are your colors signifying the asking and the receiving, and step two is the Universe's color signifying the "how" aspect of co-creation. (Adapted from *Nurturing Spirituality in Children* by Peggy Jenkins.)

- Imagination Blitz: Hold visualization sessions as a family where each person closes his eyes and imagines in full-blown detail and color what he currently desires to create. Then write down, draw, or collage the vision and share with the family and claim out loud to the Universe. Post somewhere visible in your home. It's important to recognize the *essence* of your heart's desire rather than becoming attached to it manifesting only one way. This activity is meant to assist your children in recognizing their own power to co-create their future reality.

- Manifestation Game: Each person writes on a slip of paper an object to manifest into physical reality for the week. Put each written suggestion in a hat or a bag and have someone pull out one slip of paper identifying what the object to manifest will be for that week. (A red ball, a purple hat, a blue feather, etc.) All week each member of the family keeps track of how often they see this object out in the world. Note each person's sightings on a shared piece of paper or posterboard. Have fun! (This game was taught to me by Debbie Mackall.)

- Emotional Scale: This is a scale which encourages all family members to utilize their emotions to *feel* their way to a higher state of being, while reminding them that state of being is the cause of reality, not the effect. Hang a copy, either posterboard size or standard, somewhere in your house. It's a great way for family members to determine how they're feeling and what they need to process in order to raise their vibration. (The Emotional Scale can be found in the book *Ask and It Is Given* by Esther and Jerry Hicks.)

Books:

Picture: *Because Brian Hugged His Mother* (David L. Rice)
Chapter: The *Sara* series (Esther and Jerry Hicks)
Adult: *Ask and It Is Given* (Esther and Jerry Hicks), *The Secret* (Rhonda Byrne)

Movies:

Pay It Forward (2000)
Chariots of Fire (1981)

Songs:

Be Good (Hothouse Flowers)
Man in the Mirror (Michael Jackson)

Chapter 10

Soul to Soul Parenting *Spiritual Theme*

Authenticity and Joy

Authenticity and joy go hand in hand. Being truly authentic, by making the choices and living in a way that most accurately reflects your deepest beliefs, always brings joy to the soul. Speaking your truth with compassion and conviction, while following the beat of your own heart, is the surest way to experience true joy within your soul. Saying yes when you mean yes and no when you mean no defines authentic living. Authenticity should be encouraged with every choice that a child makes so that he can live in personal freedom and true joy. Authenticity and joy come quite naturally to children, but as they get older they must be encouraged to *continue* to go within and really *feel* a choice in their deepest space.

Speaking your truth with compassion and conviction, while following the beat of your own heart, is the surest way to experience true joy within your soul.

Experience the joy that rises up from within each time you remain true to your unique authenticity. Engage in the things that you love to do as often as you can. Surround yourself with other authentic individuals. Find out what makes your eyes sparkle and *go there* frequently. When you feel joy moving freely deep inside your soul, don't hesitate, for this is God expressing joy through you, and there is no greater gift.

In order for one to be fully joyous, one must be fully authentic. Likewise, in order for one to be fully authentic, one must be totally joyous on a deep inner level, even in the face of seemingly bad events and circumstances. Authenticity is about living true, living true to your truth, your dreams, your joys, and your passions. Teach your children to

> Share your feelings and expressions of joy with your children. Model a life filled with passion and authenticity. A child who witnesses joy and authenticity regularly in a parent will find it easier to live her life authentically and joyously, too. Support all family members as they engage in the passions and pursuits that bring them joy.

ground themselves in their own authenticity by modeling and speaking often of what this means. Encourage them to zipper themselves up in their truth each and every day.

Authenticity comes in all shapes, sizes, and forms. This is where wondrous, miraculous, and beautiful variety expresses itself within the Oneness. Most human beings are very much in touch with their authenticity and joy as children, but ever so quietly, they conform to parental, peer, and societal expectations, losing what they know to be true about *them* along the way. Don't allow your children to lose themselves in conformity. Encourage them to heed the voice of their soul and to resist the temptation to rely on outside sources for personal truth. It's never too late to reconnect with your most authentic and joyous inner space, your soul. The voice of your soul will *always* lead you home.

Being truly authentic, without fear, guilt, or apology, has perhaps been my greatest challenge in life. Looking back on my early years, I see that I began to fly under the radar, so to speak, at a young age. I didn't allow myself to be too smart, too pretty, too athletic, too spiritual, too authentic, or too joyous for fear that if I shone too brightly, I would no longer be loved and accepted by others. It was this self-sabotaging fear that I would somehow become *separate* from others that

> *It's never too late to reconnect with your most authentic and joyous inner space, your soul. The voice of your soul will always lead you home.*

held me back for much of my life from living true. So I trod along my path rather quietly, always holding back just a little and hoping not to attract too much attention. Yes, I could sometimes be the life of the party, but that's not really what I'm talking about here. I'm talking about sharing my authentic self proudly, confidently, and joyously with the world, knowing that I can be openly passionate towards life in any way that I choose.

I now understand that the only time I feel separate is when I separate myself from my soul energy and begin to resist the divine flow of my own life. It's when I hold back my true essence and deny my authenticity out of fear that my joy dissipates and feelings of separation take hold. I see now that I can never be separate from All That Is because that is who I am. The intricacy and beauty of God that I am here to express is my divine flow, and it looks, sounds, and feels like no other. There may be similarities in my outward expressions with another, but my soul imprint is uniquely mine, and it is to be cherished, acknowledged, appreciated, and loved at *every* turn.

Trust Annieness, Jimness, Aidenness, Piperness, and Peteness

When you trust the voice of your own soul, you're led to the perfect choices for your own unique path, and no matter what appears externally in your reality, all really is well.

The above is a Soul to Soul Reminder that's received many curious looks and interesting comments from visitors to our home. This originally appeared as simply *Trust Annieness* as a personal reminder to me to be authentic without self-doubt, fear, or apologies. Trusting *me* has been my biggest block to acknowledging and nurturing my inner being; self-doubt and fear of separation have been my greatest karmic work in this lifetime. So, trusting Annieness, in all my glory, has become a celebrated choice in my life. After a family discussion on the topic of authenticity, we added all of five of our names to this reminder. When you trust the voice of your own soul, you're led to the perfect choices for your own unique path, and no matter what appears externally in your reality, *all really is well.*

We continually focus on this topic of trusting yourself—trusting your perceptions, life experiences, and deep inner resonation. Even within one's own family, many individuals often have a difficult time living authentically and expressing joy. In fact, sometimes, one's own family unknowingly imposes the biggest hurdle to living true. Often roles are created within families, keeping members locked and trapped into appearing a certain way. These roles may even follow them for an entire lifetime, years after leaving the nest. Giving another human being permission to feel totally and completely at ease with his unique personal truth is perhaps the greatest gift that you can ever give to another, especially to the members of your beloved family.

In our family, we do our best to celebrate each other's passions. This doesn't come without challenges, but we're willing to see each family member clearly and consciously without hidden agendas or motives. We are willing to stand as *souls* with one another and strip away outer masks. To the best of our ability in each moment, we encourage one another to follow her truth and her bliss.

My older daughter Aidenn is quite grounded, with a strong sense of her own inner beauty. She trusts herself in a way that is mature for her age. She rarely looks to others for approval and makes decisions based on her own feelings and perceptions. She's extremely confident, yet in no way craves attention or the spotlight. She loves peace and quiet, doing well in school, writing, playing soccer, interacting with others in an in-depth way, and being with her family and close friends. She possesses the gift of expanded perception in that she is able to observe her surround-ings and acknowledge and appreciate many aspects of a larger picture; she is open to the divine whole rather than simply her small window of reality. Teachers consistently point out Aidenn's maturity and capacity to understand situations beyond her point of view or her age. She is a child to be trusted and appreciated for her sense of fairness. Her generosity of spirit is perhaps one of her finest attributes. She's extremely comfortable in her own skin and unafraid to speak her truth in a kind, but firm way.

Our middle daughter Piper is quite different from her older sister in many ways. While she too is empathetic, she's not as grounded and perceives the world from a unique, ethereal vantage point. She lives more in her imagination and prefers smaller groups to loud, crowded environ-ments. Piper shares a deep relationship with the natural world beyond simply enjoying nature and animals. She is able to experience oneness and quiet in this world in a way that eludes many others. Her authen-ticity is most apparent in settings where she is very connected physically to the wonder and beauty of our natural world. Catching a frog or collecting rocks in a field brings to Piper a sense of wholeness and peace that can be seen in her entire being. The faraway smile and gleam in her eyes expose a joy in her deepest space that is palpable.

Pete, our third-born and only boy, could not be more authentic if he tried. Even as young as six months old, Pete's favorite toy has always been a ball of any kind, but especially a baseball. To this day, Pete continues to be an intense, competitive sports lover and displays tremendous control of his physical body. You can sense in the way he moves, focuses his energy, and smiles that Pete is living true when he participates in or observes sports. He shines and expresses his true self to the world in this arena. That is not to say that he has no other interests or is a singularly faceted guy, and we would never encourage him to be so (unless, of course, that is what he chose). Whether Pete is hip-hop dancing in the family room or playing soccer on the field, he relishes the inner workings of his beautifully agile, God-given physicality.

A funny thing happened one summer day when our whole family went to see the movie *You, Me and Dupree* starring Owen Wilson and Kate Hudson. Owen Wilson, after much difficulty, ends up finding his way and becoming an inspirational speaker. As he begins talking to a standing-room-only crowd, he states that the only thing you really need to do to be happy is to trust yourself. He points to an audience member and says, "You know, trust Joeness!" We all looked at each other in disbelief and smiled broadly. This movie embraces the exact theme that we utilize to encourage authenticity and joy in our family. It was a divine wink at its best.

Is This Who I Am?

It is not for us to judge another's path to authenticity and joy. Bliss is always a personal choice. The question *Is this who I am?* was first posed to me in the *Conversations with God* material, and it always reconnects me to my higher self. It's important to check yourself as you move through the day. Ask yourself: *Am I thinking, speaking, and behaving in accordance with my truest self? Are my choices reflective of my highest thoughts about myself? Am I expressing myself authentically? Am I in alignment with the voice of my soul? Am I swimming in divine flow?*

Help your children answer these questions for themselves as life situations and relationships present opportunities to live their truth. From the choice of whether or not to pick up a tin can littering the street to take home and recycle or how to react to your best friend's sad news, the choice to live true is always yours. Begin to contemplate on a regular basis how you choose to move through this world. Reconsider when you are behaving in a way that doesn't accurately reflect your inner belief system. Be fully present in each moment. Notice everything. Consciously and joyously move with the divine flow that is your life. Choose to live a truly authentic, joyous, and spirited life and model for your children what this looks like.

Be Courageous, Listen to Your Heart's Desires, and Assist Others on Their Path

This Soul to Soul Reminder is about leaving our comfort zones and living our truth with an awareness of not only our own path, but also the paths of others. It's always worth attempting to achieve something that you truly desire because ultimately the joy is in the journey, not the prize. We encourage our children to reach beyond all perceived limitations and expect the best. We teach our children to rely on God to assist them on whatever path they choose. We support our children in viewing themselves as multidimensional beings who possess the capacity within them to create the seemingly impossible. We encourage our children to bless the whole journey as they consciously seek guideposts along the way. And always, always, we remind our children to help others on their individual paths in anyway that they can, for to empower another lights up the whole world.

Come Out!

These two words on a Soul to Soul Reminder remind our family to *come out* with our true selves. Authenticity keeps you connected to your spirit. Announce yourself to others. Show the world your uniqueness. Speak your truth with love, honesty, and compassion. Don't hold back from being beautiful you. Refuse to "hide your light under a bushel" out of fear that you'll somehow become separate and unlovable. It's so important to model authentic living to your children. If they observe you being uniquely you out in the world, then it will come quite naturally to them to live in this same way. Speak truth about who you are. Authentically and joyously share yourself with others. Hold the space that was carved out in this world especially for you. No one else can fill that space. Come out with yourself and occupy your sacred space *fully*. Invite others to join you in your quest to live true. Trust me, others will come out of the woodwork, basking in the freedom and glory of their own newfound wholeness and desiring to assist you on your path.

Allow your children to live authentically and joyously. Usually at a very young age, children show strong signs as to which path comes most naturally to them, highlighting the path of their soul. Listen to your children and pay attention to where they're leading you. Look, and feel, for their authenticity and their joy. When children are observed carefully with an open heart and an open mind, these two things will be hard to miss.

How often do you allow yourself to express free-flowing joy, even to your closest friends? Are you sometimes afraid that showing too much joy will somehow diminish another? I say let your joy ignite joy in the other. Rather than hide uninhibited joy, help others to find their joy, too. There is all too often an abundance of joy-stomping in the world and not enough joy-expanding. Seek to find out which of these you do when it comes to your own joy and the joy expressed through another. Are you a joy-stomper or a joy-expander? Encourage all family members to assess this same aspect in themselves and seek to change patterns of interaction that no longer feel right.

It is such a gift to the child *and* to the parent when a child's authenticity is easily and undeniably revealed. So many people spend their entire lives almost as *lost souls,* without an inner knowing of what it is that makes them feel most alive as spirit-embodied living here on this planet. It is my strong feeling that passion, at any age, should never be squelched. While as a parent you do have an obligation to guide your children in the balancing of many aspects of life, you must allow your children to lead authentic lives at all costs. Help your children understand the importance of true living to their total well-being.

Call Your Spirit Up Every Day

"Calling your spirit up" is the way in which one of my favorite teachers describes reconnecting with your spirit. Only you can know what places you in vibrational alignment with your soul. Reconnecting with your spirit is a personal, intimate process. It's your responsibility to get to know yourself from the inside out. It's up to you to *allow* yourself to lead a spiritually driven life. Find out: What lights you up? What fills your tank? What feeds your fire? What touches your heart? What stirs your soul?

Reconnecting with your spirit is a personal, intimate process. It's your responsibility to get to know yourself from the inside out.

These are the things that will: Awaken you each day to the glory of God. Create in you a beautiful channel of grace. Enable you to navigate the challenges in life. Expand your heart to a greater capacity for compassion, understanding, and forgiveness. Inspire you to become your best self. Assist you in your ability to give and receive love.

Feel the energetic shift in your vibration as you engage in what you love. When you begin to pay attention to how you *feel,* you can easily discern where you stand energetically each day; and therefore, consciously assess the energy that you're offering the world. This energy that emanates from your being is your point of attraction at any given moment. Be conscious of the energy that you are in, always feeling and accepting exactly where you are, while at the same time, seeking to move to higher ground as quickly as possible. Understand that a shift in energetic output rarely happens all at once, but rather is a gradual working through and releasing of emotions that are not beneficial to hold onto longer than needed.

Teaching your children to become responsible for assessing where they are in relationship to their own access to free-flowing joy is imperative if they are to liberate themselves from a life filled with resistance and fear. Work with them on recognizing emotions as signs and guideposts showing them exactly where they're standing in relationship to their personal divine flow. Empower them to learn for themselves how to call their spirit up and move up the emotional scale towards hope, contentment, peace, and joy as quickly as possible. Model for them how *you* process anger, frustration, and disappointment; and thereby, move

Some days I wake up feeling totally connected to the Divine Presence that is in me and in all things. I don't really need to call my spirit up; I'm already there. I can feel that I'm vibrating at a high level and know that I will move through my day with joy, divine flow, surrender, and ease; on other days, not so much. I know from the moment I open my eyes that I'll need a little help reconnecting with my spirit. For some reason, I'm feeling anxious, worried, or simply off. I accept those feelings and begin to assess the internal cause. Slowly, I begin to navigate the suddenly choppy waters that are disturbing my interior peace. It may take minutes, it may take hours, or it may even take days for me to move back into my natural state of ease and alignment with my soul. It may prove to be quite challenging or easier than I had anticipated, but I now understand without a trace of doubt that the only individual who can scale my emotional ladder is me. I am responsible for my own vibrational frequency. I am responsible for calling my spirit up to heighten my movement towards greater peace, love, and joy within my own inner being.

into emotions that reflect the pure energy of your spirit. It is possible for a family to live together consciously assisting one another in this way. It is possible to experience anger as not something that should be hidden or denied, but rather something that should be safely expressed and worked through. It is possible to become aware moment-to-moment of the changes in your own energetic output which greatly determine all that will become manifested in your future reality. It is possible for children to begin to understand these *advanced* universal teachings at a young age because they are deeply aware of them on a soul level. It will resonate as truth if the parent allows true resonation and utilization of these teachings.

While it hasn't always been the case in my life, I now choose to give myself permission to live from my spirit more than ever before. For example, writing this book has been one of the first times in my life where I have fully allowed myself to be utterly engaged for long stretches in the work that I love so much. This newfound capacity within me to allow myself to be enraptured in my work has been life-changing. The freedom to be doing whatever it is that I choose to do, and being however it is that I choose to be, is nothing short of joyous exhilaration.

It is extremely important that you provide your children every opportunity possible to become enraptured in their own passions and choices. When a soul is called to create in a specific way, resisting that call is "hell on earth" for the soul and leads to unhappiness and resentment, for the psychic attraction to create in a specific medium reflects an individual's core truth. Ignoring the call inevitably leads to a feeling of separation from the divine source within. While I agree that some balance is necessary in a child's life, when a child discovers what truly lights her up, I see it as a beautiful gift that has fallen into the *entire* family's lap.

I am deeply in touch with the call of my spirit and assist my children at every turn to be in touch with the call of their spirit, too. I reach for my passions and my truth as I seek to release negative emotions and allow more contentment and appreciation into my reality. Take some time and ask each person in your family to compile a personal list of what truly brings him joy. Jot down everything that comes to mind in a five-minute period. It's amazing to see when the lists are shared how many simple pleasures you can engage in every day to call your own spirit up and raise your energetic vibration. These are things that will assist you each and every time you desire equilibrium in your thoughts and alignment with your soul.

I find that creating these love lists is much more difficult for adults. Many adults have lost touch with their passion and no longer acknowledge or even recognize what really lights them up. As an adult, if you are unsure of your passions, the easiest way to assist you in gently unfolding them into your awareness is to rediscover what you truly loved to do as a child. This will give you great clues as to how you can lead a more authentic life, filled with passion and fulfillment.

*   *   *   *   *   *   *   *   *   *   *   *   *   *   *   *   *   *

Here are a few items from my personal love list. I've shared *big* examples and *small* examples, but to me, they all have personal meaning and share the same purpose, moving me always towards greater peace, love, and joy.

I love to **swing**. I never miss a chance when I'm at the park with my family to swing really, really high so that I feel as I did when I was a little girl, that my feet can actually touch the sky. Sometimes my children swing with me, but many times now that they are much older, I remain on the swings while they roam about the park doing the things that they love to do. We also have a swing that hangs from a huge oak tree in our backyard, and I spend a lot of time on that swing, weather permitting. It brings me much joy to immerse myself in this activity.

These are the things that sustain me. This is the spiritual well that I return to time and time again to access my divine reservoir.

I love to **dance**. I was a serious ballerina as a child and dancing still rocks my soul just as it did then. I was four years old when I began taking dance lessons and fell in love with ballet. My passion for ballet throughout my entire childhood reminds me of my passion for spirituality now; I am both a dancer and a spiritual journeyman in my heart of hearts. With dance, I love the music, the poise, the grace, and most of all, the fluidity of movement that can be expressed through my body. If I'm feeling out of sorts and disconnected, it can usually be remedied with dance. I put the music on and let the healing begin. One day before I was to work lunch duty at my children's school, I remember feeling very flat. Nothing in particular was *wrong*; it was just a feeling of discontent, the winter blues. I knew I didn't want to serve lunch to hundreds of wonderful schoolchildren and extend this feeling of malaise towards them. The solution was to call my spirit up by turning on the music and dancing my way back to a joyous energy vibration. I danced around my house for a full thirty minutes, and with each move, I could literally feel the shift throughout my body and emotional output. I felt a release. I felt joy. I began to soar. By the time I reached the school, I was on such a natural high. I felt tremendous love for the children and created the space to be wide-awake and fully present for the whole experience. I knew I had created this energetic shift through my dancing, and I was grateful to recognize how important dancing is to my well-being.

I love **my morning ritual of a warm mug of coffee or tea**. I look forward to starting my day this way. Most times I don't even finish the whole cup. I enjoy quietly making it. I enjoy holding the mug in my hands. I enjoy the steam. I enjoy moving it around with me as I move about in the morning. It makes me feel happy. I'm not sure why, but I know that it does. This morning ritual calls my spirit up and helps me awaken to the infinite possibilities in my day.

I love **large bodies of water**. I grew up in a city surrounded by water, and I now live less than a mile from Lake Michigan. Water rejuvenates my spirit. It calls me back to God. As I leave my house for a long walk, my spirit always turns me in the direction of water unless I have a specific destination in mind with a stop to make. I feel close to Mother Earth around water. As a family, we choose to vacation around water. Walking a beach or swimming in a lake stirs my soul. I am very conscious of what water does to my vibration. It lifts me up and inspires me to live more authentically.

I love **my chocolate brown straw cowboy hat**. Several years ago, I was leaving Nordstrom on a gorgeous spring afternoon after doing some shopping when this great hat caught my eye. I loved the color. I loved the shape. I loved everything about this hat. My *spirit* called out to this hat. I purchased the hat and wore it around all spring and summer. I wore it out to dinner, to parties, to the pool, and even just on a regular day around the house or picking my kids up from school. I *feel* good every time I put this hat on my head. I listened to my spirit and bought something that I adored. Believe it or not, this hat represents in many ways my shift to living true to Annieness without fear or apologies.

I love **deep conversations with friends**. Almost nothing excites my soul more than really *going there* with a close friend. Soul to soul interaction is contagious. It only takes one individual to open the door and lead another into the green pastures of deep sharing and connection. Through deep conversation, internal shifts can begin to take shape and flourish. Taking the time to engage fully with a friend brings me great contentment and joy, providing true nourishment for my soul.

I love **sunny days**. Give me some vital vitamin D and make my day. I sleep with unshaded windows so that I can sense what kind of a day it will be before I even open my eyes. Living in Chicago, a city that I adore, one puts a high premium on sunlight and warmth. Lifting my face towards the sun for a few minutes, even on a cold day, does wonders for my spirit. The energy of the sun's rays lifts and centers me. I choose to exercise outside whenever possible, even putting my membership to the gym on hiatus for six months a year, so that I can fully utilize my enjoyment of sunny days. I'm not a big tanner; I simply use the sunlight for raising my energetic vibration and enhancing my day. When a sunny day comes a-calling, I will call to *it* right back. I create space on those beautiful days to connect with the beams of light streaming down upon me in any way that I can.

I love **being silly with my family**. Those closest to me know that my inner child is always along for the ride, and when she feels compelled to come out, there's no telling what she'll do or say. As a young child, I was an absolute paradox: on the one hand longing for depth and on the other, the clown of the family. I've always felt a giddiness towards life deep within. I greatly enjoy cutting loose and expressing myself with a child's delight. While silliness may occur in a public place, these moments of glee almost always occur alongside my family or close friends. I can actually feel my cellular body shift gears as my spirit explodes outward, reflecting a wild-eyed, happy child.

Other items on my love list include singing, coloring, working with clay, swimming (especially in the ocean and lakes), going to a bookstore, walking, hiking in the mountains, sitting on a park bench, playing games, cooking out, being with family, biking, rollerblading, lying on the couch under a blanket, al fresco dining, riding the rides at an amusement park, flowers, butterflies, eagles, traveling, hanging out listening to music, driving, dressing up, dressing down, playing kickball, going to movies, good food, good wine, snow days, making soup, mowing the lawn, smoothies, light beer, meatballs, laughter, a full moon, reading a great novel, sleeping in on cold dark mornings, picnics, porch swings, jumping waves, huge trees, beautiful paintings by local artists, live music, farmhouses, open fields, waterskiing, family dinners, kayaking, local diners, Christmas Eve, writing, sitting quietly . . . and that's just the beginning.

* * * * * * * * * * * * * * * * * * * *

Once you get started, the list just grows and grows. Everything on this list, and more, can be utilized to call my spirit up. These are the things that sustain me. This is the spiritual well that I return to time and time again to access my divine reservoir. These are the things that I rely on to move me through my more negative emotions, allowing me to return to harmonic alignment with my soul. You never know the openings that may occur when you follow your divine spark and let your soul lead the way.

Many of our family discussions revolve around what we adore, appreciate, and love in this world. We share what moves us deep in our core. We continuously remind our children to embrace what they love and to follow the voice of their own soul. We encourage them always to check in with their inner being and assess how something makes them *feel*. As spiritual leaders of our own family, we model, through our own lives lived, how to effectively call our own spirit up and raise our energy vibration. It's been wonderful for our kids to observe that my husband and I feed our fires in very different ways, but the result is the same:

expressed joy. The bottom line is to teach children to know themselves as no other ever truly can and to adhere to Shakespeare's sage advice, "To thine own self be true."

At age seven, my daughter Piper quickly stood up after one of our family discussions on this topic, got out the bright yellow paper and a black marker, wrote *Live full-out* in her sweet, little-girl handwriting, and taped this spiritual reminder up with our Soul to Soul Reminders. *Live full-out* reminds you to live true, to leave your comfort zone, to think outside of the box, and to celebrate life. Don't hold back the joy that desires to leap from your whole being. Don't hold back the love that naturally wants to burst forth from your heart. Let go of fear with truth and light. Share yourself freely by being generous of spirit in *all* ways.

Stretch yourself. Step outside of the box. *Leap* outside of the box if you want to. As I heard metaphysical teacher Caroline Myss once discuss, there is no greater liberation than freeing yourself from the fear of humiliation; releasing that fear opens up everything. Let your spirit show you how to stretch. Stretching yourself exponentially expands the number of doors that may open for you, *and* it expands your heart.

Spiritual artistry takes many, many forms. A dear friend of mine, a true spiritual companion, emailed me the following quote titled *High Art* by Henry David Thoreau. I wept when I read it.

High Art

It is something to be able to paint a particular picture, or to carve a statue, and so to make a few objects beautiful; but it is far more glorious to carve and paint the very atmosphere and medium through which we look, which we can do. To affect the quality of the day, that is the highest of arts.

We all have the capacity within us for High Art, just like we all have the capacity within us to be artists. Learn how to call your spirit up and stretch yourself. Do whatever it takes. Move, dance, sing, garden, or write. Consciously create your own heaven on earth. Listen to your heart. Follow your bliss. Your authenticity and joy await you. Choose it! Claim it! Bless it! Live it! Share it!

Integrate It into Your Own Family!

Parent Contemplations:

- Name at least twenty things that bring you exquisite joy. How often do you allow yourself to experience them?

- Name three things that you do on a daily basis to raise your vibration.

- What attributes constitute your authenticity, making you uniquely you? Assess your ability to think, speak, and act your truth. Cite recent examples where you were able to do so. Cite examples where you were not.

- In what ways do you most often experience joy with your family?

Activities:

- Love Lists: Create your own personal love lists of earthly activities, choices, experiences, people, and places that bring you joy and express your authenticity. The list becomes your "toolbox" for raising vibration as needed throughout your day for optimal co-creation. Young children can create a "ME Bag" or a small "trinket sack" that holds small representations of what they love, which they can carry around with them. The toolbox can also be drawn or collaged. This activity reminds us of what brings us peace and joy in our own unique way.

- Review your week at family discussions. Each person writes out and shares five aspects of their week that brought true joy and/or expressed their unique authenticity. Likewise, make note of the five areas in your week where you would now make changes and why. This activity teaches children to become conscious of their reality and empowers them to create change. Point out to your children that this is a daily/weekly process; there is no finish line in becoming more conscious. This exercise helps children discern the "shoulds" (often dictated by society and others) from what truly resonates for *them*.

- Think back to a recent conversation that left you feeling lower in vibration than when it started. Name at least one thing spoken by *you* that you would change to more accurately reflect your true feelings. Likewise, recall a conversation where you clearly spoke your truth in a firm and loving way. How did this feel? Compare the two and assess the level of freedom felt with one versus the residual resentments, worrying, and perhaps anger from the other. Encourage children to become more confident in speaking their truth in a respectful way.

- Vision-map different areas of your life to create forward movement towards activating your authentic desires in each area. (Examples might be in friendships, school, work, play, family, health, spirit.) The vision map may be drawn by creating large circles with the name of each area inside the circle. Create lines like sunrays coming from each circle, with words or pictures of your grandest desires for each area. The sunrays represent your intentions in each large area of your life.

- Create collages that represent your many paths of joy. Use any and all small objects and materials such as buttons or pieces of cloth, pictures, drawings, etc., to represent the feeling of joy for *you*. It's the essence of joy that's important, not the specific form. Hang somewhere highly visible in your home.

Books:

Picture: *God's Paintbrush* (Sandy Sasso), *Unstoppable Me!* (Wayne Dyer)
Chapter: *Mandy* (Julie Andrews Edwards)
Adult: *Trust Your Vibes* (Sonia Choquette)

Movies:

The Bucket List (2007)
Buffalo Dream (2005)

Songs:

Defying Gravity (from the Broadway show *Wicked*)
I'm Coming Out (Diana Ross)

Chapter 11

Many Paths Up the Mountaintop

*W*e teach our children that their spiritual path, their inner truth, their vantage point is not the *only* way; it is simply *one possible* way. That there are many paths up the mountaintop to God stands as one of the most important messages learned on *any* spiritual journey, and one that can be easily integrated into the many layers of home life wholeheartedly. We talk about this concept almost daily in our home. Our mantra for everything in life has become *For Me, For Now.* This spiritual theme speaks to not only accepting differences in belief systems both religious and otherwise among individuals, but also to appreciating and respecting the preferences of others in regard to life relationships, circumstances, experiences, and choices. Utilize this theme on a regular basis to examine differences among family members, friends, and all peoples of the world. We cite this credo when mending hurt feelings over disagreements. We express this belief whenever we encourage another to walk his own path and find his own way. We acknowledge this truth each and every time we respect and accept the vast variety and diversity that exists on planet earth.

We hope that our children are *always* able to accept those who are on spiritual paths different from their own. Teach your children that each soul's preferences and choices are to be respected. Offer examples of different pathways to enlightenment by openly discussing not only world

Offer examples of different pathways to enlightenment by openly discussing not only world religions, but also ways in which each family member feels connected to her own soul.

religions, but also ways in which each family member feels connected to her own soul. As exemplified with our love lists, we teach our children that people feel God and know God through their very own soul in millions of different ways. An individual's relationship with the Divine is a personal and intimate experience. Even if one is deeply involved in a spiritual community, within that, the Creator will be seen, felt, and heard in a multitude of ways and through numerous inner unfoldings. It's important to continuously share your own awakenings with your family. Let them know that awakening is an ongoing and ever-expanding process to be cherished and fully integrated into their own life and in their own way.

All family members should be encouraged to express their spiritual nature in any way that they choose. One individual may feel God kneeling in prayer on the pew of a beautiful old church. That is absolute perfection. Another individual may find God riding on his Harley through the countryside watching the sunrise. That is absolute perfection. Yet another individual may hear God while planting flowers all alone in her garden. That is absolute perfection. And yet another individual may experience God unconditionally loving him while worshiping in a mosque. That is absolute perfection. Some people feel Spirit most while listening to music. Others feel Spirit most while playing a sport. And still others feel Spirit most while designing a modern building. Bowling, singing, sewing, cooking, or biking may be pastimes used to effectively raise one's vibration and connect him more deeply to God. If Shakespeare brings you closer to your core truth than does the Bible or the Koran, then by all means read Shakespeare.

Encourage your children to light their own unique path up the mountaintop. Each human life is meant to open to the acknowledgement of its spirit-embodied truth in its own way. There is not one teacher, one path, one resource, or one manifesto that is right for

> We choose to remain open and clear channels for Spirit to reach us in any way possible. I personally expect God to show up anywhere, anytime. I could never put limits or boundaries on a Presence that is infinite, unlimited, and boundless, and such an integral part of my own identity and existence. It is our belief that God is in everything and everything is in God; therefore, we expect to embrace and be embraced by Spirit in more than one place, in more than one way, and in any given moment.

everybody. In fact, with spiritual unfoldment, one ultimately realizes that while other individuals and external sources may serve as guideposts along the way, faith, trust, peace, and love, the hallmarks of total consciousness, can only truly be found from the inside out. Spiritually awakening is unique and specific to each individual. While you may share similar experiences with others, true liberation stems from inner knowing and state of being. We foster enthusiastically supporting and encouraging others on their path *whatever* that path may be. It is the height of righteousness and arrogance to think that you have the capacity to choose for another his path to God because you feel it must match your own. We encourage our children to be open to all paths up the mountaintop and to lovingly and compassionately assist others on their individual path, *only* if asked and an opportunity arises to do so.

I feel it is important to teach children from a young age that human beings tend to see the world only through their own personal lens. Children must learn to take into account another's perception of reality at all times. Everyone's perception of reality becomes her own truth. When you teach your children to accept this, it enables them to be more tolerant and accepting of another's point of view, and in this way they can experience the beautiful divine dichotomy that things don't always have to be either/or, but can instead be and/both. Understanding the reality of different perspectives in a multidimensional world also serves the purpose of liberating a child to make valid her own perceptions as truth for her.

A client's daughter, a first-grader, was experiencing some bullying at school, and she didn't know whether or not to call the other mom about it. Since the ugliness was continuing, I suggested to my client that she call the other mother to have an open, honest conversation about the events at school. I counseled that I feel it is always best to start a conversation such as this with understanding and compassion. I foresaw the conversation going more smoothly if approached as something like this: "I know that this is a difficult phone call to receive, and I also know that one day I very well may be receiving a similar phone call from another parent. I want to share with you how my daughter perceives certain situations at school. All that I can do right now is share with you my daughter's feelings and honestly relate what she is experiencing through her own unique reality. I very much hope that you are able to share with me anything that you can about *your* daughter's feelings and experiences." While there are, of course, no guarantees that the conversation will move in a direction that my friend desires, she has consciously opened the conversation in a nonthreatening, neutral way that hopefully allows the other parent to feel safe and more open, rather than immediately defensive.

You can only flow with life to the radiant beat of your own drum, your own heart. Your only obligation to others is to give them permission to do the same.

Since this long-ago advice to my client, I've been on both sides of phone conversations such as this due to my own children's relationships and behaviors. I greatly appreciate grace and honesty all around in these difficult situations. No matter which side of the conversation I land on, I assure the other parent that while we Burnsides are far from perfect, we are accountable, and we will continue our multifaceted efforts to raise kind, loving, and conscious children.

I have many friends whose spiritual beliefs are different from my own. Many of these friends are part of my daily life and bring me much joy. While some friends may find their salvation through Jesus Christ, I find mine through my own personal connection to the Universe. While some friends may believe that the Bible is the only true word of God, I believe that the Bible, Koran, Torah, and thousands of modern-day books can also be extremely helpful as one finds his own way. While some friends believe that Jesus was different from other human beings in his godliness, I believe that Jesus showed us the way by inviting all human beings to emulate his Christ Consciousness. Allow others to glean strength and joy from their personal spiritual beliefs. Differences in spiritual

While agreeing with another can seem like the easier, safer path or converting another to your beliefs can seem necessary to your ego, following your own authentic path up the mountaintop to higher consciousness is the highest choice for all involved and leads to total freedom. I do not require anyone to be anything other than who they really are. I do not require anyone to agree with me. I allow each and every individual who crosses my path the freedom to choose for herself a road map for her own life. While I love sharing spiritual ideas with others, I do not need spiritual companions. I'm open to others experiencing God in any way that they choose. I encourage others to know God intimately and personally in a way that feels right to them. That, after all, is the basis of my work.

beliefs do not have to create divisions. Coexistence stemming from true tolerance is the road to creating peace in our world.

How does one reconcile seemingly stark contrasts with others in their fundamental beliefs? It's actually quite simple, but we make it so difficult. You reconcile differences by letting go of the need to be right, by loving the individual as she is, not as you desire her to be; by appreciating the other's point of view even when it's different from your own; by allowing others to awaken to their own truth and share it with the world in any way that pleases them; and by surrendering to the fact that *you* are the only one who needs to be in alignment with your truth and live true to it. You can only flow with life to the radiant beat of your own drum, your own heart. Your only obligation to others is to give them permission to do the same.

I express love and appreciation for my friends exactly as they are. Unconditionally loving another means that you are ecstatic for her to find joy, love, and truth wherever she finds it. I support another's spiritual choices with love and gratitude that we live in a world of blessed, purposeful and glorious diversity. We are all companions of the heart, not the mind. Through your example, teach your children to celebrate their friendships with love and laughter, remembering that oneness does not mean sameness.

I invite you to explore *your* personal path up the mountaintop to God. Enjoy all aspects of your life, even the seemingly mundane or unbelievably outrageous. Live big, live small; it's always your choice. Most of all, when you feel joy moving freely inside of you, flow *with* it with every ounce of your being. That feeling of joy is God expressing itself as life through you; there is no greater gift. It's important for your children to understand through your example that one's spiritual truth can be found and felt through an infinite number of earthly means. Encourage your children to express their spiritual nature in any way that they choose, whether it be sitting in a church pew, raking leaves, baking a cake, listening to music, reading a good book, sitting quietly, or watching a sunset. And remember, *For Me, For Now* allows every individual to feel safe experiencing their joy ride up the mountaintop.

Integrate It into Your Own Family!

Parent Contemplations:
- What are your true passions?

- Do you often compare yourself to others, or do you walk to the beat of your own heart? Explain.

- How do you feel towards others who are different from you in race, religion, economic status, sexual orientation, or gender? Can you easily see beyond superficial differences among individuals?

- How often do you seek out new experiences?

- Do you listen to your inner voice when it comes to life choices or ignore the call? Why or why not? Cite examples of each.

Activities:
- Use a large jar and a bag of small marbles for family discussions. Place a marble in the jar at the completion of each family discussion to create a physical representation and memory of the soul expansion occurring with each unique spiritual exploration shared. Place the ever-growing jar of marbles in a special and visible place in your home. This jar is a constant reminder of both your family's unique path up the mountaintop (the whole jar and its contents) and the individual paths carved out by each family member (each marble). When the jar becomes full, you can place it on your spiritual altar and start another one.

- Create a list of close friends. Write down at least five unique ways that each friend joyfully expresses himself. (For example, hobbies, phrases, interests, learning styles.) Share your lists as a family. After each friend has been recognized, wish each individual many blessings on her/his path within your family circle. Of course, the friend could be contacted at a later time, as well. This activity encourages appreciation and respect for all paths. Children will quickly sense the liberation that comes from living true.

- Read passages from other religious traditions, specifically the mystical teachings of each, and explore together both the similar and unique threads. There are many ways to go about this; the internet can be a wonderful resource. (Examples: the teachings of Jesus, Buddha, the Persian poet Rumi.) The objective of this activity is to help children understand that their belief system is only one belief system, and the essence of other belief systems have more similarities than they may realize. (Adapted from *The Hope: A Guide to Sacred Activism* by Andrew Harvey.)

Books:
Picture: *Hope for the Flowers* (Trina Paulus), *Pebble* (Susan Milford)
Chapter: *Star Girl* (Jerry Spinelli)
Adult: *Invisible Acts of Power* (Caroline Myss)

Movies:
The Rookie (2002)
Swiss Family Robinson (1960)

Songs:
Unwritten (Natasha Bedingfield)
Wide Open Spaces (Dixie Chicks)

Chapter 12

Soul to Soul Parenting *Spiritual Theme*
True Eternal Nature

"*W*e are spiritual beings having a human experience, not human beings having a spiritual experience." I first saw this quote as a bumper sticker on the back of someone's car, and I grinned from ear to ear at the implications of this realization becoming fodder for the entire world to ponder while sitting in traffic. If you can remember this truth stating the totality of who you really are, then your life experiences and relationships

As you learn to trust your vibes at all times, you align yourself with the pure, absolute energy that is God.

become much clearer to you in so many ways. This quote refers to seeing yourself and all others, first and foremost, as Spirit. You can then appreciate other human beings on a much deeper level, giving others more leeway to walk their own path without judgment, and with greater acceptance and understanding in your heart. You come to accept with total faith that you can never fully know another's soul purpose or view the world through his eternal perspective. We're reminded that we are all eternal beings living *temporarily* in a three-dimensional time/space reality.

Eckhart Tolle, Deepak Chopra, Neale Donald Walsch, and many other spiritual teachers living among us today have greatly assisted humankind in more deeply understanding its true eternal nature. Although you will definitely leave your current physical body behind at some point during this incarnation, you can never, ever die, as you are eternal in nature. As energy, you may change form and transition into a different dimension, but as a spiritual being you are formless and timeless—a divine essence that is no less than an aspect of God expressing for a very brief time in this particular form called a physical body. It's important to begin speaking this truth in very simple terms to your children as early as possible. They'll have a much easier time comprehending the concept of eternalness at an early age because they haven't yet been completely conditioned to view themselves *only* as a localized "I" with the narrow viewpoint which that conditioning creates. While a child can seem very egocentric, a child's ego doesn't take full control of her existence until the latter half of childhood (beginning around age ten), thereby leaving spaces where her connectedness to All That Is can still be readily detected *by* her and accessed *through* her.

It's supremely beneficial to children as their ego becomes stronger and more defined to balance that expansion with a deep under-standing of their true eternal nature. From the beginning, you can teach children that they, and all others, are so much more than what they appear to be. You can teach your children that they are multidimensional beings living in a multidimensional Universe, and that this truth allows and invites unlimited potential. Encourage your children to transcend the limits of only utilizing their five physical senses to discern what is true for them. Let these basic understandings become a founda-tion for your child's expanded perception and growth in this lifetime.

> How wonderful for your children to learn at an early age that they are in fact not their ego, but rather ageless, timeless beings composed of divine energy who are actually consciousness itself. How wonderful for your children to learn at a tender age that the ego can coexist peacefully with the soul to create a life of toler-ance, purpose, and freedom. How wonderful for your children to be exposed at a young age to the grand-ness, magnificence, and beauty of each and every living form on the planet.

All that is called for with this spiritual theme is an opening to the idea that you are an integral aspect of something so pure, so beautiful, and so loving that even in your wildest imagination, you have a difficult time holding the truth of it. Begin this dialogue when you are cradling your children as newborn babes. Whisper in their ear the truth of their divine eternal heritage. Look deep into their eyes, and you will see that this truth already lies deep within them. Refuse to allow the truth of their true eternal nature, which they come into this world already knowing and accepting, to become covered up by the illusions of the ego and the conditional perspective of external forces.

In a workshop that I attended a while back, the teacher had us write a letter to our ego acknowledging and blessing it, but asking it to step aside and allow our Higher Self to lead. This was a very powerful exercise for me that I have since used in my own workshops. Often throughout my day, I close my eyes and invite spiritual guidance into my life and create the space for it to enter. I consciously choose to create within the influence of Spirit. I consciously choose to manifest from a place of unification with All That Is rather than from a perspective of separateness controlled by my ego. This is not to say that, every now and then, my ego doesn't try to have its say, but when I feel my ego rise up to seize a situation, exert its influence, and control my thinking, I acknowledge this shift which now immediately creates a feeling of disunity and disharmony within my core. When this occurs, I lovingly, but firmly deal with the shift in the fastest possible way so that I can return to my eternal vantage point and resume living in divine flow as spirit-embodied.

Trust Your Vibes

One of my favorite teachers, Sonia Choquette, wrote a book called *Trust Your Vibes,* detailing this important way of harnessing the divine energy that surrounds all human beings and utilizing the eternal, all-knowing voice of your own soul. Your vibes are the same thing as your intuition or your sixth sense. By following your vibes, you allow your spirit to lead the way, rather than your ego. Your spirit is *you:* the beautiful, eternal you that is the essence of God. As you learn to trust your vibes at all times, you align yourself with the pure, absolute energy that is God. At times, your vibes about something may not make any sense to you, but this is where faith comes in. Insight that comes from your soul is always the path to follow because it comes directly through your connection to All That Is. If you choose not to trust your vibes in any given situation, that's okay because there are many different possible paths to reach every destination, but know that the easiest, most synchronistic path is always the one that is directed by the spirit, not the ego.

As parents, it's your job to assist your children in recognizing and utilizing their vibes. The best way to accomplish this is to speak of your own vibes in all situations. As they witness you continuously checking in with your internal guidance system, they'll quickly recognize the importance of checking in with theirs. It's just as important to their growth to share the times when you *didn't*

In order to receive more love in your life, be more loving. To receive more generosity, be more generous. To receive more joy, be more joyful.

listen to your vibes and the consequences of those choices. Seeing your constant attempts to lead your life from a place of spirit rather than ego, and the many missteps and triumphs that go along with the continual process, helps your child integrate this spirit-centered way of life and make it an internal process for himself.

In order to hear your vibes and utilize them, you must *stop the endless mind chatter and listen to your soul*. This Soul to Soul Reminder reminds our family on a daily basis the importance of first quieting the endless drone in your mind, which takes up so much time and space, so that you can actually hear the subtle, loving voice of your soul. From a young age, we have taught our children that getting quiet and being still at times throughout the day enables them to tune into their soul and receive the guidance being offered. This leads to a deep knowing and ready utilization of your divine, eternal nature. If you fill your days with nonstop busyness, it becomes nearly impossible to receive divine guidance. Children often have an easier time hearing and acting on their vibes because they haven't yet allowed the past and the future to consume their thinking. Typically children remain much more present in any given situation because they are closer to remembering the soul reality of the Eternal Moment of Now.

Be the Source

Remember that who you *really* are is a creative, divine, eternal being. *You* are the creative source for all that occurs in your life. Never forget the infinite power that you possess to shape what you perceive in your world. In order to receive more love in your life, be more loving. To receive more generosity, be more generous. To receive more joy, be more joyful. Teaching children to see themselves as the *cause* of what occurs in their own life, rather than the effect, is vitally important. One need not go too deeply into metaphysics to explain to children that what they are indeed *being* in every moment is what they'll see reflected back to them in the world. We teach our children to focus on their state of *being* first, and their *doing* second, rather than the other way around. As human beings, we often have this creative truth backwards. In understanding and utilizing the universal truth that state of being is the cause, not the effect, the effect comes to *you* effortlessly as you follow inner impulses to take action when needed. It's entirely possible for your inner state to remain unperturbed by outer circumstances, and the intention can be for this to occur more and more frequently throughout your day.

I Am Deeply, Deeply Loved

We keep this Soul to Soul Reminder above our kitchen sink. It reminds us every single day that we are deeply loved spiritual beings. All That Is, of which you are an integral part, unconditionally loves you with a capacity that is beyond your wildest dreams. In fact, this Universe loves you so much that the second you send out any type of vibrational signal via thought, word, or deed, it begins reflecting that signal back to you on some level of your physical life experience. Your job in the physical dimension is to openly receive the impenetrable love that's being offered to you moment-to-moment, and to offer that same love to another. Your job is to openly allow the divine gifts that flow freely to you each and every day, and to feel and trust this deep universal love even though it may seem unfathomable to the human mind alone. All you have to do is remember that you are deeply loved, and in your heart, you will know that all is well.

Death and Rebirth

Death is a difficult subject for most people to discuss, but one that's vitally important in the spiritual work with your family. Death and rebirth exist all around us in nature. In the natural world, the transition from death to rebirth, over and over again, of living forms is accepted as truth. With humans, however, one's ego often does not allow him to accept that death and rebirth are the natural way of things. We resist this divine flow, believing that death actually exists and that it is the end of "I". Unfortunately, humans' enormous fear of death is perpetuated from generation to generation, keeping most people from truly living in the divine, peaceful inner state of nonresistance, nonattachment, and nonjudgment that is liberation for the soul.

Speaking openly about death and rebirth can become a normal part of your family's spiritual practice. The change of seasons offers a wonderful opening every three months to revisit this topic. If a human death occurs, I feel that you greatly serve your children by speaking gently, yet truthfully, about the transition from physical to nonphysical. It is my belief that as human beings, we actually confuse our ideas of birth and death. Being born into a physical body, while gratefully chosen by the soul, is actually the *death* of the soul's natural state of being for the short period of time that a soul inhabits a body while seeking to expand consciousness as spirit-embodied in the physical dimension. Likewise, physical death for the soul is a much-desired *rebirthing* back into the familiarity of its natural state and an ecstatic joining once again with All That Is.

My spiritual exploration over the past twenty years has led me time and time again to what is now a deeply held inner belief that there are no victims in life, and this includes the timing and details of death. A soul recognizes when a physical incarnation is complete and co-creates with All That Is a death experience and time of physical departure. While extremely sad and difficult for loved ones left behind, physical death is the most magnificent moment in one's incarnation, representing a return to total knowing and oneness with All That Is.

At the times in my life when I have been in close proximity to death due to a loved one's passing, especially when working with a terminally ill patient and visiting him regularly, I could feel

We teach our children that as with nature, this cycle of death and rebirth, the joining and rejoining with the totality, continue for us throughout eternity. We use the infinity sign to express our eternal, timeless nature. The center of the infinity symbol is the core signifying complete immersion with God. The right side of the symbol represents the nonphysical realm and the left side represents the physical realm. You move through infinity the same way, following the lines of the symbol, passing in and out of the core as you make your transition from death to rebirth over and over again.

the nonphysical realm more acutely during these periods. I sensed the light. I sensed the love. I sensed the peace. It never felt scary, but rather familiar to me as I once again surrendered to divine flow and glimpsed the fullest aspect of them *and* me. Many individuals who have experienced near-death experiences describe similar feelings about death. While I do not fear death in any way, I understand that this perspective is not necessarily shared by the general population. It is my grandest hope that through the expanding of a parent's own perspective on death and through the sharing of that with her children, all human beings can overcome the enormous fear of death and begin living their lives in a less fear-based and more unlimited way.

Our family recently experienced the death of a classmate's father. Two of our children were in the same grades as the two children whose father had died. Thankfully, we were encouraged to bring our children to the visitation where a special room was set up for his beautiful daughters in first and fourth grades to greet their classmates and accept their condolences. I found the inclusion of children to be a progressive, honest, and loving way to deal with death. Teachers and parents from the school attended, as well as many students, to honor these children and support them as they began to accept their father's death. We allowed our children to bear witness to grief and loss. We allowed our children to bear witness to the process of life, *including* physical death. We have gifted our children with our belief that they are capable of enduring the cycles of life. In doing so, we prepared them to practice surrendering to what is so and accepting the inevitable transition from the physical dimension.

> We have gifted our children with our belief that they are capable of enduring the cycles of life. In doing so, we prepared them to practice surrendering to what is so and accepting the inevitable transition from the physical dimension.

We discuss death and rebirth with our children quite often. We explain that different lifetimes offer different types of growth. We teach our children to have faith in their soul's knowing when the purpose of each lifetime has been fulfilled. We share that we have no way of ever *fully* consciously understanding every aspect of our soul's agenda and so have no way of ever fully consciously understanding when a specific soul agenda has reached completion. We encourage our children to move with the unique and beautiful flow of their own life, knowing that while life on earth is sacred and a tremendous gift, each incarnation is simply one aspect of their eternal identity. We encourage them to trust that each life experience will be varied, beneficial, and purposeful to their individual soul evolution and the collective evolution of the human species; and therefore, should not be judged. The potential for expanded consciousness in every incarnation far outweighs any perceived pain while inhabiting a physical body. As a nonphysical entity you fully understand the choice you make when entering a physical body, knowing that the length of time you spend in a specific incarnation is of no importance, for you are timeless. It is participating fully in the life that you've created that is of far more importance to the soul. Choosing to remain fully conscious and feel blissfully alive while in the physical body in each eternal moment of now leads to an acceptance and deeper understanding of both life *and* death.

I once read an article speaking of the Dalai Lama being able to remain in total ecstasy and bliss *even* as he cradled a dying child in his arms. The Dalai Lama knows the truth of who he is with every fiber of his being. He feels it in his deepest space. He lives it without fear or apology. He understands that we are *all* divine, eternal beings, and that death is not possible, only transformation. Although you may continue to grieve the physical death of loved ones, there is no reason to fear your own physical death. As you assist your children in developing an expanded view of death and rebirth, you simultaneously heal your own fears surrounding death and allow yourself to bask more fully in the joys of life.

Angels in Disguise

On a beautiful October Sunday our family headed out on bikes to hang out on the rocks that jut out into Lake Michigan by Northwestern University. These rocks have become a sacred place for our family. We love to climb along the shore and find the perfect spot to sit and relax. On this day, my oldest daughter Aidenn suggested that we have our family discussion on the rocks. (I had secretly planned the same thing and was thrilled that she had also thought of it.)

From the beginning of our ride, I felt total joy. It was that kind of picture-perfect fall day where in the back of your mind you know it could be one of the last ones to feel this wonderful and warm again for a long time, especially in Chicago. I remember feeling happy and centered as we neared the lake, and I took this whole day in with big gulps. I just couldn't get enough of it, *all* of it, as I kept saying to my husband and children.

Settling in on our rocks, we began our family discussion. We talked about our belief that as human beings, we are actually angels in disguise, every single one of us. We asked our children to really contemplate what that meant regarding their true nature. We then discussed how God is actually not a bigger version of humans with human characteristics, but that we are actually a smaller version of God with God characteristics. This perspective of the true nature of human beings is very subtle; it evokes a profound difference in how one perceives not only himself, but all of humanity.

We continued to discuss our eternal nature as spiritual beings for several minutes before the children went off to play on the rocks. Jim and I remained on the main rock and continued to talk on this subject a bit longer. I remember feeling grateful that the two of us had the opportunity to speak together on such a deep topic as we sat listening to the water lap up against the rocks and watching our precious children playing nearby. Eventually, however, the peace was broken when Aidenn and Piper began to fight on one of the large rocks. They'd been playing house and were fighting over who had rights to one of the rocks as her dining room! We had to separate the girls and send each one to a neutral rock. As you can see, even after a delightful family discussion, no family is perfect and must remain accountable for their choices.

While the family discussion was wonderful, my favorite part of this story comes at the end. As we gathered our things and readied ourselves for the bike ride home, I noticed that Piper was not at her bike and sat pouting on a large flat rock several feet away from us, so I climbed down to try and pull her out of her mood and get her moving towards her bike. As I reached for Piper and looked down at the rock where

It is we who must become conscious and simply take the time to be here now and pay attention to each moment and all that it offers.

she was perched, I began to get my divine flow energy feeling. I excitedly asked Piper to stand up. Like many rocks down by the lake at North-western, this one had been painted. Piper had unknowingly sat on a huge rock with a painting of a beautiful naked woman with enormous angel's wings. I couldn't believe what lay before us on that rock. My heart beat wildly as I called the rest of the family down to take notice of what Piper and I had discovered. We had just discussed our belief that all human beings are actually angels in disguise, and here, right before our eyes only minutes later, was an enormous painting depicting exactly what we had just discussed. Now that's what I call a divine wink! I explained to our children that this was divinity at work in a Universe where Spirit is ever-present and orchestrating on our behalf. It is we who must become conscious and simply take the time to be here now and pay attention to each moment and all that it offers.

What about People Who Do Bad Things? What about Terrorists? Are They Angels, Too?

These are really tough questions that can be explored in family discussions. Metaphysically speaking, I believe in individual and group soul commitments, and I believe in the magnificence of physical death. We never know the purpose and agenda of another's soul. We never know when or why a soul transitions back into the spiritual realm. We must trust that on a soul level we are all very aware of our commitments. You choose a soul path before you enter into a physical body that offers you and others spiritual evolution. Once on earth, your inner guidance system gives you clear direction and reminders of your soul work, but it is up to you to listen and receive these signs.

I would explain in simple terms to children that these individuals who do *bad* things sadly *appear* to be totally unconscious and discon-nected from the voice of their soul; and therefore, totally disconnected from God. They are individuals who *appear* to no longer remember who they truly are. They are individuals who *appear* to have lost their way and who *appear* unable or unwilling to listen to their inner guidance system. Although God still speaks to them all the time through the voice of their own soul, for some reason, they *appear* to have shut off their own natural ability to hear God. I would explain that there are always natural conse-quences in the Universe for *all* types of behavior. I would discuss that ultimately there are no victims and no villains in any given situation. We all call forth on some level our present reality, with no exceptions, whether we do so consciously or not. Above all, I would encourage your children to trust the process of life and to focus their energy on the purposeful and beautiful unfolding of *their* own life.

It is important to teach your children to see God and themselves in every circumstance, person, and condition. For children, I speak in terms of how, without darkness, we would not know light; without cold, we would not know hot; without pain, we would not know joy; without hate, we would not know love. Remind children that they are in this world, but not of it. They can perceive to be hurt by another in the physical dimension, but their true state of being can never be harmed by another; their true home is not a dualistic world of contrast such as earth, but rather the eternal, divine realm of Spirit which is infinite and absolute. It's important for children to understand their eternal movement throughout infinity, and to realize that both realms are completely necessary for their soul's growth and should be acknowledged and blessed.

If you were to do a past-life regression today, you might immediately recognize those individuals who currently get *under your skin* or even the *enemies* in your life who led you to a pivotal shift in consciousness as a dear husband, brother, or daughter in a previous lifetime. Account after account of past-life recall has detailed that those souls with whom you are closely tied incarnate with you again and again to propel you forward in your soul's evolution. Sometimes, it is the most difficult situations, *caused* by the most difficult individuals, which are your greatest tools for growth this time around. That's why you must *bless* every person and condition, and offer gratitude and appreciation for the role that they play in your script. Trust that your beautiful spirit is leading the way. I invite you to keep healthy boundaries if that's what is needed, but do your best not to judge. That *horrible* person may in the nonphysical realm one day be recognized as your former lover or best friend. Be open to all of the possibilities. Who knows how some of us have danced together throughout this vast Universe? I love to imagine my spirit dancing *out of body* timelessly and eternally, and oh, the freedom and ecstasy of that!

All Knowledge Lies Within

If you teach children early on the importance of going within to receive answers, you will be granting them such a tremendous service. When you become reacquainted with your soul, you see that your soul guides you right to where you need to go to expand your perspective. Your soul will guide you to the next logical step on your path. Your soul will lead you to the answer. You need not seek answers from the outside world unless your soul leads you there. It is so important to go within first and take direction from your own inner being. Your inner being knows your soul's purpose and is privy to the bigger picture. It is for this reason that going within is always the best starting point in all situations. Teach your children how to feel their way to an answer. From a young age, they can begin to understand that the language of the soul is feeling-based, not thinking-based. Allow the feeling to come forth uninhibited by the mind, and then use your mind in adjunct with the feeling. External proof is not needed when inner resonation is accepted and allowed.

If you teach children early on the importance of going within to receive answers, you will be granting them such a tremendous service.

How do you know if something resonates with your soul? You look to how you *feel* about it. Learn to view your deeper feelings as an incredible inner guidance system assisting you in listening to your own soul. If you feel joy, appreciation, contentment, or peace then you know that you are in alignment with your soul and the divine flow of your life. If something makes you feel resentment, anger, disappointment, or frustration then this is a sign that you're out of alignment with your soul and have some inner work to do to move through and release these negative emotions, and as quickly as possible, turn in the direction of ease and flow. Your feelings offer a continuous guidepost as to the energy that you're offering to the world; and therefore, your alignment with the voice of your soul. Rely on these feelings to create the best possible outcomes in your life. They'll always let you know exactly where you stand and point you back in the right direction if you give them value and meaning.

I suggest always heading in the direction that brings authentic joy, love, happiness, and peace. It may be a slow turnaround from wherever you currently sit, but energy is never static, and shifting to a higher feeling is always possible. You may have to go within frequently throughout your day to uncover what your true feelings are in any given circumstance. It takes practice to discern the voice of your ego versus the voice of your soul. Your natural soul state is one of bliss and joy; you'll know that you are in alignment with your eternal source when your feelings reflect this state of being. Your true eternal nature, the greater part of you, can be your internal compass, if only you allow it to be.

Many masters advise simply being with a problem for a while rather than immediately trying to solve it with the mind. Your best insights typically come to you out of the blue, when your mind isn't trying so hard to figure it out. I found this to be true time and time again while writing this book. It was when I relaxed and got out of the way that my best ideas came to me. I often wake up early in the morning with answers on the tip of my tongue. Let your Higher Self run the show. The outcomes in your life will reflect more accurately your truth if you allow your soul to lead the way.

Let your Higher Self run the show. The outcomes in your life will reflect more accurately your truth if you allow your soul to lead the way.

How do you begin to experience more fully your true eternal nature? Stay present and pay attention to everything. Notice things as signs, guideposts, answers, and gifts. See yourself as an individual expression of the divine whole. Begin to see everything as Spirit. Accept that there are no coincidences. Sense the interconnectedness in all physical forms. Recognize that all of life flows in cycles. Experience the ebb and flow of your process with grace and trust. Learn to commune with nature. Be quiet and still every so often throughout your day. Perceive the earthbound world, and your physical reality within it, as tiny slivers of what is actually so in the broadest sense of who you really are. As you begin to experience your true eternal nature more fully in life, death and rebirth become a natural aspect of reality, no longer feared, but seen as a continual process in your eternal evolution.

Through close observation of the natural world and discussion of these observations within the family, children can begin to view death from a broad, nontraditional vantage point. While physical grieving over the loss of a loved one or a pet is to be expected, the eternal soul language used within the family can help children accept death as a transition rather than an ending, and propel them forward in their ever-expanding, conscious perspective of reality.

Integrate It into Your Own Family!

Parent Contemplations:
- What are your views on death and rebirth? Do you believe in reincarnation or in the system of one physical life only? Explain.

- Are you afraid to die? If so, why?

- Do you feel that you are eternal? In other words, do you see yourself as a spiritual being having a human experience or as a human being having a spiritual experience every now and then?

- Are you comfortable discussing physical death with your children? If so, how have you explained it to them thus far? If not, why?

Activities:
- Name at least three ways you connect to your deepest space within—just you and your innermost feelings. (Examples might be watching a sunset, lying quietly in bed, drawing.) What does that connection *feel* like for you? What does it look like? Where does it usually occur? Get to know where, when, and how you most easily connect to your soul.

- Think of a loved one or a pet that has died. Write him or her a
  love letter of gratitude and appreciation for all that you shared
  together. Invite this energy to connect with you often so that you
  can feel its presence. You may also place a photo with this letter
  in a special place that you can visit anytime you desire soul to
  soul connection.

Books:

Picture: *All I See Is a Part of Me* (Chara M. Curtis)
Chapter: *Conversations with God for Teens* (Neale Donald Walsch),
    Looking Beyond: A Teen's Guide to the Spiritual World (James Van
    Praagh)
Adult: *Many Lives, Many Masters* (Brian Weiss)

Movies:

Field of Dreams (1989)

Songs:

Shine Your Light (Robbie Robertson)
This Is It (Hothouse Flowers)
Wondering Where the Lions Are (Bruce Cockburn)

Chapter 13

Soul to Soul Parenting *Spiritual Theme*

Forgiveness

*F*orgiveness is simply another word for peace, trust, faith, empowerment, and love in the language of the spirit. We teach our children that forgiveness, one of the most important aspects of creating a spiritual life, really has only to do with them, not the other person. When you move through life holding negative feelings towards another in your heart and mind, it is only you who is actually affected by it. We remind them that their perception of a situation is *their* reality, not the reality of another. Their truth is *their* truth, not the truth of another. Ultimate reality is, of course, Oneness, and forgiveness is a foregone conclusion, unnecessary when the process of life is viewed from a macrocosmic perspective, but from the human perspective, you and only you can be responsible for any and all of your feelings. In the physical dimension, learning the practice of forgiveness heals perceived hurts and wounds, allowing for the free flow of energy throughout your body once more. It's entirely up to each individual to reap the vast benefits of forgiveness for himself. No one else can make this spiritual leap, opening and expanding the heart while simultaneously expressing the soul, but *you.*

> *When you move through life holding negative feelings towards another in your heart and mind, it is only you who is actually affected by it.*

We often remind our children that *enemies* can be their greatest teachers. The individuals and situations that cause you the most angst can also provide you with the greatest opportunity to shift into a new perspective and deepen your spiritual well. Once a difficult situation has passed, we ask our children to imagine finding in their heart the capacity to actually thank those involved on a soul level for assisting them in their soul's evolution. Through the centuries, it's often been said by spiritual masters that it is in your darkest moments and through your most difficult situations that you expand to your next highest version of yourself. Over and over again, I've found this to be true in my own life: the most disappointing and hurtful situations propel me forward in my inner work, eventually leading to a greater awareness of my own soul and an expanded perception of reality.

Encouraging your children to see hardship as both co-created and an invitation for expansion will greatly assist them with the process of forgiveness, a process that must be modeled continuously in the home.

Encouraging your children to see hardship as both co-created and an invitation for expansion will greatly assist them with the process of forgiveness, a process that must be modeled continuously in the home.

Teaching children at the youngest possible age to view the world from a place of nonjudgment, nonattachment, and nonresistance is a wonderful starting point to teaching forgiveness. These patterns of thought will greatly assist your children in accepting the contrast and variety that surrounds them in the physical world. One can never know all that another spirit has encountered on the earth plane. One can never fully understand another soul's beautiful history and soul purpose in a single lifetime. One can never fully uncover all of the outer layers that cover another angel in disguise. When you come from a soul to soul perspective, forgiveness becomes a natural process, and eventually a moot point, because you view all people and situations from a spiritual perspective—a heightened perspective which changes everything.

As you work towards a more forgiving heart, it's important to love the *difficult* ones as they are, not as how you think they should be. Accept what is so in every single individual and in every single situation because in doing so you accept the inevitable moment of now. To resist what is showing up is to resist the process of life and create disharmony with divine flow. Every circumstance must first be met with acceptance to create the opportunity for the best possible outcome to spring forth. Resistance is not an optimal starting point to create the next moment that you desire. Surrendering to what is actually occurring is the always the

In all instances, we encourage our children to accept where they are in the eternal moment of now and begin to slowly, but surely, feel their way forward as each new moment presents itself.

first step in the creative process that is your life unfolding.

Teach your children that surrendering doesn't mean that they become doormats, but does mean that inner acceptance of wherever they are in the current moment is the best course of action to create change. From that starting point, you can follow your inner guidance system and move forward moment-to-moment. This means that you speak your truth with honesty and compassion, maintaining boundaries where necessary, while also viewing the other individual in your deepest space as an eternal spirit just like you. At times, the best course of action is to separate from difficult circumstances and individuals. You may need to move in a completely different direction. You may need to work through anger and change course. Wherever you find yourself emotionally in any given situation is okay; the important thing is to accept where you are so that you're not resistant to the moment at hand—which is always futile because the moment is indeed at hand. Resistance serves no purpose other than holding you in disharmony with reality. In all instances, we encourage our children to accept where they are in the eternal moment of now and begin to slowly, but surely, *feel* their way forward as each new moment presents itself. If the situation involves a difficult interaction with another, we encourage our children to speak their truth firmly, but with compassion and a deep understanding that the other person is simply expressing himself from his own vantage point in reality. We encourage our children to bless the other in their heart, forgive, and move on *for now* as soon as they are able. We always say *for now* in order to remain open to all future possibilities. It's important that children understand the creative power in always remaining open to the ever-changing divine flow that is life.

Teaching children at a very young age the power of acceptance gives them permission to embrace their own spiritual nature and utilize it to create the highest possible outcomes in all situations. Acceptance always leads to self-empowerment because you create the necessary space for peace, calm, and stillness to connect you to the universal wisdom that lives and breathes inside and around you.

We talk a lot about acceptance in our home. Learning to accept people and situations as they are because that's what life is showing you in that particular moment can save your children the unnecessary suffering that occurs when one denies and attempts to resist reality. Once the person or situation has been accepted just as it is, then you can invite your soul with its heightened awareness to lead you in a new direction of both understanding and action.

We acknowledge that we are all in different stages of soul development. Every individual on this planet is awakening at his own pace and in perfect timing with the rhythms of his own soul and the Universe as a whole. The variations of awareness among human beings are infinite. While we are all part of the same overall consciousness that is God, one's level of consciousness in regards to this differs greatly. It's important that children begin to realize that it is not the divine essence of another hurting them, but rather the other's affiliation with ego. Wakefulness is really the only consideration when it comes to forgiveness. The more conscious one is, the more he understands his connection to a divine whole, and his choices and decisions reflect this understanding. A less conscious individual sees the world from a more narrow perspective that stems from the ego, and his choices and decisions reflect that understanding. You must trust that natural universal consequences occur for all choices and all individuals, no exceptions. These natural consequences serve all, especially those who are awakening from a solely ego perspective. In other words, it is not your job to *judge the dreamer* for her continued sleep; every individual awakens to an expanded perspective of reality in her own time.

It is important to teach your children that no stage of wakefulness is superior to another; it's simply different. Remind your children that every stage exists within the divine presence and the divine presence exists within every stage. Each individual soul charts its own course within the divine presence and is totally aware on a soul level of the course charted. An analogy often used involves beautiful flowers in springtime. One flower may open earlier than another, showing its glorious, blossoming self to the world in early April. On the other hand, the flower right next door may remain closed for a while longer, not opening its full beautiful self to the world until late April. Finally, there may even be a precious flower in the same yard that never opens its majestic, magnificent self to the world at all. You trust that each flower has followed its true path for *this* spring. You accept each flower as it is and are only concerned with *your* feelings and choices regarding each one. You deeply understand that the closed flower will eventually open, and it will be every bit as beautiful in its own way when it does. In fact, its inner beauty can be detected in its closed state if observed lovingly and carefully. You would never accuse the closed flower of being *less than* simply because its time of blossoming has not yet arrived. All of the flowers contain within them the same divine essence that lies within us with a pattern of growth and opening unique to them.

There are many processes that one can utilize to move through anger and work towards forgiveness. I share three of them as activities at the end of this chapter. In my forgiveness practice a few years back, I closed my eyes and trusted Spirit to present me with the image of an individual whom I needed to forgive. A friend immediately came to me in my mind's eye. I focused on her face and then began to look deep into her soulful eyes. What I saw in them astounded me. I didn't see in her eyes a desire to hurt me. I saw inner beauty, love, tenderness, pain, joy, God, fear, and a deep longing to be accepted and loved for who she really was. And probably most importantly, I saw *myself*. I saw myself in her eyes as I recognized that we were both of the same essence, simply incarnated in separate physical bodies here on earth, doing the best that we can to navigate our soul's path.

I was absolutely amazed at my feelings after participating in this

> Forgiveness invokes compassion and empathy within us, which invites a capacity for healing that is powerful beyond words. The first direction in which you should extend forgiveness is always towards yourself. Look deep into your own eyes and see what truly resides there. Connect with your divine essence and realize that you've been living in an ego-induced dream. Invite your soul to take the reins of your life and then get out of the way and allow it to do so. As you awaken, understand that others don't necessarily perceive themselves in this same way. They may still be vigorously attached to their ego persona, but that shouldn't stop you from transforming your perception of reality. Forgive yourself and move with grace towards a future you.

exercise. I instantly forgave this woman for having *wronged* me in some way. Our ego relationship with one another became utterly secondary, almost nonexistent, compared to our divine connection, now so apparent to me. Interestingly, it didn't matter to me whether or not she'd be able to see me in the same light. I knew that my work in forgiving this woman was complete. After having peered so deeply into her eyes, I understood that her *soul* forgave and loved me, too, even if she never became conscious of that in this lifetime. I was grateful beyond measure to feel such peace and to have received this well-lit path to forgiveness. I could now move forward from this relationship with love in my heart.

Discuss as a family the importance of beginning to practice forgiving the little everyday hurts that occur so that it's easier to forgive the *bigger,* more rare instances of suffering that may come your way down the road. There's really no difference in forgiving the little things and the big things. Although often not perceived by us as the same energy, they actually are; each simply creates a different level of feeling *separated* from your soul and All That Is. Belief in separation from God is really the only true issue in any given situation creating suffering; all other issues stem from that. As your ego becomes more and more undone, taking up less space in your perspective, this truth can more readily be received by you. Negative emotions stem from the degree to which you believe you are separated from life and All That Is. It's important to realize that you are never separate. It is impossible to be separate from something of which you are innately a part. Masters such as Jesus and Buddha understood this to be true; they knew that nonresistance, nonattachment, and nonjudgment are the pillars of peace in earthly reality.

Forgiveness, just like every other aspect of your spirituality, is a choice. Choose to be forgiving and guide your children to be forgiving, too. Talk through the process of forgiveness with your children. Together, role-play difficult life circumstances as they arise so that children can more easily see that a difference in perspective doesn't have to be taken personally, even if it seems like a personal attack. Help them understand the freedom and peace that forgiveness brings to their heart and mind. Forgiveness reunites mind, body, and spirit in the magical field of transcendence where miracles are free to flourish.

Integrate It into Your Own Family!

Parent Contemplations:

- How easy is it for you to forgive others? What processes/beliefs do you typically rely on to assist you in forgiving another?

- How do you make forgiveness a top priority in your life?

- What do you view as the major benefits of forgiveness? Name at least three.

- Do you speak often of the importance of forgiveness to your children?

Activities:

- Make a list of people whom you would like to forgive and do one of the following exercises. This can be done as a family with each individual doing their own forgiveness work at the same time. Share findings/feelings with the family.

  EXCERCISE ONE: Close your eyes and imagine looking into the eyes of the person you desire to forgive. For several minutes, peer deeply into her eyes using your imagination. Look carefully. What do you see there in the windows to her soul? What images or words appeared for you? What did you feel? (Learned by Carol Miller at a Byron Katie Workshop)

  EXCERCISE TWO: Imagine that you are sitting across from someone whom you desire to forgive. Close your eyes and trade shoes with that person. Wear his/her shoes using your imagination for several minutes. What images or words appeared for you? What did you feel? (Learned by Sharyl Noday, www.sharylnoday.com)

- The Anger Process: This process can be used to help family members resolve residual anger. The release of anger, rather than holding it inside, is extremely important to overall well-being and co-creativity. This technique teaches children how to release anger that blocks them from moving forward in certain areas and opening to their highest vibration and potential. The following exercise offers a step-by-step approach to working through anger so that an individual can move towards a greater self-love.

   Step One: Choose an object to represent the issue or person with whom you are angry; be as creative as possible here. Place the object on a bed or a chair. While hitting the object over and over again with a plastic baseball bat or a pillow, express your anger through speaking, yelling, or screaming. *Use your body! Use your voice! Express your deep-seated anger!* The point is to release the anger from your energy field so that you can move on. Do this in your own home and when you are alone. (Parents will need to assist younger children with this process.) Keep at it for as long as the anger continues rising up and out. You'll know when the anger has been released through an exhausted, yet content feeling.

   Step Two: Sit in front of the object and in your mind's eye hold a conversation where the person or situation speaks to you, asking for forgiveness and expressing that they see your perspective, offering numerous ways to "right" your feelings of being wronged. Use your imagination! Cover all possible bases/angles here that you desire to be made right in your eyes. Create in your imagination a total completion and acceptance by the other that *your* feelings and perspective have validity. Imagine the scenario to be just how you wish to create it.

   Step Three: While still in your house and near that space, do one self-loving act for yourself. Dance, sing, journal, look deeply into your own eyes, wrap yourself in a bear hug, enjoy tea, or simply sit in solitude for at least ten minutes.

Repeat the whole process on another day if the anger was not completely released. (Anger Process originally introduced to me by my spiritual teacher Sharyl Noday, www.sharylnoday.com.)

Books:
Picture: *The Little Soul and the Earth* (Neale Donald Walsch)
Chapter: *So B. It* (Sarah Weeks)
Adult: *The Four Agreements* (Don Miguel Ruiz)

Movies:
Where the Red Fern Grows (2003)
The Journey of Natty Gann (1985)

Songs:
The Heart of the Matter (Don Henley)
The Scientist (Coldplay)

Chapter 14

··

Soul to Soul Parenting *Spiritual Theme*

Self-Love

Self-Love is one of the most important things to encourage in and exemplify for your children. *Everything* stems from an interior love of self. True change always occurs from the inside out. Self-Love is a term used frequently in modern times, but what does it really mean? Self-Love means acknowledging and appreciating *every* single aspect of you: the light, the dark, the happy, the sad, the sick, the well, the courageous, the fearful, the lazy, the conscientious, the quiet, the bold, and every other universal trait and its polar opposite that *all* human beings share the capacity to express. Self-Love is being gentle and loving towards *you* at all times. It means always considering yourself as deserving of your best efforts, even and especially when you are offering loving service to another. It means factoring yourself into every choice. It means not slapping yourself on the hand for a perceived mistake, and recognizing when it's time to turn a page and move forward. It means releasing the need for approval by others and holding on to your own power. It means no more people-pleasing and diplomacy for diplomacy's sake, but rather offering soul nurturing and loving service when you hear the call to assist another. It means constantly paying attention to the subtle shifts in your vibration and seeking to always move towards the highest vibration possible for *you* at any given time. It means continually assessing the energy that surrounds you and protecting yourself from

> *When you love yourself, you accept all past choices with grace and forgiveness, knowing that they were guideposts on your journey, and you are moving towards a future self of your choosing.*

unwanted, negative energies. It means seeing you as a divine entity that is an intricate, perfect, and beautiful part of the Universe entire. It means nurturing yourself in both internal and external ways. Truly loving yourself comes down to remembering your true nature and allowing full outward expression of it. You are a spirit residing temporarily in a human body. You hold every possible human characteristic within you, and yet you are formless, shapeless, limitless, and eternal. When you surrender to your own authenticity and allow your humanity to merge with your spiritual nature, you demonstrate the highest level of Self-Love by fully blessing your very own spirit-embodiment and fulfilling your unique divine purpose.

Self-Love is found deep within your own consciousness and is experienced as impenetrable joy, appreciation, inner knowing, and eternal bliss. These moments of intense Self-Love become more and more frequent as one accepts her own divinity and interconnectedness with All That Is while simultaneously expressing an authenticity in one's humanity that stems directly from the soul. Once one has pierced this inner dimension, living true to the voice of the soul becomes the top consideration in every life experience. In these moments, the *whole* self is felt as unimaginably pure and sacred.

Teach your children through your continuous example all that Self-Love requires. Self-Love is a deep understanding that there is no right or wrong direction on your path. Some turns may take you down an arduous, steep slope where the learning curve seems more difficult, whereas others may indeed take you to a brightly colored field, but *every* turn must be accepted and blessed all the same, for every choice leads to a greater awareness of self. Each and every experience offers a gift in its opportunity to know oneself more deeply. When you love yourself, you accept all past choices with grace and forgiveness, knowing that they were guideposts on your journey, and you are moving towards a future self of your choosing.

Explain to your children that Self-Love requires remaining present and wide-awake as they sift through the contrast and variety on their path to find their own unique way. They are *whole* just as they are and hold all universal traits inside of them to express as they wish. No aspect of themselves should ever be denied, but rather looked at closely to see if expressing this trait feels good in their deepest space. Every choice can be viewed as either self-loving or not. Every choice must matter, as it leads you to your next moment.

Loving yourself and really feeling that love in every cell in your body, and to the depths of your soul, is the greatest thing that you can do to change your life and also to change the world.

The initial encounter with truly loving yourself is the biggest step. It may take months of looking deeply into your own eyes in the mirror and gently reminding yourself of who you really are. It may take a tremendous amount of inner work. The shift into loving yourself more deeply requires, for many, a complete interior overhaul. You must change a self-doubting interior dialogue that has become habitual. Often, an abundance of quiet, stillness, and solitude is needed to make the transition from self-doubt to self-love. Take the time to do this. It is time better spent than any other. Model this transition for your children. Once you've made the enormous human leap to loving yourself on the inside, everything in your external world will shift to mirror that Self-Love right back to you. Loving yourself and really feeling that love in every cell in your body, and to the depths of your soul, is the greatest thing that you can do to change your life *and* also to change the world. This should be the primary goal on any path because all else will stem from it. Life experiences and relationships are directly determined by the love felt from within first. I am not saying that loving oneself more deeply will be an easy task for everyone, but isn't it worth the energy and effort to make Self-Love a top priority in your life? Loving yourself fully gives your children permission to love themselves in a similar way.

For the longest time, I held the erroneous belief that Self-Love was all about *doing* rather than a state of being as well. It wasn't until I came to understand the twofold nature of Self-Love while in a channeling class* that I came to see I was missing the most important part of the equation. Initially for me, Self-Love was solely about nurturing myself through the act of taking the time to do the things that I enjoyed doing. I felt this was a big step; I made the conscious decision to make Self-Love a top priority in my life and began the process of discovering what brings me joy. I slowly began to nurture myself more and more through the doing of these things and released commitments and habits that were no longer a fit for me. While on a certain level this felt good, I still felt that there was something missing in the equation.

One day I realized that the act of doing wasn't enough; it was merely the first step towards fully loving me. A deep understanding washed over me that Self-Love must flow from the *inside* out to truly effect personal growth and change. Yes, I had changed the output, but the input hadn't much changed. Yes, I was allowing myself more time to do the things that I loved, but that didn't translate into peace and acceptance *on the inside*. Yes, I was enjoying many life experiences, but I still didn't love myself fully and completely where it really matters, which is in the mind and heart. I discovered that while the masculine aspect of Self-Love, the

In order to practice Self-Love, you must be willing to go within and see what's there. Beliefs, thoughts, attitudes, habits, patterns, and entire paradigms must be evaluated as to whether or not they truly serve your deepest desires. Old wounds must be reopened, worked through, and accepted as valuable parts of your total journey. Excavating the roots underneath the persona that you show the outside world is the first step into a deepening well of Self-Love. It doesn't happen overnight, but rather it is a lifelong process. While at times the process can be uncomfortable, painful, and time-consuming, I can tell you from firsthand experience that the journey within is the most wondrous, exhilarating, and unconditionally loving thing I've ever done for myself. The uncoverings and understandings are continual, and with a little effort, can become joyously integrated into an expanded you that had previously been imperceptible. Do you feel truth in your choices? Can you learn from regrets and forgive yourself all past grievances? If true Self-Love is deeply desired for your children, it becomes imperative that you begin the inner journey yourself so that you can lead your children by example and through personal experience to their own divine kingdom within.

doing, is extremely important, it's in the weaving of that with the feminine aspect of Self-Love, the *being,* where one fully begins to comprehend the seemingly incomprehensible: the possibility to live in total love, peace, and joy within one's own skin.

The feminine aspect of Self-Love exists internally. It's a deep inner feeling of acknowledgement, appreciation, and unconditional love of the *whole* self, and all of its individual aspects, in every waking moment that represents true Self-Love. No matter what is appearing in the external world, the doing of enjoyable pursuits or mundane tasks, the experiencing of pleasure or terror, the interior dialogue remains the same—an interior dialogue of love, compassion, and understanding for all aspects of self, the good, the bad, the pretty, and the ugly. True Self-Love is a tenderness and gentleness with self that few people imagine possible. True Self-Love leads to an intimacy and gratitude for your own essence that is nothing short of sacred ecstasy. You recognize in your deepest space that there is no source for outer approval. Internal approval and acceptance beckons as the only path to true freedom. While you share your journey with others, your journey becomes deeply personal and unique to you.

I began to understand the feminine nature of Self-Love during a time when I was working with my body to heal itself. At a channeling forum*, I was advised to create a deeper relationship with the cells and different parts of my body that make up the whole system. I've never viewed my body in the same way since that recommendation. I had never before fully viewed my body and all of its miraculous aspects as an aspect of consciousness in its own right. I'd never thought that much about the tissues and organs of my body as entities with which I could actually create a two-way relationship. Boy, has that changed. During this healing period, I began feeling an intense love for *all* parts of my physical body. Regularly as a healing process, I deeply acknowledged and expressed gratitude for each body part and its miraculous function. One day, the inner dialogue I began having with the cells of my body as I invited them to heal struck me as the most loving way that I had ever spoken to myself. I noted that it was such a tender, compassionate, and accepting way in which I was communicating with my body. Through this loving communication with my body over the course of several weeks, suddenly I comprehended the true meaning of Self-Love. I realized fully for the first time that Self-Love is not just allowing me to *do* the things that I love; but more importantly, it is the expressions of love to me on the *inside*, the being with me in a loving and kind way, that creates true Self-Love.

I realized with clear sight that for much of my life, I had used my inner voice as a tool for self-sabotage and self-doubt rather than as a tool to help me flourish as a human being. My interior dialogue had abused me more than any outside force ever could. It was in bringing this realization out of the darkness and into the light that propelled me forth on a journey of self-discovery and Self-Love that has often left me breathless. While at times I fall back into old patterns of self-sabotage, I now know what it *feels* like to love myself with the same profound tenderness and compassion that a mother has for her child. I have learned to mother *myself* in this way, and this high-frequency inner feeling is what I continually strive to move towards day in and day out as I choose both loving thoughts *and* actions to create my own reality. Nirvana is found deep within your own consciousness. It is here where I have experienced heaven. In those rare moments of complete and utter Self-Love, which become more and more frequent as you journey within, there arises a deep understanding that nothing exterior to yourself can ever bring you such bliss. Heaven is indeed an inside job.

The internal passage to loving yourself more deeply may seem like a foreign concept to many people until you begin to recognize life choices and relationships that reflect this interior feeling. How do you begin to love yourself from the inside out? It may be a slow process of simply reaching for a more positive thought about yourself here, a bit more appreciation for yourself there, some gratitude for yourself here, and an ounce more acceptance of yourself there; always remembering that true Self-Love stems from an inner feeling, not an outside focus. Begin to monitor your thoughts and your choices. Do these thoughts and choices reflect an inner belief that you are a sacred, divine, and much-loved spiritual being? Do these thoughts and choices inspire and enhance your overall feeling of well-being? Do these thoughts and choices feel good to your soul? You will treat yourself the way that you *see* yourself. Allowing the *doing* and the *being* aspects of Self-Love to join forces creates the space for love, peace, and joy to flow freely throughout your whole being uninhibited, and becomes the point of power and creation in your life. Allowing the masculine and feminine aspects of Self-Love to merge completes the circle and transports you to a higher level of intimacy with both Self and All

Much has been written on shadow work, and it's something that eventually must be considered as you move towards a deepening Self-Love. While it may seem scary at first, acknowledging and owning all facets of your interior is the only path to wholeness. Debbie Ford is a true pioneer in this area, and I highly recommend her work and books on this topic. She details a shadow process in her book *The Dark Side of the Light Chasers* that opened me to a me so vast, so human, and so divine that I am forever changed in my perception of myself as spirit-embodied.

That Is than ever before experienced.

This process may also lead you to do some shadow work where you literally dig through your interior and uncover hidden aspects of yourself that you have denied for years. Within each uncovering, whether it be a dark shadow or a light shadow, lies a gift. This denied aspect of yourself has taught you many things that are now yours to decipher and integrate.

As you move into a greater love of self, you release the need for approval by others. You begin to experience the joy and liberation that comes from truly being yourself. This life-changing release frees both you *and* others to show up in all life experiences in any way that feels right. It frees you to unconditionally love yourself and all others without need or expectation that reality be anything other than what it is. When you fully love yourself, you can simply enjoy and love others without the need to change them or receive something different from them. You are no longer dependent on validation from another, so you can accept him as he is rather than as how you think he should be to best suit your needs and gain approval. You begin to surround yourself with those who allow you the highest degree of freedom. You no longer give the opinions of others much thought or power. You begin to take full responsibility for every choice as you live deliberately and purposefully. The external world is much less of a priority than your inner world. It becomes obvious to you that while acknowledgement by others is certainly icing on the cake, true freedom can only be found within the cake itself.

Once the inner feeling of Self-Love becomes evident within you, it will be much easier and much more enjoyable for you to nurture yourself outwardly by doing the things that you love to do on a daily basis. While many things that bring you joy have been a mainstay in your life since you were a young child, be open to new desires that come to you and see where they lead. What connects you to your joy may evolve depending on where you are in your life. The question becomes how can you nurture yourself right now, in this moment, on this day, during this season, from the inside out? Are you willing to experience your inner joy even while performing the more mundane tasks and the *must-do* tasks of your life? You will come to realize that joy is a state of being; it is the cause, not the effect.

When my youngest child headed off to first grade a few years ago, it was the first time in ten years that all three of my children were in full-day school, and I decided to take that fall to really nurture Annie like she had never been nurtured before. While I had loved my time at home with young children, the time had come for a new phase in my life, and I wanted to breathe deeply and begin by nurturing myself first.

It's absolutely thrilling to the soul to ride the wave of passion, completely free to engage enthusiastically with life in its own unique way.

I suddenly felt an overwhelming desire to expand my horizons, but wasn't sure where to begin. So I simply got quiet and listened for the voice of my soul to lead the way. The following are but a few ways that I gently transitioned myself into my new life over the course of that first fall when I began to perceive myself once again beyond the role of mother.

• • • • • • • • • • • • • • • • • •

I fell in love with my bike. We were fortunate to have beautiful weather in Chicago that fall, and I took advantage of it in so many ways. On those gorgeous days, there was no greater joy for me than riding my bike from my home in Wilmette all along the shore of Lake Michigan to downtown Chicago. To this day, I continue to love everything about these solo rides. I love the feeling of freedom and exhilaration of being on a bicycle again. I love the adventure of heading into the city with the feel of the lake right beside me, along with the blue sky, beautiful colors, and sunshine. It takes me about an hour and a half to reach my destination where I picnic, staring at the Chicago skyline and Lake Michigan. I usually allow myself an hour to relax; I meditate, people-watch, journal, swim, or simply bask in the sun.

I took long walks in nature and along city streets. Walking is something that I have enjoyed for many years. Taking the time for them has been an act of Self-Love throughout my entire life. Both walking and riding my bike ground me to this earth *and* connect me to God at the same time, making me acutely aware of my co-creative existence.

I put my glorious face towards the sun whenever possible. I often took breaks from my "to do" list to sit on my lounge chair in the backyard, shut my eyes, and feel the heat of the sun on my face and body.

I found those moments by myself in my own backyard to be absolutely delightful. Sunlight with its warmth, light, and source of vitamin D has always been essential to my sense of well-being. Sunshine brings me great joy as it raises my vibration and elevates my spirit.

I enjoyed my little dog, Mia Moon. Ever since she came into our lives, I'm amazed at the incredible amount of joy that this ten-pound life force has brought to me personally. I knew that my children would adore her, but I hadn't anticipated my own adoration. Mia and I thoroughly enjoy each other's company. Time spent with her at the dog beach or on long walks are often highlights of my day.

I discovered an exercise class called *Nia*. Nia combines the expansion of body, mind, and spirit into one class utilizing harmonic movement. It includes chanting, fluidity of movement, strength, free-form dancing, reaching, asking, and receiving all rolled into one spirit-embodied experience. It promotes self-love through self-healing, and I highly recommend it to anyone who dares to give it a go. You must leave your ego-based inhibitions at the door and allow yourself to zoom into a space of infinite possibility.

I wrote down the inner linings of my heart. Writing has always been a benefit to my soul, but it hasn't been until recently that I view it as a courageous act of Self-Love. Writing feeds me. Whether simply writing an email, writing in my journal, writing a lecture, or writing a book, writing widens my heart and stirs my soul. Writing has also proven to be one of the most effective ways for me to channel Spirit; it connects me to my internal source, so write I must if I desire a fulfilling life.

I read my beloved spiritual books. I now allow myself to do so freely whenever I get the urge to be with myself and Spirit in this way. I used to feel that reading my spiritual books was not a large enough act of *doing,* as many of my friends embraced more active hobbies. At times reading my books used to seem more passive in some way. I now realize that my acts of Self-Love need not look like anyone else's. Every path is perfectly valid for each individual in its own way. Self-Love is absolutely bound to authenticity. The two go hand in hand when living a spirited, extraordinary, ordinary life.

Through the years, I've discovered that Self-Love means making the life choices that feel right to you, no matter what the outside world presents. Along with inner feelings of unconditional love towards the self and self-nurturing acts, allow yourself the freedom to deliver a high-quality yes or a high-quality no, free of guilt or apology to another. Answers are high-quality when they are delivered by you with utmost respect for yourself *and* for the other person. A *yes* means that you are committed, available, and present to what's been asked of you. A *no* means that your total presence isn't available for that particular endeavor at this time. Allow your soul to make all decisions based on a deep inner knowing of what's right for you in each moment. Always allow room for flexibility and adaptation, but trust that *you* know better than anyone else what feels right for you. Commitment to Self-Love means that you *consciously* decide how to spend the hours in your day. On some level, whether it seems to be true or not, you are choosing everything that is occurring, so you might as well choose wisely for you. If you're not fulfilled by your current choices, then you must release what occupies your time and presence so that you can reach enthusiastically for some-thing different in your day. Become available to the creative surges flowing through you. It's absolutely thrilling to the soul to ride the wave of passion, completely free to engage enthusiastically with life in its own unique way. Self-Love empowers you to choose your own path consciously without guilt or apology to any other. I no longer give anyone or anything permission to stand in the way of my heightened vibration. I simply love myself too much for that.

Teaching your children the breadth and depth of Self-Love is best done through the living of your own life. As the spiritual leader of your family, model how to live a life filled with choices that are best for yourself. Share with your children what leads you to make different choices in your life. Explain to your children the ways in which you continually factor yourself in when making a life choice, big or small. Help them examine their possible life choices with a greater awareness of their internal feelings and beliefs. Assist your children in becoming conscious in that they assess all choices according to their effect on state of being.

Speak to your children in a way that shows tenderness and compassion towards yourself and them. Role-play interior dialogue so that they understand the subtle, yet enormous difference between a critical inner voice and a loving inner voice. Share your intimate moments of internal joy and bliss. When you make a mistake, speak of it openly within the family, allowing your children to view the inner process of self-forgiveness. Help your children move through hurts and disappointments consciously by analyzing the life choices and beliefs that lead to the situation at hand. Construct new choices together that will lead to a different experience that feels better to them. The ultimate goal is to assist your children so that they can become conscious that every choice matters and makes a difference in not only their physical reality, but in their state of being. The key is to remain conscious and extremely present as you converse and sit with one another. Often the tendency is to fall into ego patterns and go unconscious when things get difficult rather than to speak truth with serenity and compassion.

Self-Love is a call to yourself and to your children to understand on the deepest of levels your true spiritual nature, while simultaneously owning and accepting your universal humanity.

Encouraging your children to follow their bliss encourages them to acknowledge and appreciate their core. Their bliss very well may not be your bliss, but with openness and truth, bliss can be navigated healthily together. Try to remain open to your children's ideas of who they are and who they choose to be in any given moment. This doesn't mean that you neglect to point out aspects of their choices that they may want to reconsider, but it does mean enthusiastically encouraging your children to always move in the direction of inner joy. Self-Love stems from being authentic and living true. Yes, you assume all of the responsibility that comes with being a protective parent; it's just that the older your children become, your primary focus becomes spiritual guidance as you assist your children in seeing the bigger, broader, grander version of their story.

Self-Love is a call to yourself and to your children to understand on the deepest of levels your true spiritual nature, while simultaneously owning and accepting your universal humanity. The path within that leads to a deepening of Self-Love will clear out old patterns and wounds that keep you from fully experiencing your own divinity. It's a lifelong process that becomes a sacred journey through the depths of your interior. The sooner conscious living is modeled for children the better. When challenges, obstacles, patterns, habits, and wounds are dealt with honestly and openly, the psychic baggage won't build up for your child and turn into an emotional thread in his vibration that will need to be excavated at a later date. The path to wholeness can begin at any age. Deal with the "holes" as they occur, rather than allowing them to become lodged and hidden within the human psyche.

Self-Love stems from a deep intimacy with your own soul. Eventually, every single choice will flow from this interior connection to your true self. Your outer world may appear exactly as it has always been, but your inner world will be a completely different experience. Today my divine flow energy moments rise up from a place deep within whereby I can feel my own indescribable magnificence as I merge with the Oneness of All That Is.

Recently, I was driving down the street listening to a pop song called *Love Song* by Sara Bareilles, and I had one of my moments. As I listened to the words and felt the cascading music, intense feelings of Self-Love began to wash over and through me. My divine flow energy feeling enveloped my entire being in a rush of warmth and love. I recognized the divine energy specifically as Self-Love, with no differentiation between my true self and the larger field of consciousness. After my glorious experience with this song, I realized that each and every day I must *choose* to write *myself* a love song in the living of my life; not an ego-based love song, but one of acceptance and appreciation for the beautiful essence currently in physical form that I am. I recognized that if I was able to see and feel and live a love song *for me*, deep inside of me, than I could freely express my acknowledgement, love, and gratitude for all other souls as well. In that moment, I knew in my core that loving kindness and forgiveness towards oneself would always be the first step in changing the world, for it is through an intimate, interior love that we are ultimately able to love *truly* externally.

*Annie mentions a channeling class in this chapter. She credits her work with Siria Family channeled by Sharyl Noday as being a huge catalyst for deepening her understanding of Self-Love.

Integrate It into Your Own Family!

Parent Contemplations:

- In what ways do you regularly nurture yourself? Name at least ten.

- Are your interior conversations typically of a negative or a positive nature? Describe a typical inner dialogue.

- Do you base most of your life choices on pleasing others or on pleasing yourself? Cite examples.

- Do you self-evaluate relationships, priorities, beliefs, habits, and patterns often? If so, how does this usually occur? If not, why?

- How do you model Self-Love for your children?

Activities:

- Coin Flip: List five negative beliefs that you hold about yourself. Flip the coin over and turn each negative perception into a positive perception. For example: *I am lazy*…flip coin…*My ability to sometimes do nothing allows for much-needed quiet time with my soul.* Or: *My good friend no longer wants to spend as much time with me…flip coin…I now have clear, open space to create new friendships.* This exercise teaches your children that there are always two sides to every coin.

- List ten attributes of yourself that you'd like to share with the world on a daily basis. Under each attribute draw or write ways that you can share it more fully with yourself, others, and the world at large.

- Choice Challenge: Analyze a typical day and categorize in a "T" chart (Draw a large T on top of a piece of paper with each side of the T representing an opposite) as many aspects as you can as either self-loving or self-defeating. (For example, habits, food, conversations, how you spend your time.) Self-loving aspects raise your vibration and expand your sense of well-being; self-defeating aspects diminish your enthusiasm, hope, and overall sense of well-being.

- Dance and sing—together as a family or alone—as often as possible!

Books:

Picture: *The Goodness Gorillas* (Jack Canfield and Mark Victor Hansen)
Chapter: *The Patron Saint of Butterflies* (Cecilia Galante)
Adult: *Oneness* (Rasha)

Movies:

Rudy (1993)
Stand and Deliver (1988)

Songs:

The Greatest Love of All (Whitney Houston)
Strength, Courage, and Wisdom (India.Arie)

Chapter 15

Soul to Soul Parenting *Spiritual Theme*

Truth and Perception

*A*conscious family is comfortable looking at every angle of a situation. Family members recognize that their particular truth, the perceptive lens through which they view the world, is not necessarily more valid than the truth of another. They realize that their perception of the world will rarely match the perception and truth of another. That is, they understand that the interpretation of reality has everything to do with individual perspective. In fact, they fully expect and accept differences in perspective. A conscious family understands that truths may blend and overlap, and they look for those integrative aspects in every circumstance. They understand on a deep level that this is where compassion and empathy for the other can be found.

A conscious family member is someone who doesn't need to be right, but someone who desires to be heard. She is unable to hide her truth because she lives it authentically and transparently, day in and day out. Her consciousness arises from an awakened awareness of her own divinity. An inner *allowance* of each member's own divinity enables a conscious family to flow with life more easily, as they're better prepared to accept what is so; while at the same time they remain eager and enthusiastic for what is to come. Spiritually conscious individuals respect, honor, and validate their own truth and allow others the same privilege. Your personal truth and perceptions make you uniquely you, adding a beautiful facet to Total

Spiritually conscious individuals respect, honor, and validate their own truth and allow others the same privilege.

Consciousness as a whole. Once this is fully recognized for yourself, it becomes obvious that the same is true for every other individual, too.

We practice acceptance in our family on a daily basis. The perspective of always accepting reality in a given moment leads to greater self-empowerment. Tremendous personal power is derived from surrendering to what is so because what has already shown up cannot be changed, and one's energy can then be spent on creating the next moment to come in his future reality. Acceptance stems from a deep understanding that physical reality constitutes what is *called forth* by you on some level. As many masters have stated, *Nothing is good or bad, only thinking makes it so. If you do not want something in your life do not think it in your mind.* In the next moment, you are free to choose again, but the moment at hand is upon you, and acceptance leads to peace and greater insight within the present moment.

In all situations, we encourage our children to remain in nonpersonal awareness as they assess the situation and invite the voice of their soul and Spirit to light the best possible path. Nonpersonal awareness keeps you in a keenly awakened state, but without resistance or attachment to external forces. No matter what the outer circumstance—losing a job, receiving a promotion, going on a cruise, experiencing a hurricane, holding a dying person's hand, or rocking a newborn baby—your willingness to accept what is so determines your inner state of being. Your inner state of being then determines how you experience each situation; and therefore, also the next situation that is called forth by you into your awareness. Your capacity for peace and calm need not ever change when you have a deep understanding of your true nature. The outer world may shift beneath your physical body, but your inner world can be a constant, stable source of serenity and joy.

Many individuals have a difficult time feeling total joy and peace in *any* of the above mentioned situations. Even when the outer world presents you with something that you perceive to be *good,* you often question whether or not you actually deserve the gift. Loving what is so can be hard for humans no matter what is showing up, *good* or *bad,* because one tends to question his worthiness either way.

We encourage our children to be unafraid of what is showing up in

Openness to all of life, along with a confidence that you are steering the ship in a co-creative simpatico with the Universe, enables you to move forward, forgiving everything and choosing again.

their life. We see everything that shows up in life as a gift. It's shown up in the present moment for a reason and was created on some level *by* and *for* us. Yes, indeed, some paths are more arduous, some turns more painful, but you never know exactly where each path is leading you. Higher ground could be just around the corner and only possible after a trek through the swamp. Openness to all of life, along with a confidence that you are steering the ship in a co-creative simpatico with the Universe, enables you to move forward, forgiving everything and choosing again. You choose your personal relationship to any given person or situation. There are no victims and no villains, only those who are consciously making life choices and those who are not.

Divine Dichotomy/Divine Paradox

When I first learned the meaning of a divine dichotomy many, many years ago in the *Conversation with God* series, I was absolutely floored. I was floored because I had finally recognized in my heart and mind how one can acknowledge two seemingly opposite perspectives as truth. This newfound understanding freed me to actually pursue a life of nonresistance, nonattachment, and nonjudgment rather than simply pay lip service to living more consciously. While not always easy, there exists within me now a deep understanding of differences in perception and truth that assists me greatly in my desire to experience peace and tranquility throughout my day.

I love a good divine dichotomy, and life is full of them. In fact, I really enjoy searching for them and literally grinding them out of my personal perception of reality. A divine dichotomy or divine

Probably my most favorite divine dichotomy and Soul to Soul Reminder is one that greatly expanded my perspective when I began to really understand its meaning. It states: *Everything has meaning and nothing matters.* I know in my heart that every word, thought, and gesture has beautiful divine meaning and purpose, and yet I also clearly see that from the broadest of spiritual perspectives, ultimately nothing matters because we cannot make a wrong choice. We are in the divine presence and the divine presence is within us, and nothing can ever separate us from this truth. This clear sight enables you to live in peace, knowing that your choices reflect your current state of consciousness, not your true state of being.

paradox is a truth that can be viewed from multiple perspectives. The truth illuminates as not simply either/or, but rather as and/both. Oftentimes humans are so very black and white in their need to be right that they're unable and unwilling to view life circumstances from any other vantage point than from their own perspective lens. Many individuals are quick to condemn others as being wrong so that they can prove themselves right. In reality, more often than not, there are many different perspectives that are true and accurate for any given situation or idea. Teaching your children to be open to an enlarged paradigm invites them to see the world from a more expansive perspective and encourages them to openly explore their own life perspectives and inner truths.

When teaching your children the power and beauty of different perspectives, utilize the many divine dichotomies that can be found every day in life. Explain the importance of diversity and variety in the world by depicting the blandness and inability to acquire preferences that would exist if all people and experiences were the same. Teach your children that differences in their world are extremely purposeful from a spiritual perspective in that they allow them to choose and create their own unique reality. Encourage your children to perceive Oneness not as sameness or singularity, but as multifaceted and multidimensional. Children follow their parents' lead at the earliest stages of life, making it imperative that you allow your children to flow with their natural appreciation for differences and diversity. We've included *Remember the Divine Dichotomy* on a Soul to Soul Reminder to highlight the idea that everything in life doesn't have to be perceived in only one way. There are many facets to every person, condition, and situation. It is your job to seek the broadest perspective possible so that you can accept the reality of what is so. Some life examples that our family shares are: Participating on a soccer team can be both draining *and* exhilarating. Getting the flu and staying in bed for four days can be both taxing *and* an opportunity to rest mind and body. Writing a thesis for school can be both exhausting *and* satisfying. Hidden within reality there exist infinite paradoxes. Many individuals so often choose to resist rather than rest peacefully *within* the paradox. To encourage the latter in your children will assist them greatly in their desire for internal peace.

As things come up with your children, within your marriage, and in all relationships and life situations, always seek to understand the under-lying *unseen,* yet often deeply felt divine dichotomy. It does exist and can be a most healing, light-filled truth serum as it enters your frame of refer-ence. Teach your children to look for the divine paradoxes as they seek to understand different life experiences. Encourage them to open themselves to *all* perspectives and *all* possibilities as they learn to accept with grace what has shown up in their life.

As you grow in awareness and begin to greatly diminish the role that ego plays in your life, it becomes easy to detect when you are keeping yourself from seeing a larger truth in any given situation. You can feel the resistance in your body as you strive to move headlong through a tunneled perspective. When you sense light at the end of the tunnel, in comes a rushing sense of relief that more space has once again been created for an expanded vision of reality and truth. It takes work and commitment to monitor thoughts which aim to keep you in a close-minded state of consciousness, but you are, at your core, an infinite, eternal being that cannot be confined in any way. Eventually, despite all resistance, your formlessness and shapelessness will lead you to a greener pasture.

Author Cynthia Bourgeault writes in her book *A Wisdom Way of Knowing,* "In any situation in life, confronted by an outer threat or an opportunity, you can notice yourself responding in one of two ways. Either you will brace, harden, and resist or you will soften, open, and yield." The first reaction is from your limited ego self, and the second is a spiritual surrender to divine flow. We discussed these two possible reactions during a family discussion, reiterating with our children that an everyday spiritual practice is a moment-to-moment openness to what is so: a surrender to and love of what is true for *them,* coupled with a deep understanding that their truth may not be right for another. We feel that this spiritual perspective brings the gift of peace—a gift that keeps on giving reflected in every cell of your being.

Teaching your children to live in nonpersonal awareness frees them to make moment-to-moment decisions and change course whenever they choose. They're no longer dependent on anyone or anything to make

A wonderful spiritual teacher in my community, Ramaa Krishnan, uses a superb analogy when discussing nonresistance, nonattachment, and nonjudgment with her students. She describes how you often have unrealistic expectations of what another individual should be prepared to give you. Others do not necessarily hold the capacity within themselves to appear in the way that you want them to appear. In order to maintain peace in your life, you must accept what shows up and then freely make your choices as to how you choose to relate to the situation at hand. Any disappointment that you feel is really based on your need for the other person to deliver to you what you feel they should. Ramaa humorously shares the notion that you wouldn't walk into a grocery store and demand that they sell you some furniture. A grocery store doesn't carry furniture, so furniture is not available to you in this venue, and you fully accept that without question. You may either enjoy a shopping trip to the grocery store to purchase your food, and choose to appreciate the fruit and vegetables along the way or not. Or you may leave the grocery store and look for furniture elsewhere. Likewise, if another human being isn't capable, in that moment, of giving you what you imagine you need from them, then it becomes your job to change course and move in another direction, not the other person's job to change what they choose to be offering you at that time.

them happy. You consciously create your own happiness through the utilization of your very own inner guidance system. You expand your perceptions by opening up your limited perspectives. You accept and include another's truth as *part* of your own reality, but at the same time maintain your personal inner truth. You accept what shows up and acknowledge your deep desire and capacity to steer your own ship.

Encourage your children to sense the energies that surround them so that they can accurately direct their own course. Help them sense the energies of individuals and groups that come into their physical awareness. Teach them to ask themselves the following to assess all situations: *Do these energies feel stressful, calm, volatile, neutral, or balanced? Do I feel energized, tired, upbeat, or drained while interacting with certain energies?* Support your children as they learn to listen to their body and inner senses so that they can integrate the internal feedback and guidance that comes to them. Encourage them to make their choices accordingly. You don't want your children to fall into a pattern of simply being reactive to the energies that surround them day in and day out. Instead, invite them to respond to all energies with a sense of self-empowerment and compassion.

We teach our children to look for wisdom first inside of them, but to remain open to what resonates with their soul in the outside world. Your inner voice can lead you to find wisdom in unlimited and unique ways. There are many sources in the outer world that can serve as guideposts on your path. Wisdom could resonate from a scholar with a Ph.D., or it could resonate from the boy skateboarding down the street. Wisdom could resonate from a minister, or it could resonate from a teller at the bank. Wisdom could resonate from the waitress at your favorite restaurant, or it could resonate from the president of your company. Wisdom may resonate from a film, an article, a book, an advertisement, a neighbor, or a song that speaks truth to you.

The only question necessary in any given relationship or life situation really becomes what speaks truth to you?

Who knows? Who cares? Remain open and aware. We encourage our children to *feel* for the answers. If something resonates with their soul and raises their conscious awareness, then that is truth for them, no matter the source. The only question necessary in any given relationship or life situation really becomes *what speaks truth to you?*

What You Resist Persists!

I learned this oft-spoken truth long ago from my body. Through the years, minor health issues remained with me until I was able to uncover and face the underlying emotional cause. Unresolved issues will remain with you until you honestly delve into the deeper meanings behind them. Often you are inundated with clues as to what truth you must cease denying and accept, but you refuse to shift thinking and remain stuck in old patterns of thought. Your dreams, your body, your intuition, your spirit guides, and your subconscious all try to assist you in unfolding whatever it is that you are resisting paying attention to. We encourage our children to accept what is so, embrace it as something that has entered their reality for a reason, and then stay open to creatively move forward in a different direction, if desired. We encourage our children to remain open to new truths, even ones that are different than what was expected. Once the resistance to the problem itself is gone, the energy is free to flow smoothly again, and you're able to call forth a different reality.

Recently I realized that I am no longer afraid of truth, even raw, painful truth. I thrive on discerning the truth that is within me because I now understand that the truth really does set me free. One way or another, no matter how deeply you've been able to bury it, truth will rear its head, and you must face the music. I find that it's much easier to deal with things in a wide-awake state of consciousness *when* they arise rather than wait for another reason or another season.

One way or another, no matter how deeply you've been able to bury it, truth will rear its head, and you must face the music.

We teach our children that they can run, but they cannot hide. You must eventually stand in the fire and experience life just as it flows to and through you in the here and now. Life is a constant dance of catch and release. It's a continual balance of holding and letting go. Your soul provides the perfect guidance as to when it's time to anchor and when it's time to swim. Greater intimacy with the part of you that *knows* is what living in divine flow is all about. Your soul recognizes the impermanence of all outer forms and accepts change as the natural way of things. The Universe remains in a constant, vibrant state of eternal fluidity, and your very existence here on earth is a beautiful reflection of that truth.

Journaling has greatly assisted me in my ability to embrace clear sight when it comes to my own life and things that can be difficult to look at. My many spiritual mentors and teachers have also tremendously encouraged my quest for truth. They've helped me to see that I must do my own inner work to uncover my blocks and barriers. With loving insight they have guided me to my own reflection in the pool. Their gift to me has been the acknowledgement within myself of my own capacity to realign myself with the divine flow of life. It is through their guidance that I realized, in the deepest sense, that healing must take place from the inside out.

Downstream Versus Upstream

The idea of flowing downstream versus upstream in your boat (your life) was first proposed to me at a workshop led by Esther and Jerry Hicks, authors of many bestselling books. Many individuals, due to their own uncompromising resistance, attachment, and judgment, spend the majority of their lives paddling their boats upstream in a river that naturally flows downstream. The Hicks refer to God as Source Energy or the

Stream of Well-Being coursing through all things. When you resist the stream, you resist remaining in alignment with God and with your soul purpose. Ultimately, even though at times it may not appear to be so, flowing downstream in perfect alignment with Source energy is *always* the way to go. As they state in their lectures, "Nothing that you truly desire is ever upstream."

You are continually guided by Spirit as to *how* to turn your boat around; these are the guideposts, intuitive flashes, and synchronicities which continuously appear on your path, but ultimately it's up to you to make conscious choices, do your own inner work, and move through emotions to remain headed in the downstream direction that is divine flow. The first move in any *turnaround* situation is always an acceptance and an appreciation for where you already are in your present reality. After full acceptance has occurred, then you are able to slowly, but surely, get your boat turned around and moving once again in its natural direction. It is your resistant thoughts and inner beliefs emanating from your energy field that cause you to continue paddling upstream. The energy that you're currently in is what you offer to the world and becomes your point of attraction. There's no getting around this universal law no matter how hard you paddle upstream. The sooner that your children become informed of the stream of well-being that is their birthright, the easier and more peaceful their life will unfold for them. It's important for them to understand that they are an integral part of the stream, whether they remain conscious of it or not. *Upstream vs. Downstream* is another loving Soul to Soul Reminder in our home. We often refer to our choices as either an Upstream Choice or a Downstream Choice, and we help each other to discern between the two.

Stay Loose

It's easy to get so caught up and mired in the details of your day that you forget to stay loose and go with the flow. You begin to lose your flexibility and adaptability when what you're *doing* becomes more important than what you're *being*. Sometimes I really need to remember to loosen up and have more fun. There really are very few emergencies in life. Yes, focus is important, and I do like to accomplish things in my day, but in the realm of Spirit, none of it much matters. I've learned that my days run much more smoothly when I choose to lighten up. Lightening up is about both lightheartedness *and* allowing more divine light to enter your physical body. I notice that perfection surrounds me as life divinely flowing *through* me with love and joy. I don't need to create perfection on a daily basis in my surroundings; life is perfection, and therefore, so am I.

Lightening up is about both light-heartedness and allowing more divine light to enter your physical body.

Speak *often* to your children of differences in perspective and why they are more than okay. Help them sift through the variety and contrast that is inevitable and necessary on every life path so that they may better perceive what is true for *them*. Most important, encourage flexibility and tolerance in your children as they live their truth.

Integrate It into Your Own Family!

Parent Contemplations:

- Are you able to easily accept another's point of view as valid? Can you perceive multiple angles of any given situation?

- Do you believe that individual perspective creates reality? If so, explain.

- How do you determine what is true for you in life experiences? Do you feel resonation deep inside? Do you typically assess based on external effects?

- How do you express your truth to others? Is it typically communicated with compassion and ease or with a strong need to persuade and to be right?

- Do you speak often to your children of valuing different perspectives?

Activities:

- Recall a painful, disappointing, uncomfortable, or tragic situation
  or experience and write out at least three positive, soul-directed
  understandings to be gleaned from it. This activity encourages
  children to recognize underlying meaning, purpose, and overall
  soul expansion derived from universal life challenges.

- Identify five weak spots in your energy field where you typically
  give your power away. Find the holes/areas where you attempt to
  please others versus living true to yourself through your thought
  patterns, voice, choices, and specific actions. Likewise, identify
  five strongholds in your energy field where you typically hold
  onto your power and live your truth no matter what.

- The Right Questions: The book *The Right Questions* (Debbie Ford)
  offers ten questions that can be used with every decision to help
  you determine whether a choice is life-enhancing or life-defeating
  for you. Post the questions near your emotional scale (as
  discussed earlier) to help family members make choices that
  reflect their highest, truest self.

Books:

Picture: *Because Nothing Looks Like God* (Lawrence Kushner and Karen
     Kushner), *I Think, I Am* (Louise Hay)
Chapter: *Monsieur Eek* (David Ives)
Adult: *The Right Questions* (Debbie Ford)

Movies:

The Truman Show (1998)
Mr. Holland's Opus (1997)
Life Is Beautiful (1995)

Songs:

Angels Among Us (Alabama)
Thing of Beauty (Hothouse Flowers)

Chapter 16

....

Soul to Soul Parenting *Spiritual Theme*
Kinship

According to *Webster's Dictionary,* the word *kinship* is defined as "The state of being related by common ancestry." In my heart of hearts, I believe that we are all truly kin. As you recognize your shared spiritual heritage with another, you see that we are all of *like kind.* You are, in fact, a kindred spirit with all other spirits who reside in this Universe. You are beautifully unique, and you sing your own song, but you are undeniably connected to all others through your access to the divine wisdom that lives within all human beings and all life forms.

In kinship, alignment in overall perspective, coupled with a reciprocal exchange of energy, heralds a soul companionship that goes beyond a more ego-based friendship.

While kinship with all of humanity may or not be a conscious aspect of your life perspective, most of us are fortunate enough to acquire friends in our lives who reflect back to us the true meaning of kinship. These are the individuals with whom you share your heart's desires and your dreams. These are the people who bring sunlight and joy into your very existence. These are the friends who touch your core in a way that no one else can. These are the beloveds in your life who hold your hand as you soar to new heights. In kinship, alignment in overall perspective, coupled with a reciprocal exchange of energy, heralds a soul companionship that goes beyond a more ego-based friendship.

Friendships offer you the unique opportunity of experiencing true kinship. While some friendships may come and go, and others may last a lifetime, they all come to you with the blessed gift of assisting you in knowing yourself more deeply. Friendships are a sacred playground of learning like no other, for it is in both the superficial layers of friendship *and* within the deeper folds where we often come face to face with the active threads in our own energetic vibration. I feel that women, in particular, tend to hope that their friendships with other women will in one way or another expand them and lead them to a higher ground. In most cases, whether the friendship in its final stage is deemed *good* or *bad,* an expanded awareness has indeed taken place.

Children define themselves so much through their friendships that you must help them navigate these choppy waters. In order to assist your children as they grow and acquire friends, look closely at your own friendships. *What roles do you tend to play in your different friendships? How much intimacy do you allow? Are there any hidden agendas lurking within a particular friendship? Most importantly, what is it that you truly desire from friendship with another?* As you pay attention to your own friendships, you're better able to serve your children with theirs. Friendships are not always *pretty;* oftentimes you actually learn more along the way from *messy.*

In college, my friends and I categorized socialization into three tiers: Tier One constitutes your inner circle. These are the friends who just make life sweet. They are your comfort, your ease, and your joy. They are typically lifetime friends, but not always, as inner circles do change throughout your life. The boundaries are often thinner here than with other individuals. I have been blessed with many Tier One friendships in my life. Individuals in this core group continually grow and shift with me, on parallel paths. Physically, we live down the block from one another or are separated by hundreds of miles, but a strong heart connection exists in a mutual space. I've always felt very comfortable creating Tier One friendships. In fact, I thrive on them in many ways.

Tier Two: My college friends and I dubbed this the enormous circle of acquaintances that you acquire throughout your life. These are people that you may run into on a daily basis, but the chatting is usually quick and tends to remain more on the surface of life. These individuals change often depending on your life circumstances. They serve to keep you grounded in each phase of your life and offer a sense of community as well as guideposts and gifts in numerous ways to propel you forward on your path. They may fade in and out of your attention, but you know that they are there when you feel an impulse to reach out and make a connection. I appreciate Tier Two friendships, but in many ways, I always long for more on this tier. I prefer the deeper intimacies in a Tier One friendship, but I value the need for both just the same.

Tier Three friendships consist of the many strangers that move in and out of your life each and every day. These are people who share your space even though you may not even share more than eye contact and a smile. Once their role has been completed, they often drift out of your life, never to be seen again. I've always loved this tier because I feel such possibility with Tier Three. You never know who's going to pass through your life with a most precious gift and serve as a guidepost on your path. You never know how *you* may unexpectedly touch another. I find it rather easy to remain open and alert on Tier Three, with the expectation of a new connection on the horizon.

A friendship becomes its own divine slow dance, elegant, graceful, and purposeful in its unique vortex.

My friends and I used to discuss and evaluate these tiers frequently. We enjoyed categorizing situations as a Tier One, Tier Two, or Tier Three Moment. I've come to realize that all three tiers are beautiful and valid in their own way. I've learned to acknowledge and cherish *all* of them. Each tier is a necessary aspect of your co-creative capacity as a spirit-embodied human being. One tier of connection is not less than or greater than another; they are simply different and purposeful in their own way. While I do tend to enjoy the deeper, more intimate connections that I share with others, I understand clearly now that the short-lived relationships that offer other types of communication also offer numerous blessings.

A friendship becomes its own divine slow dance, elegant, graceful, and purposeful in its unique vortex. It's important to teach your children that a deep, loving, authentic kinship with self will lead to a deep, loving, authentic kinship with Spirit, which then leads to a deep, loving, authentic kinship with another. Fortunately, my partnership with my husband Jim and the tribe that we have created together as a family is also a divine matrix all its own. It is slow-moving, all-encompassing, and expansive in its very existence. The shared kinship in our family dynamic is palpable. Our souls have all been imprinted in a similar way as we have blended our energies in harmony with one another. This doesn't mean that our home is always peaceful, because it surely is not. It just means that we are united in our consciousness of who we really are. We understand our spiritual ancestry, allowing us to fully embrace the fact that we are truly kindred spirits.

All friendships, whether they are inside or outside of a family unit, provide you the opportunity to acknowledge the kinship that is the truth of your being. In friendship you are called to explore your own desire to love and be loved. Upon further evaluation of what you deeply desire from your friendships, you discover that you desire those same things from yourself. Friends provide soul mirrors for one another. When looked at from this vantage point, it is imperative that you assess your friendships often and encourage your children to do the same.

Help them choose to be with those friends with whom they can sense kinship. Like you, your children may have to go through the more challenging friendships to get to the gems, but assist them in being grateful for them all, just the same. Helping children navigate the ups and downs of friendships provides a grand opportunity to put into practice many of the spiritual themes being discussed within the family.

Friendships provide the perfect training ground to fully experience many of the spiritual practices being explored in the home. Assist your children in making these profound connections. Forgiveness, Connectedness and Boundaries, Truth and Perception, and Self-Love are but a few of the spiritual themes to be analyzed within a friendship. Identifying what you desire in a friendship steadily moves you towards that type of friendship with others, and most importantly, within yourself.

Kinship exists on a spiritual level between all living things. Only you can decide to make kinship a shining aspect of your earthly reality. Is it going to be soul to soul or role to role when it comes to your relationships with others? You access Spirit through

My personal desires in a friendship as recorded in my Intuitive-Gratitude Journal include the following: depth, authenticity, tolerance, trust, truth, silliness, lightheartedness, support, encouragement, enthusiasm, generosity of spirit, kindness, ease, openness, and lots and lots of joy. All of these things I also desire to give me. Ultimately, you realize that when you find these very things within yourself, you will create friendships that reflect them back to you with ease and grace.

human connections. You access God through your relationships with others. Feel this truth *inside* your friendships. Turning friendship into kinship is simply acknowledging in your deepest space the bounty of your shared spiritual ancestry. Gaze deeply into the eyes of another and allow the truth of kinship to flourish in your midst. Encourage your children to open themselves to the possibility of true kinship with others.

Integrate It into Your Own Family!

Parent Contemplations:
- What attributes do you most value in a friendship?

- Name three friends whom you most enjoy and why.

- Do you feel kinship with anyone? If so, why?

- Have you developed a strong friendship with yourself?
  If so, describe.

- Have you developed a strong friendship with God/Spirit? If so, describe.

- How do you help your children navigate their friendships?

Activities:
- Kinship Lists: Create a list of the positive attributes shared by you and another friend whom you regard as a kindred spirit. Keep in mind that a kindred spirit could be an adored pet or someone that you don't know extremely well, but with whom you feel a strong, shared essence. Note the similarities and differences that create the unique compatibility between you.

- Identify five to ten individuals in your life as *team* members on your life journey. These are persons who really *see* you and accept you for who you are. Full authenticity is allowed in these relationships. Why do you feel that they are part of your team? Why are they in your life at this point in time? Specifically, how do you feel about each one? Identify the energy exchange. How does it positively affect you/them?

- Identify at least three people whom you do not know well or know at all (for example, a teacher, an author, a world leader, etc.) but whom you desire to emulate in some way. Why are they role models for you? Which attributes that they express speak to you? How could you integrate some of their positive soul attributes into your own life? Assess the soul attributes that you hope to model for others.

Books:
Picture: *Secret of the Peaceful Warrior* (Dan Millman)
Chapter: *Charlotte's Web* (E.B. White)
Adult: *Friendship with God* (Neale Donald Walsch)

Movies:
Remember the Titans (2000)
White Fang (1991)
Fried Green Tomatoes (1991)

Songs:
Shower the People (James Taylor)
I'll Stand By You (Carrie Underwood)
On the Wings of Love (Jeffrey Osborne)
Ain't No Mountain High Enough (Marvin Gaye)

Chapter 17

Gratitude and Appreciation

*G*ratitude and Appreciation are states of being. The vibration of gratitude and appreciation is your greatest creative tool, not only for physical manifestation, but for inner peace as well. The absolute key to shifting your life into one that's infused with an everyday spiritual practice is to appreciate and become blissfully grateful for what you already have. Appreciation turns the life force

At every turn, teach your children the importance of gratitude and appreciation to their entire well-being.

that resides within you into a high-octave vibration that resounds throughout the Universe, gleefully announcing, "Yes! I am awake! I am aware! I see clearly that I am surrounded, adored, and unconditionally loved by God!" Gratitude not only serves you, but also serves the entire Universe, calling forth the expansiveness of your state of becoming. The Universe grows and expands as you grow and expand, and there is nothing more expansive than gratitude and appreciation teeming with love and joy. At every turn, teach your children the importance of gratitude and appreciation to their *entire* well-being.

I simply cannot stress enough the infinite power of gratitude and appreciation to pull all of the esoteric themes and ideas together and download them into your children's consciousness now and forever. Your spiritual nature thrives and exponentially expands on gratitude and appreciation. It is the surefire fastest way to propel your soul into the forefront of your daily living. No matter where you sit or stand at any moment, you can *always* reach towards a little more appreciation, a little more gratitude, for the bounty that is life. As long as you are breathing, you are an eternal life force in dominion with the three-dimensional physical earth plane. To be here, right now, no matter what the circumstances, is a gift.

Thank You!

These two words really say it all. Don't let a day go by that isn't laced throughout with appreciation and gratitude. Commit to having an attitude of gratitude each and every day. The mere feeling of being grateful raises your vibration automatically. As with the act of breathing, without any conscious effort you open yourself to the creative power of God, simply by feeling thankful. When I see those two words on my kitchen cabinet, I am reminded not only to thank God, but also to thank more freely every single individual and circumstance that enters into my life. Even my so-called *enemies* should be thanked on some level for providing me the opportunity to know myself more deeply through the contrast. Saying "Thank you!" and even more importantly, feeling *thankful*, has changed my life. Only positive energy can come from these two little words.

So much has been written about gratitude over the past several years. Teacher after teacher has reminded us that gratitude is perhaps the most powerful means of shifting your life into a more open, connected, and peaceful space. Writing about your gratitude can be very beneficial in that it forces you to take note and pay attention to the divine intricacies of your life. Writing down your gratitude says very clearly to the Universe that you are fully aware of the infinite number of gifts that are showered upon you in every moment of the day. I've also found that just giving a genuine nod of thanks in my own mind as I pass through life with awareness and appreciation is, in and of itself, conscious living. "Thank you! Thank you! Thank you! Thank you for all of it!" courses through my soul, day in and day out, reverberating throughout the entire Universe with its high frequency.

> *Saying "Thank you!" and even more importantly, feeling thankful, has changed my life. Only positive energy can come from these two little words.*

The Appreciation Rampage, as mentioned in Esther and Jerry Hicks's book, *Ask and It Is Given,* is an underused tool that can affect your energetic frequency as easily and quickly as meditation. It requires simply appreciating from wherever you are, whatever surrounds you in that moment. This is a spiritual tool with immense consequence. You can actually feel the shift from resistance to receptivity when you engage in this activity. It pushes you past your current threshold for goodness and pleasure and amplifies all that is *right* and wonderful in your life.

> When I find myself in a low-feeling energy pattern or in a downward spiral where I feel stressed, hurt, sad, or disappointed, I know that appreciation can turn my boat around faster than any other method. This doesn't mean that I don't acknowledge my current feelings. It simply means that when I am ready to move through and past those feelings, I know that gratitude and appreciation will be my greatest support in diminishing them to more tolerable levels, and eventually releasing them from my energetic vibration all together.

We talk frequently to our children about the importance of gratitude and appreciation to their well-being. All good things that come into their lives first stem from a loving acknowledgement of what is already there. They know that feeling grateful is one of the most potent and powerful frequencies in the whole Universe. As we sort through problems and hindrances together, they know that the first step to creating a change is always acceptance and appreciation for what's already shown up in the divine flow of life. From that point, they can begin to examine more closely their desire for change. It is in the here and now where they can offer a higher thought, a higher word, and a higher choice to create the transformation that they so desire.

The intensity and depth of the feelings of appreciation and gratitude contribute greatly to the extent of well-being derived from any given moment. *Do you truly feel the Divine Presence that exists within all things?* When deeply recognized, you can actually sense in your soul the shift in vibration that occurs when gratitude and appreciation abound. It's similar to the sensation of joy welling up within as you engage in the activities that you love. It's similar to the feeling of interior acknowledgement and compassion that accompany self-love and reside in a place deep within when it bubbles to the surface of your reality. Not only do you feel the vibration of gratitude and appreciation in your soul, but you can also feel it inside your body. Such is the power and vitality of appreciation and gratitude that you can actually feel the cells in your body vibrating at a higher frequency.

Neale Donald Walsch shares with us these words which have been a Soul to Soul Reminder in my home for many years:

> "The day will come when you will review your life and be thankful for every minute of it. Every hurt, every sorrow, every joy, every celebration, every moment of your life will be a treasure unto you, for you will see the utter perfection of the design. You will stand back from the tapestry, and you will weep at the beauty of it."

These words have been such a gift to me and to my family through the years. You are in the process of becoming, and every single step of your beautiful becoming is etched into the tapestry of your very own soul. Each strand with its unique colors and textures represents the eternal, unlimited, infinite, expansiveness that is your true nature. Nothing, absolutely nothing, should be taken for granted, go unnoticed, or ridiculed in any manner. *All* of it counts! All of it becomes intricately woven into your tapestry. The tapestry of a soul is so sacred that even God—*especially* God—salutes its magnificence.

A while back, I wrote in my Intuitive-Gratitude Journal an expression of gratitude for the different kinds of days. I realized that I love the unique vibe of each day. I expressed appreciation for the slow, more freeing type of day where there's a lot of room for contemplation and reflection, *and* I also expressed gratitude for the full, busy, action-oriented day that is jam-packed with the hustle and bustle that can be my life. I saw that I actually cherish both kinds of days and what they add to my overall reality. I choose more now to flow with each kind of day as they come and go rather than constantly

A gratitude dance created by two friends has been downloaded on YouTube, reaching millions all across the globe. We watched the different clips of it together one night on the computer as one of our family discussions, and then we each shared our own version of the gratitude dance. Now we often invoke the special dance as a reminder in difficult situations or in easy, breezy situations to express appreciation for what is so.

resist a certain type of day and wish for the other kind while in the midst of the day that has actually shown up. Teach your children to appreciate all kinds of days, for none should be taken for granted, no matter what they choose to do with it.

Teach your children to appreciate all kinds of days, for none should be taken for granted, no matter what they choose to do with it.

Gratitude and Appreciation are cornerstones in an expanding family spirituality. It is extremely easy to teach this simple, yet profound spiritual theme. These two words will become the most-used in your family's spiritual language. Speak of gratitude and appreciation on an hourly basis in your home. Their truth and power will infuse your family with a genuine sense of godliness, awe, and grace. The peace that gratitude and appreciation can provide in any situation is truly immeasurable. The Universe invites you to bask in the glory of All That Is in every single moment of every single day. Feeling appreciative and grateful simply says back to All That Is, "Yes. Thank you. I joyfully accept!" Deep gratitude and appreciation make you aware that, as a spiritual being, you sing in harmony and dance in rhythm with the *fullness* of Life.

Integrate It into Your Own Family!

Parent Contemplations:

- Are you truly grateful for *everything* that occurs in your life? Can you find positive meaning and underlying purpose in even those life experiences that appear negative?

- In what ways do you use gratitude and appreciation as creative tools for physical manifestation?

- Do you allow gratitude and appreciation to provide you with inner peace? If so, how?

- What importance do you place on teaching gratitude and appreciation to your children? Do you speak of it often in your home?

Activities:

- Circle of Gratitude: Together as a family, sit in a sacred circle to enclose the beautiful group energy with eyes closed. Circle several times around, giving each family member an opportunity to share gratitude for something. Each individual offers one thought per turn. This circle can be created at the end of every family discussion or as the grace before dinner, if so desired.

- Magical Megaphone: Create or buy a megaphone and decorate. Use it to announce your gratitude to the family and to the Universe when the feeling moves you. The magical megaphone can also be passed around at the end of family discussions. Keep handy for daily use. Gratitude works magic by being an instant vibration raiser.

- Write a family prayer together to be posted, memorized, and shared that expresses your family's unique spirituality. This will serve to keep things fresh at mealtime or bedtime when prayers are typically shared. Encourage your children to write their own prayers for personal or family use.

- Name as many things as you can that make you smile or laugh. Create your list without interruption as quickly as you're able to write. Share your lists with the family, enjoying laughs together.

Books:

Picture: *The Giving Tree* (Shel Silverstein), *Giving Thanks* (Jonathan London)
Chapter: *Mrs. Frisby and the Rats of NIMH* (Robert O'Brien)
Adult: *Living with Joy* (Sanaya Roman)

Movies:

The Kid (2000)
Eight Below (2006)

Songs:

Thank You (Dido)
People Get Ready (Eva Cassidy)

Chapter 18

Soul to Soul Parenting *Spiritual Theme*

Trust and Faith

*T*rust and Faith initiate a relaxation into the moment, a deep inner sense of ease, a knowing that all is well, a release of worry and fear, an openness to life, an acceptance of motion and change, a love of the unknown, a desire to be surprised, a belief that life itself is the ultimate blessing, a deep expectation that what life offers serves your higher good, and a complete surrendering to the divine flow of life.

You may either crawl with the caterpillars or soar with the butterflies depending on your propensity for creativity in that moment, but there is always an absolute knowingness that *all* paths are sacred and highly regarded by Consciousness itself. You surrender to your co-creative reality with the Universe and become not only the creator, but also a *witness* to your creations. Trust and faith may come to you all at once from a specific experience of divinity or may develop and deepen gradually as you embark on the journey within. Either way, you transcend from a place of inner hesitation and fear to a *palace* of inner peace. Trust and faith liberate you to live more fully, knowing that the Universe holds you in rapture as an integral tile in its beloved mosaic.

It is imperative that children understand the spiritual meaning of the word surrender. To the ego, surrender means to give up, shy away, or lose. Surrendering in the *spiritual* sense reflects an inner allowance and expansion for the infinite possibilities that exist in the Universe. The soul understands that to surrender is to merge with All That Is

Trust and faith liberate you to live more fully, knowing that the Universe holds you in rapture as an integral tile in its beloved mosaic.

to call forth the highest outcome of any situation. Spiritual surrender also means allowing your own authenticity at all times. In this way, you live true from your soul and surrender to your own truth. In this sense, surrender is the path to liberation from a reality tethered to the approval of others.

I received an inspirational email recently stating the following three possible answers from God to your heart's desires:

YES!

Not yet . . .

I have something *better* in mind.

These answers can be a very simple way to help your children begin a life of faith. They must understand fully, however, their part in the faith equation. They must hold themselves in a state of allowing and receiving in order for physical manifestation of their *true* heart's desires to occur. In other words, their thoughts and inner beliefs continually offered to the outer world must match *vibrationally* all that they desire. Children can understand early on that they are powerful creators in their own right and must do their part to receive with openness and trust what they have called forth. Once this is understood, these are perfect answers from God to add to your Soul to Soul Reminders.

Why Wouldn't You Choose Joy, Love, and Total Faith?

This question came to me while driving in my car one day. It was a moment that brought me much clarity. I realized that the choice is mine, it always has been mine, and it always will be mine. Choosing anything other than joy, love, and total faith seemed so absurd and foolish to me in that moment. It's as if for several minutes, I could no longer even fathom why I, or anyone else, would live their life in such confusion and fear. This was definitely one of my divine flow energy moments. Of course since then I have experienced many moments *without* such clarity so I added this to our Soul to Soul Reminders as a conscious cue for all of us that it is indeed possible to choose joy, love, and faith in every moment. I keep it as a question like it came to me that day in the car because I think it reminds us how really quite unimaginable it is to choose to live any other way.

Know that the Universe will open up a path for my dreams!

Stay open to all possibilities that come your way. Many times you ask God for something, but then only remain open for the exact answer that you think you need. So many times, in fact more often than not, you miss the surprises that

Allow your path to unfold naturally with the universal flow of life, and encourage this daily in your children.

the Universe flows your way because you are solely focused on one rather rigid and closed answer. The Universe can answer you in millions of ways. Be surprised, delighted, amazed and grateful for the magic that unfolds and enters your reality. Know without even a seed of doubt that God will clear the way for your deepest desires to manifest. The toughest part is getting out of the way and releasing all resistance, attachment, and judgment. Your job is to receive with wonder and grace the surprises along the way. Allow your path to unfold naturally with the universal flow of life, and encourage this *daily* in your children.

For me, a large part of moving into a more faithful life has been about trusting *myself*. Trusting Annieness, in all her complexities, dimensions, and full-out glory, has at times seemed almost too much for me to bear. My faith that I, myself, can never be separated from my own inner divine source has been perhaps my greatest hurdle in this lifetime. My faith in God has always been impenetrable, but for me the underlying fear has been whether or not I could somehow create a life of separation where I no longer could *feel* the unbreakable bond between me and All That Is. I now know in my deepest space that a life of separation can only be found in the realm of misperception.

The only thing that's asked of you in this process of claiming your innate desire to fully and joyfully trust life is to remain open: Open to give love. Open to receive love. Open to all

On my bedside table sits the Soul to Soul Reminder **Surrender to Spirit**. Every single morning I wake up and look at this personal message to myself. I thank God for assisting me in completely letting go and allowing Spirit to work through me. It's a fine balance of being fully present and aware on this beautiful and sensuous physical plane in which you live in your body, but also allowing an intimate relationship with the spiritual dimension to permeate your every choice. It's a creative dance where you coexist not only with your deepest and highest aspect that is your very own divinity, but also with Divinity as a whole. You never lose any aspects of yourself by consciously living a life of trust and faith. Instead you enhance your very existence by threading Spirit into and through every thought, word, and deed.

possibilities. Open to your eternality. Open to the true essence of your very own core. Open to a multidimensional Universe that's more infinite than your mind can even begin to comprehend. Open to simply be. The journey to total faith is always a journey of the heart, not the mind. Peace of mind has to do with the mind being at rest so that the heart can fully expand its astonishing capacity for love. Your soul desires to lead you down this path. Your soul knows exactly what will get you there. Your soul, in blissful union with All That Is, gently takes your hand and attempts to move you in that direction with every breath. If you remain closed to everything but this three-dimensional, five-sensory world in which you live, then you miss by a long shot the truth of your own identity.

I was on a long bike ride into the city not too long ago and found myself *twirling*—worrying—about a situation that involved an adverse interaction with another. The more I twirled, the more I could feel my energy become denser. I could feel that my personal power was literally draining from my energy field as I continued to focus on this situation in a negative way. The worry led to fear, self-doubt, grasping for an answer in my head, diminished vibration, a myopic focus, and an overall dimness and confusion. In this negative energy pattern, I could feel that my antennae were down and that the signal I was emitting to the outer world was weak. If music had been playing, I knew that I wouldn't have been able to sense its higher vibration. Suddenly, I realized that it was time to make a different choice. I remember the exact location on my bike where I consciously shifted gears in my mind and stopped the detrimental twirl. I asked all of my spiritual friends for help and announced out loud to the Universe that I was totally receptive to an answer. I took a leap of faith and cleared my head while focusing *only* on my beautiful surroundings with gratitude and appreciation.

Twenty minutes later, I almost fell off my bike when I heard the answer giving me the missing piece (peace) that I'd desperately searched for in my head to no avail. The release was immediate. I could feel in every cell of my body a heightened energetic vibration. The free flow of joy was back, and with it an inner contentment, enthusiasm, and aliveness, which had become unperceivable to me only minutes before. The world appeared once again shiny, crisp, unlimited, bright, and hopeful. My intuition was powerful and clear. I knew that this shift into alignment with my soul would mean fearlessness, fulfilling interactions with others, and goodness reflected back to me at every turn.

When you are in your power and refuse to give it away to anything or anyone outside of yourself, you're able to trust the process of life and participate consciously and fully. Learn to detect the differences in your own state of being and teach your children how to assess their state of being, too. You are a beacon of light; only you can allow that light to be diminished or reside in its glow. Make it a conscious choice every day.

If you can free yourself from fear, it is much more likely that you'll grasp the significance of the many, many signposts that light your way. Synchronicities and answers are always much more apparent in the vibration of trust than they are in the vibration of fear. Fear ties you down, holds you back, and keeps you from inhabiting the space of your highest potential, your gift to humanity.

Surrendering to the Universe lifts you to new heights in your Consciousness. The more you are able to surrender to the infusion of God energy in your waking moments, the more awake you actually become. Blending with God expands your awareness and potential, not diminishes them. Trust and faith lead you to a state of openness, allowing you to harness the energy of the Universe so that you can creatively dance in unison with your own divine spark.

Encourage your children to flow with life in a constant state of surrender. This doesn't mean being passive. It means trusting that each moment coming to them is sacred and divine; and as sacred and divine beings, they have the capacity to merge with the moment and create their next destiny. Speak of faith and trust in your home. Help your

> Gift your spirit with a long walk outside on a warm, sunny day. Feel the depth of God in everything that you see. Sense the vastness of All That Is through your inner senses, not simply your physical ones. Breathe it all in and let it expand into every cell of your body and into every aspect of your being. You are so much more than you perceive yourself to be. You are as vast as the Universe itself. You are forever a part of this glorious mix as a divine parcel of Creation. Sense this truth in your deepest space. Allow it to ripple through your consciousness. This deeper level awareness of your true nature caresses your soul. This inner knowing can shower your spirit in a soft rain of total trust and complete faith.

children learn to trust the divine guidance that comes to them through their inner senses.

Encourage not blind faith, but rather a conscious faith in themselves *and* the divine flow of life. Teach them to accept their own infinite capacity to perceive and create anew in each moment. Trust and faith require that you leave resistance, attachment, and judgment at the door as you enter the brightness of a *new* spiritual world. Exemplify for your children that not knowing everything in their mind is *more* than okay. Their natural state of being doesn't spring from their mind, it stems from their soul.

Practice trust and faith with your children. Show them the ease in which faith enables one to live. Express the deep joy that comes from trusting the divine flow of life. Share your experiences of trust and faith as they intertwine with all aspects of daily living. Choose to reap the benefits of inner knowing together as a family.

Integrate It into Your Own Family!

Parent Contemplations:

- How attached are you to specific outcomes in any given situation?

- Are you able to remain open to all possibilities? If so, what methods do you use to remain open? If not, why?

- Are you okay with not always knowing an answer or an outcome? Are you open to multiple answers and outcomes? Why or why not?

- What five things do you most fear? Why?

- Are faith and trust all-important and utilized aspects of your daily life experience? Describe.

- Do you typically trust that all is well no matter what may be showing up in your external world?

Activities:

- Write out or draw your dharma, your soul purpose, as you feel it to be today. Get quiet, be still, and *feel* what it is you came to earth to do by tapping into what brings you joy and empowers you. Ultimately, soul purpose offers your highest potential to yourself, others, and the world. It is your true calling and path. Use colors, words, pictures, textures, etc., to express your soul purpose.

- Recall at least one time in your life where you felt total trust and faith that all was well no matter what the physical outcome. In other words, despite exterior circumstances that can be perceived as either good or bad, you understood fully that everything was actually on course and okay. Detail the experience. What did it feel like on your *interior*?

- Think of a recent challenge in your life. List five positive outcomes that can be gleaned from the challenge and acknowledged today. Recognize your trust in the overall process of life and your ability to accept the multiple layers offered in each new life experience. Identify the different layers, if possible.

Books:

Picture: *Zen Shorts* (Jon Muth)
Chapter: *A Wrinkle in Time* (Madeleine L'Engle)
Adult: *The Laws of Spirit* (Dan Millman)

Movies:

August Rush (2007)
Miracle (2004)

Songs:

Let It Be (Jennifer Hudson)
The Climb (Miley Cyrus)

Part Four

Final Soul to Soul
Parenting Thoughts

Chapter 19

Final Soul to Soul Parenting Thoughts: Blossoming Spiritual Companionship

If we have enough courage and enough spiritual stamina, we can help to birth *within* our children a divine awareness that will illuminate their physical life experiences to an extraordinary extent. It is truly a soul calling to embark on this *otherworldly* journey as a family. To walk the spiritual path alone is to be blessed, but to witness a rising consciousness in those nearest and dearest to your heart is breathtakingly beautiful.

Inner resonance becomes the immediate clue preceding every choice. It is the acknowledgement of this truth that expands the manifestation of this truth into every aspect of their lives.

When you get down to the essence of parenting, once your children reach a certain age and the full-out physical necessities of parenting that can be so demanding in the early years have ceased, a need for loving guidance is really all that remains. If your children can come to understand the infinite power and wisdom of the Universe that lives within them, and remember how to tune *into* that knowledge, everything else will always fall into *perfect* place. By perfection I mean serving their highest good while offering them purposeful learning experiences, which may in fact include suffering and disappointment. When they're following interior guidance, educational paths, character building, extracurricular activities, relationships, and passions enter their lives at the right time and place with little resistance or fear.

Once your child aligns himself with his core, the grace of God has a clear, direct channel *through* him. As parents, you can then simply step into your intended role as a guide and assist your children in any way that you can as they begin to consciously create their reality. Challenges are met with acceptance and confidence because your children recognize that contrast and variety serve them, and they know that they are never, ever alone. Their lives are blessed with continual, nonphysical assistance, as well as an interior knowing as to what is true for them. Inner resonance becomes the immediate clue preceding every choice. It is the *acknowledgement* of this truth that expands the *manifestation* of this truth into every aspect of their lives.

In a conscious family, it's understood by all family members that each individual must ultimately do her own work. There exists a deep understanding that each human being is a creative, eternal, intuitive, divine essence who has come to earth with a soul purpose and a sacred mission to fulfill. The family that's been created holds a most intimate space for all members to begin their lifelong journey. While you are all connected in a beautiful, divine way, each individual comes into this physical world and leaves this physical world with his own chosen agenda. Give all family members the space and opportunity to explore completely what they came here to create. It is with this broad under-standing that you allow your children to begin, as early as possible, to do their own work. You give them permission to do so by exhibiting this practice in your own life.

Parenting a conscious family requires transparency, honesty, and a willingness to fully express from one's deepest space. In other words, you are unafraid to really *go there* with one another. A spiritually conscious and wide-awake family doesn't look only one way. In fact, it's fluid and ever-changing in its shape and form. Peace and harmony in the home are not necessarily the telltale signs of a conscious family. In a conscious family, you're intimate with one another in your language and emotional sharing. You speak truth even if it's difficult for another to hear. You bump up against one another as you continually exchange energy, but you are conscious participants in all aspects of life. A conscious family is not perfect, which isn't possible in the physical sense, but rather it is *accountable* and open to the authentic expression of each family member. It accepts challenges head-on with trust that they will serve the higher good of all involved. Each path is acknowledged as different and unique, while at the same time a palpable unity exists, connecting all members like a spiderweb in a beautiful divine matrix of intricate threads. No member of the family is ever left behind as the divine matrix itself evolves and shifts to accommodate all creative endeavors.

In a conscious family, an individual's passions are shared and encouraged by all members. You tap into, delight in, and derive joy from a loved one's inner fire. Each soul's preferences are cherished and respected. In this way you witness the other's light and appreciate his soul. In our family, my husband's passion for teaching and coaching along with my passion for teaching and spirituality, as well as our children's passions for sports, animals, friendships, and creative freedom, among many other things, are fully supported and enmeshed within the totality of our tribe. We explore our passions fully and openly not only as a solo mission, but also within the framework of our family network. There is an inclusive aspect to our passions thereby touching the spirit of each family member. This inclusion is very conscious on our part, used not only as a means of deepening the spiritual connection among us, but also exemplifying for our children the power of being genuine and living true.

All family members must live true to the voice of their own soul if they are to discover true joy and happiness that can only well up and burst forth from *within*. You must give yourself and each other permission to go where you are fed. A passion is actually a spiritual path that's quite intimate and personal. The sharing of it with beloved family members and friends is a true gift of self.

Tears of joy are often your greatest source of knowing in regard to inner truth. Whether or not the tears actually flow from your eyes, it is that feeling of being *choked up* and unable to speak in the moment that delivers to you an internal announcement of truth. In fact, momentarily your ego has been *choked out* and

There is no greater gift to another, within any relationship, than encouraging that individual to live and express her own truth. The best example that parents can give to their children in this regard is living true themselves and showing their acceptance of all paths. There are an infinite number of unique paths up the mountaintop to God. You simply encourage your children to be open and aware. You remind them to listen for the answers. You support them in their limitless capacity to sense on their interior the right path for them. If something resonates in that deep inner space, then that is truth for the soul no matter what the exterior world reveals.

your soul is able to speak to you in very lucid terms. It is during these clear exchanges that you must grasp the true essence of what flows from your soul and actively integrate the message into your physical reality.

Teach your children to look to themselves for the answers. Help your children learn the language of their soul. You can feel the answers supplied by the Universe deep within through your connection to All That Is. It's up to you, and only you, to recognize, acknowledge, and accept the answers that are continuously flowing through you. Allow yourself to experience self-empowerment as you swim freely in the Stream of Well-Being without resistance or shame.

Examine your life closely. Don't negate or invalidate any aspect of your life already lived. Determine how your soul has led you so steadfastly to certain pivotal moments throughout your life. In my own life, I've often been overcome with awe as I begin to recognize the understated, gentle wisdom from my soul that's guided my choices and overall path. This wisdom can most easily be detected in the handful of pivotal moments in your life that have created the most change. For example, I knew from an early age that I desired to be a young parent. I had no doubt that this would be the way of it for me. At the time I didn't know why I was leaving my teaching career earlier than expected to have three children close in age, but my soul knew exactly where I was headed. That choice provided the perfect training ground for my future work as a soul nurturer who specializes in family spiritual support. Look to see when and where your soul has guided you down a path that would eventually expand your horizons.

I am no longer afraid of my own inner beauty and power. After many, many years of hesitation, I've finally rounded the corner and find myself in the homestretch of self-love and self-empowerment. Like many women, I used to have "girl crushes" on other women whom I desired to emulate, but now, for me, it's a full-blown acceptance and love of self that leaves me breathless. Of course, I know that I am always in a state of creation and becoming, but for me the inner "Yes!" to shining my divine light has been a true milestone. The freedom derived from this shift should never be underestimated. It literally extends into every aspect of one's life: from what to eat, to the content and quality of your work, to the depth of your closest relationships. Absolutely everything shifts when you liberate yourself to live true. The surest way to ignite in your children this inner freedom to shine their bright light is to live this way yourself. That is the only permission they'll ever truly need to liberate themselves from the fear of their own magnificence.

The time has come to shift your self-perception. *Do you see yourself as a beautiful, intuitive being, as an individual expression of God? Do you see yourself as creative and powerful? Do you see yourself as miraculous and magnificent? Do you take your own breath away? Are you the love of your life?* It is time that you bellowed a resounding "Yes!" to all of those questions. Give your spirit permission to dwell in your body with this newfound confidence and freedom. Allow your spirit the creative space to accomplish what it came here to do.

As you bring yourself into a higher consciousness, you bring your children into a higher consciousness. As you allow yourself to shine, you allow them to shine. As you choose faith over fear, you help them choose faith over fear. As you soar with your own passions, you allow them to soar with theirs. Your children are sensitive souls who intuit your energetic vibration. They follow suit much more than you ever realize, not just in regards to your actions and your words, but also as far as your state of being.

Spirituality constitutes knowing yourself fully, as well as consciously recognizing the support, energy, wisdom, and love that is directly available to you at all times. It is an inner integrity needing no justification or validation from the outside world. Spirituality is *feeling* the miraculous essence of your own soul and allowing that to emanate from your physical experience here on earth. Make soul work an intricate aspect of all that you do. Let it be the guiding force in all choices and decisions. Everything, in fact, is soul work, and you are either consciously aware of this while making the highest, most loving choices possible in any given situation, or you are not. As a family, stir it all up in one vast divine bowl. Infuse family life with a balance of freedom and responsibility, allowing spirituality to spill into every single nook and cranny of your life. Don't hesitate to feel the presence of God in every

> For me now, my spiritual journey is life experience and my inner knowing of what that experience means to me. I don't need external proof from anyone or anything. I live my life and feel in my soul what resonates as my truth. I am claiming my birthright as a conscious creator. I realize with gratitude that my physical earth experience provides my soul with the perfect opportunity to evolve and expand. My spiritual evolution has been a series of all-knowing moments of luminosity that have gradually become more frequent and more intense. I recognize that enlightenment is a continuous journey, a continuous internal uncovering of the layers that enshroud my core.

situation and circumstance. Let it in! Revel in it! Say "Yes!"

Teach your children that their core identity is not their physical body *or* their mind, but their soul. This shift in perspective is an *interior* shift that then manifests in their physicality. This truth becomes an undeniable container that gently and tenderly begins to hold outer reality in sacred space. Your spirituality *lived* comes to encompass all that you think, say, and do, determining what you experience in the external world. Your spirituality becomes the bridge between inner and outer pursuits.

I cannot emphasize enough the use of the multitudinous mediums that already exist in our complex, beautiful physical world as teaching tools. Use what already surrounds you in your everyday reality to help your children remember once again who they really are. Nature exists as a constant reminder of God. Music, books, poetry, movies, and art which touch your spirit in some way are all divinely inspired and meant to awaken you to the truth of your sacred heritage. Through these physical avenues many of us are able to feel a deeper connection with Life. You can feel the magnificence of humanity and the raw, as yet unfulfilled potential that exists within all human beings. All artistic expression is ultimately about love, the most accurate depiction of the energy of which we are all made. Use artistic expression to explore universal spiritual themes, as we as humans, especially children, desire to interact with it readily and easily on a daily basis. Feel the *underlying* meaning in these forms. Take hold of what captures your children's attention and infuse your unique brand of spirituality into that. Let life experiences be the opening of the conversation. In truth, life experiences *are* the conversation because God and Life are one.

One of the greatest gifts that you can deliver to your children is your own personal example of fearless, limitless living. Set your children free as early as possible to dismiss limits and barriers as imaginary walls from bygone eras. You can only create life experiences that you deem possible. Expose your children to the true nature of our infinite Universe. Listen to your soul, follow your spirit, receive your inner voice, and *go for it!* When you open your heart to all possibilities, you create the space for life to show up in infinite ways. All doors must remain open, or life presents itself in a most unique, daring way specifically meant for you but finds no one home. Availability to Spirit falls on you. You either make yourself delightfully available to God, or you do not.

As you begin to think in spiritual terms *all* the time, the paradigm shift feels like a complete rewiring and revamping of your awareness. It is an organic shift, which always begins on the inside, spreads throughout, and then materializes into your physical reality. This individual shift from spiritual *ignorance* to a greater spiritual understanding of your extraordinary relationship with Life and All That Is can alone change the world. As Lao-Tzu taught us with his words over two thousand years ago:

> If there is right in the soul,
> There will be beauty in the person,
> If there is beauty in the person,
> There will be harmony in the home,
> If there is harmony in the home,
> There will be order in the nation,
> If there is order in the nation,
> There will be peace in the world.

This Soul to Soul Reminder has been with me for over fifteen years and rings more true to my soul with each passing year. You can try as hard as you might to *fix* and control things in the outer world, but true change stems from a change of heart, a peaceful acceptance of what is so, and a deep understanding of your own eternal nature.

This book invites you, as parents, to take ownership and become the spiritual leaders of your own precious, beloved families. Begin speaking the same spiritual language. Start from wherever you are. There is no right or wrong. There is no perfect path. There's only what *feels* right to you and your family. Take baby steps…take huge steps…*it doesn't matter!* Spiritually conscious parenting is a lifelong process that requires trust, love, compassion, patience, and acceptance of all perspectives.

Choose to see your children as spiritual companions eager to explore both the physical and the nonphysical dimensions with you. Share with your children your life experiences, your feelings, and your deeper insights that come from the space within. This encourages your children to give credence and value to their *own*. Knock on heaven's door, not in death, but in life. The door is always unlocked. Knock on heaven's door and walk through every day. Bring your family along with you! It is simply a choice in how you perceive the world.

Begin your journey together *now* creating a truly conscious, open, spiritual home where everyone is wide-awake and listening to the voice of his own soul. Focus less on the details of *how* everything will take shape in life and more on consistently aligning with the harmonic flow of life itself. Create a family where everyone *remembers* who they truly are: beautiful, limitless, shapeless, formless, light-filled, loving, intuitive, eternal spirits with their own very personal, intimate, divine connection to God. Parent your children, not only side by side but also soul to soul. As a family join together and become bigger, bolder, brighter, more brilliant, and more beautiful as you shine as one magnificent divine matrix that reflects the luminosity of each individual spirit.

Integrate It into Your Own Family!

Parent Contemplations:

- What aspects of the Soul to Soul Parenting philosophy most excite you?

- Which spiritual themes, if any, resonate most deeply with you? Why?

- What changes do you envision within your family as a result of reading this book? What are at least five new ideas that you plan on implementing?

- How do you perceive your role as a parent after reading this book? What has changed? What has stayed the same?

To all of my readers, I wish you many blessings
and much peace in your perspective.

• • • • •

RESOURCES

Children's Books:

Little Soul and the Sun By Neale Donald Walsch

Little Soul and the Earth By Neale Donald Walsch

Hope for the Flowers By Trina Paulus

The Three Questions By Jon Muth

Stone Soup By Jon Muth

Zen Shorts By Jon Muth

Emma and Mommy Talk to God By Marianne Williamson

The Twelve Gifts of Birth By Charlene Costanzo

Because Nothing Looks Like God By Lawrence Kushner and Karen Kushner

God's Paintbrush By Sandy Sasso

Becoming Me By Martin Boroso

Secret of the Peaceful Warrior By Dan Millman

Incredible You! By Wayne Dyer

It's Not What You've Got! By Wayne Dyer

Unstoppable Me! By Wayne Dyer

Does God Hear My Prayer? By August Gold and Matthew Perlman

Where Does God Live? By August Gold and Matthew Perlman

Because Brian Hugged His Mother By David L. Rice

All I See Is Part of Me By Chara M. Curtis

Giving Thanks By Jonathan London

Pebble By Susan Milford

I Think, I Am By Louise Hay

Milton's Secret By Eckhart Tolle and Robert Friedman

Maddie Moonbeam's Garden By Karen Nowicki

Be Still! By Deborah Mackall

What Happens When I'm Asleep? By Deborah Mackall

I Love You More By Laura Duksta

All *Chicken Soup for the Little Soul* books By Jack Canfield and Mark Hansen

Books for Older Children and Teens:

Stargirl By Jerry Spinelli

The Sara Series (Sara Book 1, Book 2, Book 3) By Esther and Jerry Hicks

Because of Winn Dixie By Kate DiCamillo

A Wrinkle in Time By Madeleine L'Engle

The Patron Saint of Butterflies By Cecilia Galante

Bridge to Terabithia By Katherine Paterson

Island of the Blue Dolphins By Scott O'Dell

Tuck Everlasting By Natalie Babbitt

So B. It By Sarah Weeks

Mandy By Julie Andrews Edwards

Monsieur Eek By David Ives

Mrs. Frisby and the Rats of NIMH By Robert O'Brien

Jonathan Livingston Seagull By Richard Bach

Conversations with God for Teens By Neale Donald Walsch

Looking Beyond: A Teen's Guide to the Spiritual World By James Van Praagh

****Newbery Medal Books** and **Rebecca Caudill Award Books** are terrific choices for older children and can be found in all libraries, bookstores, and on-line.

Adult Books:

Conversations with God (Books One, Two, and Three) By Neale Donald Walsch

Friendship with God By Neale Donald Walsch

Communion with God By Neale Donald Walsch

Home with God By Neale Donald Walsch

The Psychic Pathway By Sonia Choquette

Trust Your Vibes By Sonia Choquette

A Return to Love By Marianne Williamson

Everyday Grace By Marianne Williamson

The Power of Now By Eckhart Tolle

Stillness Speaks By Eckhart Tolle

A New Earth By Eckhart Tolle

Living in the Light By Shakti Gawain

Creative Visualization By Shakti Gawain

The Red Book By Sera Beak

The Seth Material By Jane Roberts

Seth Speaks By Jane Roberts

The Nature of Personal Reality By Jane Roberts

Infinite Possibilities By Mike Dooley

The Alchemist By Paulo Coelho

Ageless Body, Timeless Mind By Deepak Chopra

Seven Spiritual Laws of Success By Deepak Chopra

Living with Joy By Sanaya Roman

Spiritual Growth By Sanaya Roman

The Four Agreements By Don Miguel Ruiz

The Voice of Knowledge By Don Miguel Ruiz

The Artist's Way By Julia Cameron

The Power Is Within You By Louise L. Hay

You Can Heal Your Life By Louise L. Hay

Sacred Contracts By Caroline Myss

Anatomy of the Spirit By Caroline Myss

Invisible Acts of Power By Caroline Myss

Ask and It Is Given By Esther and Jerry Hicks

The Law of Attraction By Esther and Jerry Hicks

The Invitation By Oriah Mountain Dreamer

Journey of Souls By Michael Newton

Destiny of Souls By Michael Newton

Inspiration By Wayne Dyer

Becoming: Journeying toward Authenticity By Jill Schroeder

The Wisdom Way of Knowing By Cynthia Bourgeault

Spirit Matters By Michael Lerner

Spiritual Unfoldment 1 By White Eagle

The Dark Side of the Light Chasers By Debbie Ford

The Right Questions By Debbie Ford

The Seat of the Soul By Gary Zukav

Music and the Soul By Kurt Leland

Practical Intuition By Laura Day

The Game of God by Arthur Hancock and Kathleen Brugger

Coming Back by Raymond Moody

Embraced by the Light By Betty Eadie

Heaven and Earth By James Van Praagh

Talking to Heaven By James Van Praagh

Spontaneous Healing By Andrew Weil

The Power of Infinite Love and Gratitude By Darren Weissman

The Golden Rules By Wayne Dosick

Empowering Your Indigo Child By Wayne Dosick

Soul Visioning By Susan Wisehart

The Bridge Across Forever By Richard Bach

Edgar Cayce- The Sleeping Prophet By Jess Stearn

The Laws of Spirit By Dan Millman

Secrets of the Light By Dannion Brinkley

Out on a Limb By Shirley MacLaine

Going Within By Shirley MacLaine

Dancing in the Light By Shirley MacLaine

Conscious Evolution By Barbara Marx Hubbard

The Secret By Rhonda Byrne

Many Lives, Many Masters By Brian Weiss

Same Soul, Many Bodies By Brian Weiss

Loving What Is By Byron Katie

A Thousand Names for Joy By Byron Katie

Oneness By Rasha

Spiritual Liberation By Michael Beckwith

The Hidden History of Jesus By Kirk Nelson

Stay Tuned: Conversations with Dad from the Other Side By Jenniffer Weigel

The Tipping Point By Malcolm Gladwell

Blink By Malcolm Gladwell

The Joy of Family Traditions By Jennifer Trainer Thompson

Nurturing Spirituality in Children: Simple Hands-On Activities By Peggy Jenkins

Teaching Meditation to Children By David Fontana

Movies:

www.thespiritualcinemacircle.com
www.teachwithmovies.org
www.goddessguidebook.com
www.bestinspiration.com

Websites:

www.soultosoulparenting.com
My website which can also be reached via **www.annieburnside.com** offers
Family Discussion Topics, Hot Picks, Kitchen Cabinet Wisdom, and much more.

www.newspirituality.org
Sign up to receive one spiritual message via your e-mail each day providing beautiful material for family discussions and personal growth. I utilize these often as the starting point for a family discussion.

Other Family Discussion Ideas:

Table Topics Family Cards found at www.tabletopics.com or tel. 925.258.9901

The Family Dinner Box of Questions at www.theboxgirls.com.

All *Chicken Soup for the Soul* books compiled by Jack Canfield and Mark Victor Hansen are great for family discussions.

Many forwarded inspirational emails can been used in family discussions.

SELECT BIBLIOGRAPHY

Bach, Richard. *The Bridge Across Forever*. New York: Dell Publishing, 1989.

Beak, Sera. *The Red Book: A Deliciously Unorthodox Approach to Igniting Your Divine Spark*. San Francisco: Jossey-Bass, 2006.

Bourgeault, Cynthia. *The Wisdom Way of Knowing: Reclaiming an Ancient Tradition to Awaken the Heart*. San Francisco: Jossey-Bass, 2003.

Braden, Gregg. *The Divine Matrix: Bridging Time, Space, Miracles, and Belief*. Carlsbad, California: Hay House, Inc., 2007.

Choquette, Sonia. *The Psychic Pathway: A Workbook for Reawakening Your Soul*. New York: Three Rivers Press, 1994.

Choquette, Sonia. *Trust Your Vibes*. Carlsbad, California: Hay House, Inc., 2004.

Dass, Ram. *Be Here Now*. San Cristobal, New Mexico: Hanuman Foundation, 1978.

Ford, Debbie. *The Dark Side of the Light Chasers*. New York: Riverhead Books, 1998.

Ford, Debbie. *The Right Questions*. New York: HarperCollins Publishers, 2003.

Gawain, Shakti. *Living in the Light: A Guide to Personal and Planetary Transformation*. San Rafael, California: New World Library, 1986.

Goodall, Jane. *The Chimpanzees I Love: Saving Their World and Ours*. New York: Byron Preiss Visual Publications, Inc., 2001.

Harvey, Andrew. *The Hope: A Guide to Sacred Activism*. Carlsbad, California: Hay House, Inc., 2009.

Hicks, Esther and Jerry. *Ask and It Is Given*. Carlsbad, California: Hay House, Inc., 2004.

Hicks, Esther and Jerry. *The Law of Attraction*. Carlsbad, California: Hay House, Inc., 2006.

Jenkins, Peggy. *Nurturing Spirituality in Children*. New York: Atria Books, 2007.

Katie, Byron. *Loving What Is*. New York: Three Rivers Press, 2002.

Myss, Caroline. *Invisible Acts of Power.* New York: Free Press, 2004.

Tolle, Eckhart. *A New Earth: Awakening to Your Life's Purpose.* New York: The Penguin Group, 2005.

Tolle, Eckhart. *The Power of Now*. Novato, California: New World Library, 1999.

Walsch, Neale Donald. *Conversations with God: An Uncommon Dialogue Book One.* Charlottesville, Virginia: Hampton Roads, 1995.

Walsch, Neale Donald. *Friendship with God: An Uncommon Dialogue.* New York: G. P. Putnam's Sons, 1999.

Walsch, Neale Donald. *The Little Soul and the Sun.* Charlottesville, Virginia: Hampton Roads, 1998.

Walsch, Neale Donald. *Tomorrow's God: Our Greatest Spiritual Challenge*. New York: Atria Books, 2004.

ACKNOWLEDGEMENTS

To my parents, Lew Derrickson and Laura Derrickson, and to my sister Leigh Lazaron, thank you for a wonderful beginning…

To my in-laws Pete and Suzette Burnside, thank you for your continuous generosity…

To my many teachers, especially Julie Walker, Sharyl Noday, Sonia Choquette, and Pieter Van Heule, thank you for offering me your very best…

To all of my joyous workshop gals, thank you for your love, support, encouragement, and enthusiasm…

To my dear friends, Jennifer Beacom and Melinda Hurley, thank you for the unconditional love and for the launch…

To my dear friends Sandra and Eric Miller, thank you for always being there for me with big hearts and open arms…

To my dear friends, Kimbra Burnside, Becky Flanigan, and Alyse Rynor, thank you for believing in me so thoroughly…

To all of the wonderful souls behind the scenes, especially Debbie Mackall, Baylor Fooks, Jenniffer Weigel, and Michael Antman, thank you for providing all that I needed right when I needed it…

To my literary agent Bill Gladstone, thank you for taking on this project and for being a great quarterback…

To my editor Lisa Pliscou, thank you for your knowledge and gentle guidance…

To my publicist Dea Shandera, thank you for your loving kindness and for the most expansive vision possible for all that is to come…

To my incredible publisher Nancy Cleary, thank you for your many talents, for your continual guidance, and for saying YES…

To my beloved spiritual family, thank you for the highest guidance and assistance possible, always...

To my husband Jim Burnside, thank you for *seeing* me, for loving me so freely and completely, and for allowing me to shine in my own unique Annie way...

To my three earthly angels, Aidenn, Piper, and Pete Burnside, thank you for simply being my children and for reflecting the heart and the soul of this book...

About the Author

Annie Burnside, M.Ed., is a soul nurturer, author, public speaker and teacher specializing in conscious relationships and spiritual development. As a soul nurturer, she helps others awaken to their *own* personal truths by providing spiritual support and encouragement while offering tools to balance their inner world with the exterior world. Burnside's teachings inspire others to reconnect with their spirit and listen to the voice of their own soul so that direct divine connection can become fully accessible within daily reality. Her open, gentle approach encompasses all spiritual paths.

Burnside became especially interested in working with other parents on a spiritual level as she began to teach her own children about their divine nature. Her passion for spiritual development drives her work. The author's mission is to inspire raised consciousness in families around the world by reminding them that they are *above all else* creative, intuitive, eternal, infinite beings who consciously create their own reality. This realization empowers all individuals, families and communities to lead more authentic lives enabling them to more easily align with their highest potential.

Burnside received her Bachelor of Arts degree in Sociology from DePauw University and her Masters degree in Education from DePaul University. She taught fourth and fifth grades in Evanston, Illinois before becoming a full-time stay-at-home mom and soul nurturer to her three children now aged fourteen, twelve and ten.

Twenty years ago Burnside began her own personal growth journey. Due to her passion for conscious relationships and spiritual development, as well as her longtime study of metaphysics, others began to seek her out as a teacher inviting her to give lectures and workshops on spirituality. She created a spiritual support practice in 2005. *Soul to Soul Parenting* is Burnside's first book. Beyond workshops and working one-on-one with clients, she writes a family consciousness column for *Evolving Your Spirit Magazine* and blogs for the Chicago Tribune Media Company under *Soul to Soul Perspective: A Little Bit of Soul Goes a Long Way*. Burnside draws inspiration from her own spiritual journey, her work as a soul nurturer, and her experiences teaching her own children. She lives in Chicago, Illinois with her husband and three children.

www.AnnieBurnside.com

INDEX

LaVergne, TN USA
06 April 2011
223146LV00002B/89/P